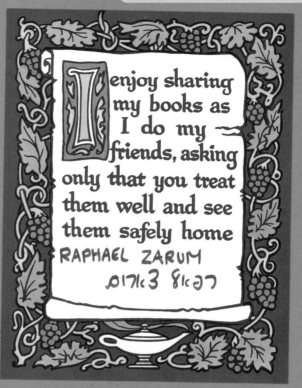

I enjoy sharing my books as I do my friends, asking only that you treat them well and see them safely home

RAPHAEL ZARUM

רפאל 3 צארום

מראה

ArtScroll Judaiscope Series

The Torah
Personality

The Torah

Collected from the pages of
The Jewish Observer
by

Rabbi Nisson Wolpin,
Editor

Personality

A Treasury of Biographical Sketches

Published by

Mesorah Publications, ltd

in conjunction with

Agudath Israel of America

FIRST EDITION
First Impression ... November, 1980

Published and Distributed by
MESORAH PUBLICATIONS, Ltd.
Brooklyn, New York 11223

Distributed in Israel by
MESORAH MAFITZIM / J. GROSSMAN
Rechov Bayit Vegan 90/5
Jerusalem, Israel

Distributed in Europe by
J. LEHMANN HEBREW BOOKSELLERS
20 Cambridge Terrace
Gateshead
Tyne and Wear
England NE8 1RP

ISBN
0-89906-850-2 (hard cover)
0-89906-851-0 (paperback)

סדר במסדרת
חברת ארטסקרול בע"מ

Typography by Compuscribe at ArtScroll Studios, Ltd.
1969 Coney Island Avenue / Brooklyn, N.Y. 11223 / (212) 339-1700

Printed in the United States of America by Moriah Offset

Table of Contents

Contributors to this volume
(in order of their appearance):

Rabbi Chaim Leib Balgley, a native of Brisk who served as *Rav* in Dubinova, Poland, now lives in Monsey, NY.

Chaim Shapiro, a native of Tiktin, Poland, who grew up in Lomza, and now lives in Baltimore, where he writes articles regarding Jewish life in Europe before WW II. The historical data in his article on Tiktin is taken from *Sefer Tiktin* published in Israel in 1959.

Rabbi Nosson Scherman is editor of the ArtScroll Series of Mesorah Publications and is a well-known educator, lecturer, and author.

Rabbi Aaron Brafman is a member of the faculty and assistant principal of the Yeshiva High School of Far Rockaway.

Mrs. Adel Engel is a daughter of the late Moreinu Yaakov Rosenheim. She lives with her family in Far Rockaway, NY.

The late *Dayan* **Dr. Isaac Grunfeld** was a former member of the London *Bais Din*, well known for his original works on Orthodox Judaica in English, especially his translations and interpretations of the works of Rabbi Samson Raphael Hirsch.

Rabbi Yaakov Feitman is principal of the Rabbi Jacob Joseph School, Staten Island, and an editor of the Judaiscope Series.

Rabbi Moshe Swift, a *dayan* (rabbinical judge) in the London *Bais Din*, studied under the Ponevezher Rav in Lithuania.

Siegmund Forst is a well known author, artist and illustrator, whose works reflect Jewish themes.

Lewis Brenner, a *musmach* of Mesivta Torah Vodaath, resides in Brooklyn where he is active in communal affairs.

Rabbi Menachem Lubinsky is director of Government and Public Affairs of Agudath Israel of America.

Beinish Rosenbaum, a businessman who lives in Brooklyn, studied in Mesivta Torah Vodaath and Beis Medrash Elyon, Monsey, NY.

Rabbi Nisson Wolpin is editor of The Jewish Observer and this volume.

Pinchos Jung was active in Agudath Israel youth work in London, and is author of several books on Torah *hashkafah: The Truth Need Not Hurt,* and *The World is My Teacher.*

Nehama Consuela Nahmoud was born in the United States, educated in Portugal, France and Israel, and now resides in Buenos Aires.

Rabbi Aryeh Kaplan, writer and lecturer on numerous Judaica topics, as well as translator of numerous works including the *Torah Anthology/Meam Loez*, resides in Brooklyn, NY.

Rabbi Shmuel Singer is a *Rosh Yeshiva* in Hebrew Academy of Nassau County and *Rav* of The Huntington Synagogue, in Huntington (Long Island), NY.

Dr. Gershon Kranzler is Professor of Education at the Towson State Teachers College in Maryland, and the author of a classic work on Williamsburg Jewry, *Williamsburg: A Neighborhood in Transition.*

The late **Rabbi Naftoli Riff** was president of Ezras Torah and rabbi in Camden, NJ.

*The biographical sketches in this book first appeared
as articles in* **The Jewish Observer,**
*a monthly journal of thought and opinion
published by Agudath Israel of America.*
The Editorial Board of **The Jewish Observer** *is chaired by Dr. Ernst
L. Bodenheimer.*

Preface

Judaiscope is a series of books founded on the concept that no area of life is outside the realm of *halachah* (Torah law), untouched by *aggadah* (Torah thought), or independent of the traditions, values, and priorities that flow uninterruptedly from the day Israel stood at Sinai. Given that conviction, the thinking Jew should take the intellectual skills and moral perspectives of study hall and synagogue and focus them upon contemporary problems and issues. What does the Torah-trained mind and heart say to modern life? How does it react to "practical" problems? How does it act in an unspiritual world?

This series, then, is an adventure in thinking — an expedition of exploration into the landscape of day-to-day events, the speculations of the academy, the experiments of the scientist, the notes of the historian, and the interactional, emotional realm of the sociologist. But because the tools used for surveying, researching, and charting are those of Torah, the findings, too, are products of Torah. In a sense, this series is a new departure for Mesorah Publications, but in a truer sense, it is an extension of our work in Tanach, Mishnah, and classic Torah literature.

It is fitting that we publish the Judaiscope Series jointly with Agudath Israel of America, for it is the organizational expression of uncompromising Torah Jewry, founded by the Torah leadership of the early Twentieth Century, based on the premise that all problems confronting Jewry can only be solved through Torah. To this day, Agudath Israel of America is led by outstanding Torah scholars, and has a wide following of members and supporters from all walks of life. And Agudath Israel is the vehicle of the Torah sages in coming to grips with contemporary problems and issues.

This volume sets the scene for Judaiscope, for it contains

many human brush strokes depicting the composite "Torah Personality" that fought for and ordered Jewish life in many countries and continents. A later volume in the series will present sketches of the prominent Roshei Hayeshivah of this century. Among other books will be studies of the Orthodox response to the need for *hatzalah*/rescue during the Holocaust; an approach to the problem of Judaism and science; evolution; prayer; and education.

The Judaiscope Series resulted from of the effort of a number of individuals, including Rabbi Yaakov Feitman and Dr. David Kranzler, who served as editor and director (respectively) of the program responsible for some of the books to appear under the Judaiscope title; as well as an advisory board composed of Rabbi David Cohen, Rabbi Joseph Elias, Rabbi Shlomo Oppenheimer, Rabbi Nosson Scherman, Rabbi Moshe Sherer (president of Agudath Israel of America), and Rabbi Nisson Wolpin.

Mesorah Publications, Ltd.

The Torah Personality

Rabbi Moshe Blau, emissary from the Torah leadership of the Holy Land, was in Vilna for the first time. His host was Rabbi Chaim Ozer Grodzensky, acknowledged leader of European Jewry between the Wars, who was anxious that his guest absorb as much as possible from this initial visit. So he instructed a young man, who was to be Rabbi Blau's companion: "Show Rabbi Blau the treasures of Vilna."

When they returned, Reb Chaim asked them, "Tell me, what did you see?"

"The shul of the Vilna Gaon, the old cemetery, the Strashun Library, ... "

Reb Chaim Ozer interrupted, "Never mind the cemetery. Did you introduce Rabbi Blau to Reb Avraham Yeshayahu Karelitz — the Chazon Ish? He is Vilna's living treasure!"

Reb Chaim Ozer was not given to extravagant praise. He was known to choose his words prudently. Yet, to him Vilna's prime treasure was the Chazon Ish — then a young, obscure scholar who rarely ventured out of his small attic apartment except to *daven*, or to discuss various matters with Reb Chaim Ozer.

It could not be because the Chazon Ish had amassed so much Torah knowledge that he had become a prime stop on the Vilna tour. The Strashun Library had more facts crowded in the volumes on its shelves, ... Nor had he undergone an unusual personal history. The silent steps of the Vilna Gaon's *shul* could, in their way, tell more tales than the tight-lipped Chazon Ish. The Chazon Ish was a rare jewel of a different type — a treasury of

Torah values that were integrated into his personality, and Torah understandings that were the frame of reference for all his judgments for *Klal Yisrael* and individual "Reb Yisraels." As such, he had few peers.

◆§ The Fruits of Diligence

One may wonder how a mere mortal can succeed in so absorbing Torah thoughts and values to the point of forming a unified entity with the Torah. The answer to this can be found in the life story of every *gadol* — every Torah giant that ever trod the earth; and it is also delineated in brief in the personal correspondence of the Chazon Ish. In apparent response to a young man's query: "How does one achieve greatness in Torah?" — he wrote: "Pursue means both rational and mystical. That is, study for long periods without interruption, do not become involved in the pursuit of physical pleasures, nor should you seek recognition for your accomplishments ... and generally be meticulous about observing all forty-eight qualifications for Torah study (*Avos*, Chapter VI) ... especially [stress such matters as] properly washing hands when necessary, and other such factors of purity" (*Collected Letters*).

There is no record as to whether this approach of total immersion actually helped the young correspondent, but *Klal Yisroel* is a witness to its effectiveness in making the Chazon Ish — like all great men who preceeded him in this course, as well as those that follow — into a *gadol beYisrael*, a towering personality.

The diligence in study of *gedolei Torah* is a matter of record: The Vilna Gaon's schedule that only allowed for four half-hour stretches of sleep — a total of two hours per day — to interrupt his round-the-clock immersion in Torah; the Chasam Sofer's passion for study that permitted him to sleep only every second night — and then, only from nightfall to 11 PM, while he kept a basin of cold water near his table, to soak his feet should he feel tiredness invading his mind; the Chazon Ish's steady perch on his sofa, with light bulb dangling overhead, as he studied Torah night after day after night, only putting his head to the pillow with any formal resignation to sleep on *Shabbos*.... immersion in Torah like the undersea swimmer's immersion in the waters of the ocean, with no separation between man and water, no surfacing except when absolutely essential.

The result has been that the individual emerges as more than a living memory bank that spews forth information on cue. A *gadol beTorah* addresses *new* problems and reduces them to their essential elements — elements that had long been defined by Torah law and practice, but are not easily recognizable in their new garb. And then he applies eternal wisdom to these "new" issues.... Thus, Reb Chaim Ozer evaluated intravenous feedings in the light of the laws of Yom Kippur fasting; the Chazon Ish dealt with complex problems of mechanized farming vis-a-vis Sabbath restrictions and the challenge of honoring the *Shmittah* restraints of the Sabbatical year in Israel's agricultural settlements, exploring the field of hydroponics, gravel farming.

⋖§ An Extra-Halachic Intelligence

This exceptional capacity to apply knowledge culled from ancient texts to modern-day problems is more than the simple sum of its parts: The endless hours of study and thought, and the brilliance of mind and intensity of concentration. Somehow, it must also encompass the special gift of ליראיו ד' סוד, the Divine secrets that G-d imparts to those who fear Him. This, too, is part of the makeup of a *gadol beTorah* and guides him in ways that cannot be reduced to scholarship *per se*. This very same factor guides the *gadol* in dealing with problems that appear to be extra-halachic in nature, appearing to belong to other disciplines, such as politics, sociology, or psychology. Yet, just as Torah, deals with every aspect of human existence, so too does the man who is great in Torah find himself equipped to address these many aspects of life. And just as the destiny of *Klal Yisrael* is intertwined with Torah — for its vicissitudes of fortune, its ascendencies and its falls from grace, are all determined by its fidelity to Torah — so, too, is the man great in Torah uniquely equipped to address the myriad problems of *Klal Yisrael* in all their facets.

> ☐ *Thus the Vilna Gaon understood the necessity of establishing large regional yeshivos, and directed his talmid Reb Chaim to found, in Volozhin, the prototype of the Lithuanian yeshiva — the institution that eventually blocked the inroads of haskalah and secularism by preserving Torah scholarship at its purest.... Similarly, the Chasam Sofer in Pressburgh of the early 1800's perceived Reform as a prime threat to the integrity of Torah Judaism, and combatted its spread with the ferocity of a lion protecting its lair; as did Rabbi Samson Raphael Hirsch in Frankfurt-am-Main of the*

latter 1800's, with his own combination of an innovative philosophy (Torah im Derech Eretz) *and the politically bold policy of* austrittsgemeinde, (separate community) *which erected unequivocal barriers between the Torah communities and those that denied the divinity of Torah.... In the same way, Rabbi Yisroel Salanter perceived Jewry's weakened ethical fiber as the primary problem to be addressed in mid-19th century Europe, and he launched what is now known as the Mussar Movement.... Rabbi Yisroel Meir Kagan saw ignorance of the laws of slander as a crucial flaw in the fabric of* Klal Yisrael's *conduct and wrote his classic* Chofetz Chaim.... *Rabbi Chaim Ozer Grodzensky invested his authority in unifying the Torah camp under the banner of an Agudath Israel to combat the splintering effects of countless secular substitutions for Judaism.... The Chazon Ish directed a multi-pronged effort to infuse the Holy Land with a Torah-life that vibrated beyond the narrow confines of select corners of Jerusalem, and Bnai Brak to pulsate in new settlements thriving cities, and even make itself felt in the halls of government.... And thus did "Mr." Shraga Feivel Mendlowitz and Rabbi Aharon Kotler each dare dream of the flourishing of an uncompromising Torah life coupled with excellence in Torah scholarship on the soil of the New World.*

How did these men divine their areas of activity — choosing targets at which to aim their mighty bows, selecting potent arrows from their well-stocked quivers? Undoubtedly, they were guided by סוד ד' ליראיו, a Divine prompting of sorts, a gift that has also been described as *"daas Torah"* — the wisdom that results from being immersed in Torah, studying Torah, incorporating Torah into one's thinking process and integrating it into one's personality.

◆§ The Gifts of Personality

Thus, there is more than excellence in scholarship in the making of *gadol baTorah*. And so do these men possess more than a unique outlook on life. A *gadol baTorah* is also a Torah personality whose very emotions and reflexes are in tune with *halachah*, and reflect (if one may) Torah sentiments. To him, the responsibilities of *Klal Yisrael do not serve as a convenient pedestal for public adulation. On the contrary, the burdens press* far too heavily on their shoulders, permitting them neither rest nor relaxation ... *Rabbi Akiva Eiger* — whose opinions on *halachah* and explanations of difficult Talmudic passages were sought by Jews living in all ends of the world — found public life to so interfere with his private service to his Creator, that he actually applied to a *talmid* for the position of *shamash* in his *shul!* To The *Sfas Emes* refused to rest his disease-racked body on a bed, while "my *talmidim*, my loyal disciples sleep in cold trenches fighting the Czar's war in Siberia." And, sleeping on the hard floor of his house in Ger, he suffered a premature death.

As a Jewish leader carries the burdens of the community at large, so does he shoulder the needs of the individual.

□ *When one of his more ascetic students questioned Reb Yisroel Salanter's caring for others' material needs to the point of indulging them, in total contradiction to his personal practice of self-denial ("You're spoiling them, Rebbe!"), Reb Yisroel responded: "Yenem's gashmiyus iz mein ruchniyus — taking care of the other fellow's material needs is my spiritual need."*

Thus, Rabbi Akiva Eiger watched in dismay as his wagon driver struggled through mud and snow to get his sidetracked horses back on the road. As the fellow climbed back to his seat, Rabbi Eiger handed him a pair of dry socks — "Take them. They're extra."

Only later, when the rabbi disembarked, did the driver notice that the rabbi's ankles were bare. He protested, "You sat in the cold, without your socks! Why did you say they were extra?"

Replied the rabbi: "When you are shivering, they're extra for me."

□ *A concerned father brought his son to the Telshe Yeshiva to study. He requested of the Rosh Yeshiva, Rabbi Eliezer Gordon, "Keep a special eye on him. I know that you have four hundred boys in your care, but he's my ben yachid, my only son. Do you know what I mean?"*

"Of course. Just like this boy, my only son," said the Rosh Yeshiva, pointing to a tall, lanky boy passing by.

Later, the parent repeated his plea. "And you understand my concern, don't you?" he asked.

"To be sure," replied the Rosh Yeshiva. "Just like my only son, over there," he added, gesturing toward a short, stocky boy.

"But I thought that the other *boy was your only son!"*
"He is. He is. And so is each of the four hundred boys
in the yeshiva my ben yachid."

◆§ Leaders For All Seasons

Such men as these have blessed *Klal Yisrael* with their gifts
of Torah knowledge, their guidance culled from Torah inspired
insights, and the glow of their Torah personalities. It is uncanny
— perhaps even miraculous in its own way — how during each
generation the leadership is of a nature that perfectly fits the
needs of that particular community at its particular juncture in
history. Truly, the emergence of *the gadol* for his generation con-
forms to the script outlined in the Midrash:

> □ *Adam despaired for the fate of his offspring. He, who*
> *had known his Creator intimately — indeed, he was*
> *fashioned by His very hands! — had transgressed His one*
> *command and eaten fruit from the forbidden tree. How*
> *could future generations fare better?*
>
> *G-d comforted Adam by showing him His book*
> *wherein were inscribed the names of* "dor, dor vedorshov,
> dor, dor, umanhigav — *every generation and its teachers,*
> *every generation and its leaders." These teachers and leaders*
> *would guide the children of Adam as the need arose.*

Notice not only did His Book contain a roster of names of
leaders for all time; the generations were listed in the singular:
every generation and *its* leaders. No generation is identical to any
other. Nor are the needs of any one generation identical to the
needs of any other. Neither are its leaders. Each is singularly
equipped to lead that generation wherein he emerges.

◆§ Penetrating the Cloak of Privacy

Military heroes celebrate their victories on the battlefield in
their published memoirs, and political leaders submit to interviews in which they reveal their secrets of success. But Torah
heroes live by "and walk modestly with your G-d" and avoid the
spotlight. They shrink from the adulating eye.

How, then, does one penetrate the self-imposed cloak of
privacy and catch a glimpse of the shafts of light that reflect the
multi-faceted Torah personality? There are ways. And they must
be pursued. Rabbi Akiva's followed his teacher, noting even
private activities when asked how he dared do such a thing, Rabbi

Akiva answered, "His deeds are Torah, and I must learn" (*Be'rachos* 62a). For indeed, his every move — even the most intimate — bespoke Torah values. There was no casual gesture or throwaway living in Rabbi Akiva's life.

This dogged following of mentor by disciple is infinitely rewarding. Did not Rabbi Yehudah HaNassi attribute his own unrivaled accomplishment to having *once* caught a glimpse of the great Rabbi Meir — from behind? And had he actually encountered Rabbi Meir face to face — had he been blessed with the opportunity to study him from close over a protracted period of time — how much greater Rabbi Yehudah would have been!

So, through the generations, have all Jews — simple Jews, accomplished *talmidei chachamim*, and spiritual giants — sought to peer into the hidden crevices of the *gadol baTorah's* personality to gain insight into his gestures, to chart the dizzying heights of his achievements, so they too might aspire for the same ... or long for it ... or at least appreciate it for what it represents.

☐ *Thus did Rabbi Levi Yitzchak of Berditchev journey from Pinsk to Mezritch to see the Maggid — the Rebbe Reb Ber.*
"*Why undertake so arduous a journey?*" *he was asked.*
"*I must see the Maggid. You see, he knows there's a G-d on earth.*"
"*Every fool knows that. Here comes Olga, the maid. Ask her.*"
"*She'll say there's a G-d. The Maggid knows it.*"

☐ *Similarly, the Chassidic leader Reb Leib Sorkes also traveled great distances to spend time with the Maggid.*
"*To see him* daven?" — *he was asked.*
"*No,*" *he replied. "To see the Maggid tie his shoelace.*"

☐ *When young Yisrael Lipkin of Salant found the saintly Reb Zundel's pretentions of ordinariness too fascinating to accept at face value, he shadowed the hidden tzaddik on his lonely strolls to wooded retreats, to penetrate those veils — until finally Reb Zundel gave him but a momentary glimpse of his formula for greatness ("Learn Mussar, Yisroel'ke," he bade him) — a glimpse that set him on his course for leadership, as the revered Reb Yisroel Salanter.*

Dorothy Thompson, the celebrated American Journalist, had wanted to include the Chofetz Chaim in her series of interviews with key European leaders between the wars.

☐ *"Sorry, the Chofetz Chaim does not have time for interviews," she was told.*

"Then let me at least see him," she begged.

This was arranged — through an open window that revealed the diminutive frame of the saint and sage of Radin seated on a simple chair, bent over a yellowed text resting on a simple wooden table, in a sparely furnished room. She peered through the window and watched ... and watched ... for fifteen minutes.

When Miss Thompson finally turned to leave, a companion asked her what had caught her fancy for so long.

She replied: "I have just seen the Jewish G-d."

Can we look and see less than G-d's wisdom as it graces our leaders? Can we pass up an opportunity to look at such a presence, given the opportunity?

☐ *A newly enrolled student in Lakewood's Beth Medrash Gevoha was overwhelmed by the Rosh Yeshiva Reb Aharon Kotler's rapid-fire delivery of highly complex material in his weekly lecture. When he complained to his previous Rosh Yeshiva who had suggested that he go to Lakewood, the man said, "Even if you fail to understand him, it pays to go to his shiurim, if just to look at his face."*

Reb Aharon is no longer with us. Nor is Reb Akiva Eiger, the Mezritcher Maggid, or the Chofetz Chaim. Their writings and teachings are very much alive, but how do we get a glimpse of their faces? — or at least their backs?

The stories of their deeds and doings, little acts and gestures, were studied, repeated, and recorded. True, the printed word is sterile when compared to Reb Aharon's fiery visage or the celestial glow that surrounded the Vilna Gaon. But at least the typed words tells us something that otherwise we would not know.

❀ ❀ ❀

The various chapters in this volume take many forms. They range from formal biographies to sketchy reminiscences, from full-blown eulogies to contemporary newspaper accounts. Some focus on political and social problems of time and place (Rabbi Jacob Joseph, New York's first and only Chief Rabbi), others to the geography of the soul ("Dvinsk" of the Ohr Someiach and the Ragatchover; "Brisk," as recalled by Rabbi Chaim Balgley).

These give the reader an appreciation for the setting that nurtured the development of greatness in men — the devotion to Torah, the trust in G-d, the fidelity to Jewish values that so prevailed in these places.... Some stories recount in detail a Chassidic Rebbe's *Tisch* (Vizhnitz; Reb Itzikel). Others may seem to target in on refuting the spurious reporting of secular historians ("Lomza"). Do not be sidetracked by polemic. That, too, helps us understand that viewing a *gadol* to study him and gain inspiration from his ways — this, too, calls for a Jewish sensitivity, which is unfortunately in such short supply today.

Focus on the man ... or the angel in the guise of man. Take note of the lacing of a shoe, or the unslept-on mattress. These — each in its own way — give us a glimpse of the dazzling riches of the Jewish People, not to be found in any other national treasury: *The Torah Personality.*

Nisson Wolpin

ঙ্গ Of Places and People

*The spiritual landscape
that nurtured greatness in men*

The Brisker Legacy

*The Lithuanian city of Brisk is celebrated as a home
of Talmudic scholars, notably the famous Soloveitchik
family — Reb Yoseif Dov ("Reb Yosha Ber," 5580/1820-
5652/1892), Reb Chaim (5613/1853-5678/1918), and Reb
Yitzchok Zev ("Reb Velvel," 5647/1887—5719/1959),
זכרונם לברכה, who in succession served as rabbis of Brisk.
In addition to their lomdus (analytical approach to
Talmud study) and their kano'us (zeal), there is yet
another tradition, equally ingrained, but not as widely
known: the exceptional Brisker generosity.*

*On these pages, Rabbi Chaim Leib Balgley שליט״א
shares his reminiscences, relating several incidents regarding outstanding rabbinical leaders of Brisk through the
ages — incidents that exemplify the Brisker legacy.*

◄§ The Bach's Formula for Recovery

WHEN the *Bach*, Rabbi Yoel Surkis (16th Century scholar
whose redactional notes appear in the margin of Talmud and
Shulchan Aruch) was Rav in Brisk, he directed a Yeshiva that attracted students from all over Eastern Europe. His graduates
became outstanding rabbinic leaders in a number of prominent
communities.

One morning, when the *Bach* was on his way to the yeshiva,
a woman came running toward him crying: "Rebbe, help me. My
one child who attended your yeshiva is sick and was hospitalized
for a full month. Now the physicians have given up on him and
sent him home. Rebbe, help me!"

The *Bach* explained that his medical knowledge was in no
way superior to that of the physicians, adding, "In what way can
I possibly be of help? Even our forefather Yaakov told Rachel
(when she pleaded with him 'Give me children'): Can I substitute
for G-d?"

She begged: "Rebbe, I have not come for your personal aid
in my son's behalf, but rather for the merit of your Torah study at
the yeshiva."

"This is an altogether different matter," said the Rabbi. "What is your son's name, and what is your name?" He recorded these names and sent her home with his blessings.

At the *shiur*, the Rabbi related the incident to his students and asked them to concentrate on the Torah discourse he was about to deliver, in which merit G-d should send a complete and speedy recovery to that sick boy. Upon the conclusion of the Torah lecture, the Rabbi recited the customary *Mi Shebeirach* prayer for the sick.

The following day, the mother entered the yeshiva, and with tears of joy, related what had transpired several hours after her street-side plea with the Rabbi — how her son had opened his eyes, then asked for water, and later for some food; and shortly afterward got out of bed and played about on the floor. The mother then publicly — before the assembly of students and teachers — expressed deep gratitude to G-d and took leave.

Later in the day, after she had returned home, the family physician stopped by to check on the child. When he saw the boy walking about and playing, he exclaimed: "This is beyond all wonders! We had expected his life to end in a matter of days. What in the world happened since he came home from the hospital?"

Upon learning the sequence of events, the physician exclaimed: "This is truly *t'chias hameisim* — a revival of the dead! I am now a convinced man of faith."

(This incident is recorded in the Book of Records in Brisk.)

⋅§ Protector of the Schools

Rabbi Yehoshua Leib Diskin (5577/1816-5658/1896) was a young man when he became Rav of Brisk. At that time, the *maskillim* were attempting to reform the Jewish educational system, assuming that once they have taken over the schools all other aspects of Jewish life would fall into place, gradually eliminating the older folks with their "old-fashioned ways."

At that time, the mayor of Brisk was a well-known anti-Semite. He especially could not countenance the Orthodox Jews and their way of life. Hence, when young, inexperienced Reb Yehoshua Leib became spiritual leader of Brisk, the *maskillim* seized the opportunity to meet with the mayor and attack the religious Jews and their schools. They faulted the instructors as being totally inconsistent with the spirit of the times, the classrooms as unhygienic — plus several other "undesirable features."

Without much difficulty, they convinced the mayor that he should force the new young Rav to toe the line.

The mayor sent for the president of the *kehillah* and insisted that he update the Jewish School, but the president protested that all religious, spiritual, and educational matters were in the Rav's domain, and under his sole jurisdiction. The mayor then invited the Rav for a discussion, congratulating him upon assuming the exalted rabbinical leadership of Brisk. He then informed him that a new educational system was being instituted for the benefit of the entire Jewish community, which the Rav, as supreme authority, was now to set into motion.

The Rav instantly explained that when the Creator gave the Torah to the Jews, He commanded them to study this Torah in accordance with a prescribed method and system, which has been going on for some three thousand years — generation after generation. No temporal authority had the right to change this educational system.

The mayor was enraged at the Rav's calm independence, not aware that the Rav was merely conforming to: "Thou shall not fear any man."

This was the first time anyone had dared disobey the mayor, who rose in a fit of anger, paced back and forth excitedly in his office, and barked: "I'm busy right now and in a hurry to attend an important meeting out of town. When I return, I expect you to sign this document [with the order to modernize the educational system explicitly spelled out] on the dotted line and carry out its terms." — At which he exited in a fury, slamming the door behind him.

The Rav followed him out calmly.

The mayor mounted his large white steed, and rode off. While he was crossing a bridge at full gallop, the bridge collapsed and horse and rider were plunged into the raging river below, and drowned.

The Jewish community of Brisk maintained their Torah educational system, while the *maskillim* continued to plot against it at their meetings. Today, we still speak of Brisker Torah with awe, while the *maskillim* of Brisk have long been forgotten.

◄§ The Road to Brisk

Prior to assuming the *rabbanus* in Brisk, Reb Yosha Ber was Rav in Slutsk — a position he relinquished on account of the following incident:

The Czar had a policy of conscripting young Jewish children into the army for a twenty-year term of duty. These children-soldiers were called "Cantonists." This decree of whisking away young Jewish children deep into Siberia, isolated from other Jews, was in essence *shmad*. The government set a quota for each community, affecting rich and poor families alike, without exception. The rich paid high ransom fees to avoid the decree for their sons, but the quota still had to be met, so children of poor families were kidnapped.

A young boy from a nearby town was studying in the Slutsk elementary yeshiva. Some wealthy citizens had this child snatched, and locked up in an out-of-the-way hut. Reb Yosha Ber learned of this and was deeply disturbed. He pleaded with the abductors for the boy's release, but was ignored. Seeing that he could accomplish nothing with negotiations, he investigated and found out where the boy was being held. He gathered some of his loyal followers and, at midnight broke through the door with a hatchet and freed the boy.

The wealthy group was infuriated at Reb Yosha Ber's arrogance in overriding them, and had him dismissed. Others says that in view of the unsavory element to be dealt with, he simply resigned.

After the bitter incident in Slutsk, Reb Yosha Ber did not care to remain in the rabbinate. However, the rabbinical post was open in Brisk and a delegation was sent to Reb Yosha Ber to ask him to accept the position. He declined.

I had heard from the Chofetz Chaim that the community of Brisk was extremely anxious to obtain the rabbinical leadership of Reb Yosha Ber, and delegated a larger committee to entreat him not to reject a city of 50,000 Jews praying for his arrival. Reb Yosha Ber was so impressed that he and his Rebbetzin set out at once for Brisk. At this, the Chofetz Chaim declared: "Master of the Universe! Behold Yosha Ber! Upon hearing that a community of Jews are prayerfully awaiting his arrival he went there forthwith. All Israel has been awaiting *Mashiach* for so long. Isn't it surely time that You immediately send us the Redeemer?"

(Such was the Chofetz Chaim's way of imbuing every event with spiritual significance.)

◄§ Brisk — A Spiceshop of Goodness and Zeal

A number of years ago, a visitor from Jerusalem brought me regards from the Brisker Rav, Rabbi Yitzchok Zev (Reb Velvel).

Reb Velvel had related to the visitor that my father had been respected by the *bais harav* (the *Rav's* family) as an individual who had absorbed both the *ahavas chessed* (selfless generosity) and *kano'us* (zeal) associated with his family: On the one hand, Reb Velvel would send sick people to my father for his blessing, even before sending them to Reb Chaim. On the other hand (according to a magazine article about Brisk), my father was well-liked, and used this popularity to influence others to come closer to Torah.

After World War I barber-shops were for some reason very lax in Sabbath observance. A *Shmiras Shabbos* Society was organized, including in its membership *dayanim* (rabbinical judges), *roshei yeshiva*, and other *talmidei chachomim*.

On Friday afternoons, members of this Society would visit half the city's Jewish shops (especially the barber-shops!), while my father visited the other half — they were successful in persuading virtually all the shop-owners to close their stores in time for *Shabbos*. Apparently the would-be Sabbath violators recognized that their visitor's *kano'us* for *Shabbos* was motivated by genuine *ahavas Yisrael*.

A particular incident during the War demonstrated for me how my father had absorbed the *chessed* of Brisk to the point of risking his life for others: We had been driven out of Brisk, site of a large army encampment, and we settled in Vayazma, a town near Moscow, whose population was 99% non-Jewish. My father sent me to Lubavitch to study. Some time later, as the war progressed and the Germans were advancing toward Moscow, my father came to Lubavitch to take me home.

One day, when I was at the railroad station, a soldier approached me: "*Shalom Aleichem*. Do you recognize me? I was in an advanced class in Lubavitch when you were in the yeshiva ... I'm awaiting an army train, which should be arriving in about an hour. I'll be leaving for Minsk, on the front lines."

Minsk was not far from Moscow, and the Germans were advancing with heavy artillary, tanks, and their comparatively modern airforce, which was mowing down men like so many weeds. — The men? The Czar had given the order that they fight to their death. "New people are born," he said, "but not land. Fight for every yard of land!" Soldiers sent to Minsk were known not to return.

My father joined us and listened to our conversation. I introduced the soldier: "This is a *yeshiva bachur* I know from my days in Lubavitch."

There he stood, with a rifle on his shoulders, white as chalk — a picture of fear. My father thought for a moment, then said to him, "Don't go on the train. Don't stand around here. Follow us home."

When he arrived home, my father set up temporary sleeping quarters in the basement and said: "To stay in the army and follow orders is absolute suicide. The Czar has said as much himself. You're my guest, but you mustn't go out or be seen. All our neighbors are non-Jewish. The Czar issued a decree that any soldier deserting the army or anyone sheltering a deserter will be executed. So don't leave this basement!"

We kept the boy hidden there until the war was over.

What amazed me throughout was my father's calm in the face of the daily danger involved — his matter-of-fact manner, as if we had simply invited a guest to stay overnight. I was even more moved by my father's profound respect for the young man as a Torah scholar — both attitudes reflecting the heritage of Brisk. It was precisely as the *Gemara* says: When one enters a spiceshop, sweet fragrances cling to his clothing.

Remembering Reb Chaim Brisker

*the celebrated
genius of
boundless
generosity,
innovator of
the "analytical
approach" to
Talmud*

Rabbi Chaim Soloveitchik זצ"ל
5613/1853—5678/1918

*What was it like to grow up in Brisk? What was the
nature of the leadership of this city, their personalities? One
can only guess — unless one has the rare opportunity of
speaking to someone who did grow up in Brisk. Rabbi
Chaim Leib Balgley was born and raised in Brisk, where his
father, Reb Mordechai Yaakov, was an intimate of Reb
Chaim.*

*In these pages, Rabbi Balgley shares with the reader his
recollection of incidents involving Reb Chaim — incidents
that he personally witnessed or heard from authoritative
sources: Rabbi Chaim is celebrated in yeshiva circles for his
innovative analytical approach to Talmud study — known
variously as "der Litvishe derech" (the Lithuanian approach), "der Brisker derech," or "Reb Chaim's derech." His
exceptional generosity as well as his uncompromising
staunchness in religious matters — both in personal conduct
and in communal leadership — were legendary in his day,
but have faded somewhat from public knowledge in recent
years. These stories reveal some fascinating facets of Reb
Chaim's personality.*

৵§A Ba'al Habayis in Brisk

R EB MOSHE GUTTMAN became a *dayan* in Brisk when he was yet a young man. After several years in the position, he was approached by Reb Chaim regarding his financial status. Reb Chaim asked him how he was managing, in view of the growth of his family. When he replied that the situation was very tight, Reb Chaim offered him the post of secretary for his yeshiva, Etz Chaim — which he accepted.

Reb Chaim then told him that since he would be dealing with a broader public, he would like to acquaint him with the *ba'alei battim* (laymen) of Brisk: As an example he pointed to a simply-dressed man — Mr. Zelcer, by name — standing by the bookshelves in the library, looking at a *sefer*. Reb Chaim called him over and asked him a halachic question. Mr. Zelcer answered, quoting hosts of *rishonim* and *acharonim* (earlier and later commentaries) — the *Rosh*, the *Rambam*, *Tosefos Yom Tov* — and went on, explaining a pertinent *Mishnah* in various ways, according to the different *shitos* (interpretations). Reb Moshe was astounded by the *beki'us* (vast knowledge) and clarity with which the man answered — as if he had just finished studying this particular subject.

Reb Chaim later told Reb Moshe: "This is our typical *ba'al habayis* in Brisk."

৵§ Brisk Recovery

It is well-known when someone was sick on a *Shabbos* or *Yom Kippur*, and it was questionable as to how seriously he required medical attention, Reb Chaim would decide in favor of meeting the needs of the patient, even if it meant overruling the day's restrictions. (Reb Chaim would say: "I'm not lenient in regard to Shabbos or Yom Kippur. I'm stringent in the *mitzvah* of guarding one's life.") In my own experience, one *Erev* Yom Kippur, when I was very young, I was on the way to the *dayan* Reb Simcha Zelig.* Reb Chaim stopped me and asked me where

---

* Reb Simcha Zelig, the *Rosh Bais Din* of Brisk (head of the rabbinical court) lived in the upper flat of the *Rav's* house. I often saw the two studying together, with *Gemaros*, *Rambam* and countless other *sefarim* open all over the house. The two were constantly occupied in Torah discussions, even when travelling together. As great as he was, Reb Simcha Zelig was extremely humble. He dressed simply, with a plain hat and an ordinary jacket (rather than rabbinical frock). Whenever he saw us boys coming home from school, he would come down the steps and ask what we had learned, pat us on the cheek or hold one of us on his lap and kiss us on the brow when he was pleased with our answers. His simplicity offered a stark contrast with his celebrated greatness.

I was going. I replied, "I'm going to ask a *she'aila* about a weak person with regard to tomorrow, Yom Kippur."

Reb Chaim listened to my description of his condition and told me, "He is permitted to eat."

Generally, Reb Chaim referred halachic queries to the *dayan*, but in his deep concern for each and every member of his community, he wanted to decide on health matters himself.

❧ Father to the Foundlings

One *Shabbos* morning in 1910, I joined my father at Reb Chaim's private *minyan* in his house. We noticed a baby carriage in the living room and Reb Chaim seemed very concerned. The child was not Reb Chaim's own, but one that was left abandoned at his doorstep. (It was widely known that a child that would not have a normal upbringing for one of any number of reasons would find a warm welcome in Reb Chaim's home.) The child was ill and the Rav summoned a doctor, who examined the child and found him more dead than alive. He suggested that a lit candle be held close to the baby's eyes. "If the child reacts, then there *is* some life left in the child; if not, all is lost."

We stood by, watching. Said Reb Chaim to my father: "Reb Yaakov Mordechai, get a candle and a match," whereupon my father went into the kitchen. In the meantime, Reb Chaim turned to his son Reb Velvel (who later succeeded him as Brisker Rav; a young man at the time) and instructed *him* to go quickly and bring a candle and match. Reb Velvel ran, snatched the candle and match from my father's hand and brought them into the living room. The doctor held the candle near the child's eyes and reported that there was no sign of life in the child. Reb Chaim was, of course, terribly upset.

On our way home, I asked my father, "Why did Reb Chaim tell Reb Velvel to bring a candle and match when you were already in the kitchen for the same purpose?"

My father answered: "We all know that if a person's life is in danger on Shabbos, halachah demands that we do any of the prohibited labors necessary to save him. The *Rambam* says that one should do anything that would be done on a weekday for a sick person. He says further that one should not delegate the task to a non-Jew, a child, or a servant, but *gedolei yisrael ve'chachameihem* (great and wise men) should do it. One is not permitted to hesitate in such a situation. Reb Chaim realized that I was not running to bring the candle. I was calculating: First, I had heard the doctor say that this was an experiment to see whether or not there is any hope for the child — this was not a cure. Also, I knew that this child was one of those that had been abandoned at Reb Chaim's doorstep — a child of dubious parentage. But I did as I was told. Reb Chaim, with his sharp eyes, perceived this reluctance. Since one is not allowed to make *cheshbonos* (calculations) in such cases, he sent Reb Velvel and told him to run. Which he did."

The Sweetness of a Mother's Concern

These children that were brought up in Reb Chaim's house were cared for by hired wet-nurses. Once, Reb Chaim did not have money to pay one of the nurses and asked her to return the following day. The woman became excited and exclaimed, "Rebbe, just because you want to bring up *mamzeirim*, doesn't mean that I have to suffer!"

Reb Chaim immediately quieted her down: "One is not allowed to speak thus of Jewish children. I promise you, I'll pay you tomorrow."

The woman accepted his assurances and left. Shortly thereafter, Reb Chaim ran outside and called the woman back. Said Reb Chaim: "I see that you are excited. If you nurse the child now, it might be harmful to him. Please sit down until you calm down, and only then feed the child."

Recording the "Chiddushim"

Reb Chaim did not write down his *chiddushei Torah* (original interpretations) himself. The task was performed by Reb Noach, one of the *shochtim* (ritual slaughterers) in Brisk — a Slonimer chassid, who was an accomplished *talmid chacham*. On one *Shabbos Erev Chanuka*, Reb Chaim instructed his *Shammos* to ask Reb Noach to come to his house right after *havdalah*, for he had some *chiddushim* to record.

Reb Noach came at the appointed time and sat down to write. While Reb Chaim paced the floor, talking without pause for several hours, Reb Noach wrote. When Reb Noach seemed to tire, Reb Chaim gave him a glass of tea, and then started talking once again, until he had dictated a full twelve pages.

Suddenly, Reb Chaim reached over to the writing table and took hold of the notes and began to rip them into shreds. Said Reb Noach: "Give the pages to me. Why should you bother tearing them?"

When Reb Chaim heard this, he tore the pages into even

smaller strips, to make sure that they could not be pieced together later. Reb Chaim wanted to start dictating again, but the hour was late, and Reb Noach was without the strength to write anymore.

Said Reb Chaim: "False Torah explanations are not permitted to exist. The world needs only true, authentic Torah."

In view of the scrupulous attention Reb Chaim gave to every word written, it is not surprising that his published *chiddushim* earned the recognition of being *Toras Emes.*

◆§ Yom Kippur Rescue

The Jewish "Bund" had played a large role in the 1905 laborers' revolt against the Czar's government. The Czar suppressed the revolt and had all the offenders shot. Furthermore he issued a decree, that if a "proclamation" should be found in anyone's possession, that person should be shot on the spot.

Once, *Erev Yom Kippur,* two Jewish Bundists were caught, bearing "proclamations" on their persons. They were arrested and placed in jail. Their trial — and certain death — was scheduled for the next day. When Reb Chaim learned of this, he immediately contacted some wealthy men who had connections with the army, instructing them to arrange for food to be given to the prisoners; in addition, they should use all their contacts, and make every effort to save these youths.

The men did as Reb Chaim requested, and notified him that there was a possibility of freeing the men with 10,000 rubles. Where does one get 10,000 rubles — a huge sum of money, especially in those poverty-stricken times? Time was running out, and the lives of these unfortunate youths were hanging in the balance. Reb Chaim dispatched messengers to all *shuls* and *yeshivos, batei midrashim* and *shtieblach,* to convene a meeting of the *gabboim* (trustees). At the meeting, Reb Chaim established a fixed amount for each *shul* to raise by that very same evening, and also decreed that *Kol Nidrei* not be said until he would give the word.

That evening, the money was brought to Reb Chaim's house. When they had collected the entire amount, Reb Chaim sent the *shammos* to notify the various *shuls* that *Kol Nidrei* could be said ... and the boys were, of course, freed.

◆§ Boundless Generosity

An uncle of mine who was in business had once made a large shipment deep into Russia. Through some mishap, his merchandise was apparently lost, which could have thrown him into bankruptcy. He sought help from Reb Chaim, who advised him whom to see and what to do to recover his money. My uncle followed Reb Chaim's suggestions and he succeeded in recovering his money.

On his way home, my uncle stopped in to thank Reb Chaim, who was extremely happy with the results. My uncle took out a large sum of money, placed the gold coins in a kerchief, and gave it to Reb Chaim telling him that it was *ma'aser* (a tithe of his gains). Reb Chaim thanked him and then shared a *dvar Torah* with him. In the midst of their conversation, a poor man came by and told him of his desperate need for a large sum of money, asking for a donation. Reb Chaim took the entire sum of money and gave it to the poor man.

◄§ The End of Days

Reb Chaim noted that after the Torah enumerates the curses of the *tochachah*, which will befall *Klal Yisrael* if they abandon their covenant with G-d, the Torah tells us: "And the last generation — your children ... and the stranger from a distant land will say... 'Why did G-d punish this land so?' " *(Devarim* 29:21,23).

Reb Chaim asked: If the person who asks is a "stranger," why describe him further as coming "from a distant land"? It would seem to be redundant. He answered: The Torah is describing the situation that will prevail during *Ikvesa d'Meshicha* — the era just prior to *Moshiach's* coming, when ignorance will be so prevalent in the world that a Jew will ask the same questions as a Gentile from a far off country. A Gentile that lives among Jews knows that Jews do not work once a week, on *Shabbos* ... that they have a festival in which they do not eat bread ... one when Jews leave their homes and erect huts, to eat and sleep in them. However, a Gentile from a distant corner of Asia or Africa probably never saw a Jew in his life. He has no conception of their customs. Thus, the Torah describes the time just prior to *Moshiach's* arrival: There will be such ignorance in the world that "the last generation — your children" the *Jewish* people will be so far from Torah, as to be comparable to the "stranger from a distant land" — a Gentile that never lived among Jews, and is totally ignorant of their customs. ... This is what the *Gemara* means when it says: "Torah is destined to be forgotten from Israel."

Unfortunately, we have seen much fulfillment of this prophecy — may G-d have mercy on us and speedily usher in the next era.

Tiktin, Poland

✒ The Early Years

TIKTIN was founded in the year 1437. In 1522, ten Jews from Grodno, Lithuania, petitioned for permission to be the first Jews to settle there. At that time, Lithuania, the last pagan state on the continent, was a vast country, three times the size of Poland, stretching from the Baltic almost to the Black Sea, including areas known today as White Russia (where Minsk is located) and Ukraine (Kiev). Even though Tiktin was on the Polish side of the boundary, the Jews of Tiktin considered themselves "Litvakes," speaking a pure Lithuanian Yiddish, betraying their Grodno origins.

✒ Rabbanim

In America, the contemporary rabbi tends to mold the congregation in his image. By contrast, in Europe of old, the reflection worked in reverse: the *kehillah* selected a Rav in *its* own image. As a result, one could gain a good insight into the workings of a *kehillah* by the personality of the Rav and his stature in Torah.

Thus, we take note of the appearance of the name of the first Rav, Reb Mordechai (1538), as judging a *din Torah* (legal case) together with the renowned *Maharshal* (Rabbi Shlomo Lurya) sixteen years after the first *minyan* had settled in Tiktin. In 1590 we find a record of a *takanah* (ordinance) regarding the rabbinate signed by Benjamin Aaron Charif, Rav of Tiktin, together with the *Maharam M'Lublin*, Rabbi Mordechai Yeffes (הלבושים), Rabbi Ephraim Lunshitz (כלי יקר), Rabbi Yeshaya Hurwitz (של"ה), Rabbi Yehoshua Falk (סמ"ע) and Rabbi Shlomo Eidlish (מהרש"א). On other documents are found other rabbis who served as *Rav* in Tiktin: the *Maharam M'Tiktin*,[1] then the *Maharsha*, and the *Pnei Yeshoshua-Moginei Shlomo*.[2] These are followed by: Reb Moshe

---

1. נמוקי יוסף, יבמות, חדושי אנשי שם מוהר"ן שפירא — מהר"ם מטיקטין שליט"א.
2. That is, *Sheilos Uteshuvos Pnei Yehoshua*, grandfather of the *Pnei Yehoshua* on *Shas*.

Zev (מראות הצובאות, ואגודת אזוב) and the באר היטיב who served as *dayan* there. From 5609 (1849) to 5613 (1853), the Rav was Rabbi Yehoshua Isaac Shapiro, known as "Reb Izele Charif," who published eleven *sefarim*, including the עמק יהושע ונועם יהושע. From Tiktin, he went to Slonim and became known as "Reb Izele Slonimer." In 1689, Reb Aryeh Leib, the son of the *Taz* and the grandson of the *Bach*, became Rav, to be followed by Reb Moshe Ziskind Rutenburg, who left Tiktin to become Rav of the famous three *kehillos* Altuna-Hamburg-Wansbeck, where he served together with the *Chacham Zvi*, Rabbi Zvi Ashkenazi.

In our generation, Rabbi Avrohom Kalmanowitz was Rav, from 1931-1937.[3]

How did Tiktin merit such outstanding *Rabbanim?* Perhaps the following legend may shed some light on the matter: In the early days of Tiktin, various members of royalty would sell, trade, and lease huge tracts of land; indeed, they owned literally dozens of towns and villages. On one occasion, the legendary Count Potocki was involved in a trade with Count Barnicki and they could not come to terms. Finally Count Barnicki made a wager with Potocki:

"I'll accept your price if you'll find one Jewish home dark on Thursday night in Tiktin!" The old Pole knew his Jewish citizenry — Thursday nights, every Jewish home was illuminated, for in every house in Tiktin, someone was learning a *mishmar* (an all-night Torah session).

◆§ "Vaad Arba Ha'aratzos": The Committee of Four Lands

In the fifteenth century, the Polish Kings granted autonomy to the Jewish communities, recognizing the organized *kehillos* as both the internal authority and the representatives of the communities vis-a-vis the King. The rabbis also gained the authority to enforce judgments in money matters and to punish sinners. The country was divided into four lands; "Great Poland," with its seat in Posen (Poznan); "Small Poland," seat in Cracow (Krakow); "Podolye," seat in Lemberg (Lvov); and "Vollin," seat in Ostrog (Vladimir).

Then Polish Queen Jadwiga married the Lithuanian Great Duke Jegello, thus establishing the Jagello Dynasty in Poland, eventually becoming the Polish-Lithuanian Union (and the conversion of pagan Lithuania to Christianity). Lithuania followed

---

3. Rabbi Kalmanowitz is well-known as the founder of the Mirrer Yeshiva in Brooklyn after World War II.

the Polish example, granting the autonomy to its Jewish communities: A committee of five lands was established, representing the *kehillos* of "Brisk," "Vilno," "Grodno," "Pinsk" and "Slutsk." Hence Grodno and Tiktin were for the first time paying taxes to the same king, resulting in friction between the two communities.

In those days, individual taxes were unknown. The *kehillah* collected taxes from member-families and paid a lump-sum tax to the king. The more member-families, and the more communities in a province, the lighter the individual tax load. Grodno wanted Tiktin to belong to her "land" as part of its tax-base. But Tiktin had developed spiritually and financially, and was invited to be part of the Committee of Four of Poland proper. Rivalry increased between Tiktin and Grodno over four smaller *kehillos* located between the two communities, each one claiming them for herself.

Representatives of all these "lands" and their representative rabbinates would convene at the yearly *yarid* (international fair) where they drafted *takanos* (ordinances) for all member lands, and major *din Torahs* (disputes) would be adjudicated. The dispute of Tiktin vs. Grodno was brought to the annual *yarid* and the decision was in favor of Tiktin. Grodno bickered and hesitated in accepting the *psak*, but the threat of *cherem* was enough to force the issue. Thus, Tiktin became recognized as a major *kehillah* in Poland.

◄§ The Psak of Reb Chaim of Stuchin

One of the Committee of Four Lands' *takanos* limited a local Rav to deciding on *din Torahs* not exceeding 500 gulden. A case of greater magnitude was to be brought before the district *bais din*. A *kehillah* was founded in Stuchin (in the Tiktin district) by Rabbi Chaim Shenberg. A recognized *talmid chacham* and wealthy businessman, he served temporarily as Rav of Stuchin. Reb Chaim once decided a *din Torah* of 800 gulden and was immediately summoned before the *bais din* of Tiktin, to explain his breach of conduct. Reb Chaim justified his actions as follows: "The judiciary in *Klal Yisrael* was organized on the advice of Yisro, Moshe Rabbeinu's father-in-law. Notice, Yisro advised 'They shall bring every *great* matter to you, and every *small* case they should judge themselves.' However, Moshe Rabbeinu ordered, 'Every *difficult* case be brought to me.' Why the change from *big* to *difficult*? Yisro had planned that Moshe's *psak-gelt* (legal fee), based on percentage, should yield him more money. However, Moshe Rabbeinu's concern was elsewhere. He knew that the same legal principle applies to a penny as to a hundred gulden. The amount at stake does not make *psak* difficult, it is the *halachah* (legal principle) that can be formidable."

"I," concluded Reb Chaim, "concur with Moshe Rabbeinu."

ⰶ The Shul

Tiktin offered many places for *tefillah*. Every *chevrah* had its own *bais hamidrash* — for Torah study and prayer. In addition to the *Chevrah Shas*, which met in the big *bais hamidrash*, Tiktin had a *Chevrah Mishnayos*, *Chevrah Chumash*, *Tehillim*, *Chayei Adam* (later switching to *Mishnah Berurah*). Even the butchers had their own *minyan*, called *Zovchai Zevach* where a rabbi would teach *Ein Yaakov* every day. But the crown of the city was the 400 year old *shul*, one of the oldest in Poland.

It was a huge building, shaped like a fortress, with a long spiral staircase leading to a roof-top turret for scouting approaching enemies. Entering the *shul*, one had to descend three steps, corresponding to the words: ממעמקים קראתיך ה׳ "From the depth I called to You, O G-d!" Four more steps led to the *amud* — totaling seven, representing the seven letters of the word ממעמקים. The *shul* had a brick floor surrounded by white walls, covered with various *tefillos* and verses from *Tehillim*. Next to the entrance, the wall had a wide slit covered with iron bars, which was the opening for the *tzeddakah* box. Over it was posted a poem by the Ibn Ezra:

אדם דואג על איבוד דמיו,
ואינו דואג על איבוד ימיו.
דמיו אינן עוזרין לו,
ימיו אינן חוזרין לו.
צדקה תציל ממות!

A person frets over the loss of his money,
But does not fret over the loss of his days.
Yet, his money will not help him,
And his days will not return to him.
Charity redeems from death!

Came winter, no one *davened* in the huge central hall, for it would have been impossible to heat up. The front room, called "the *polush*," had entrances to smaller rooms that were a beehive of activity. One led to the *vaibersher shul* (ladies' section), which had small curtained windows looking out into the *maariv* (Western) side of the *Shul.* A small room to the side, furnished with a low bench and a leather strap, was used only on *Erev Yom Kippur.* In earlier times, when the *bais din* sentenced offenders to *malkos* (flogging), the *shamash* would execute the *psak* in that room, using the leather strap. In our days, people would come there voluntarily before the *Erev Yom Kippur Minchah* to perform symbolic *malkos,* saying *Vidui* (the confessional prayer).

The *mizrach* wall contained *kameyos* (scrolls containing mystical inscriptions) built in by various *tzaddikim.* One *kameya* was placed above the huge *aron hakodesh* by the *Maharsha* when he was Rav in Tiktin. Many miracles recorded in the official records *(Pinkes Tiktin)* are credited to those *kameyos.* Among them: A huge bronze chandelier, branching out with a hundred candle-holders, hung from the center of the ceiling. One *Kol Nidre* night, when the *shul* was packed to capacity, the chain snapped and the chandelier crashed down — yet, no one was hurt!

The city of Tiktin — strategically located on the River Narew, crossed by important bridges — was a battleground in numerous wars. Since the *shul's* extraordinary thick walls provided protection during the attacks, the *shul* served as a shelter for the Jewish population. During World War I, the Bolsheviks attacked Tiktin with a heavy artillery barrage from across the river. While the Jews said *Tehillim* before the open *aron hakodesh,* a number of shells hit the *mizrach* wall. The Torah scrolls shook as in an earthquake, but not one shell penetrated the walls! The many cavities on the outside of the *mizrach* wall remained as a remembrance of these miracles; throughout all the renovations and exterior paintings that were performed, the holes were left as they were. From the window in my grandfather's house facing the *shul,* I would often gaze at the amazing holes in the *mizrach* wall.

❧ Governing the Kehillah

Although the Jews lived for generations under the tyranny and the absolute rule of the Russian Czars, and later under the semi-fascist government of Poland, democracy reigned within the Jewish community.

Annual community elections were held every *Chol HaMoed Pesach* for a *Rosh Hakahal* (president of the community) and a number of *parneisim* (councilmen). They were charged with directing the *kehillah's* affairs as well as representing the community to the outside authorities. Selecting a Rav was another matter. A committee of *talmidei chachamim* travelled to all corners of the land, interviewing and *reden in lernen* (discussing Talmudic subjects) with the candidates, and then made their decision... (The elections of a rav described by law of the Polish fascist government, insisting on "democracy" among the Jews, was merely a formality.)

The *kehillah* would determine the Rav's salary according to the size of his family. In addition, he was provided with a spacious apartment equipped with a *bais din shtub* (hearing room for litigations) — rent free. The *kehillah* budget was funded by a family head-tax and a *shechitah* tax, sufficient to pay the Rav, *dayan*, *shochtim* and *chazzanim*, plus funds for various charitable activities. In Eastern Europe, it was customary to supplement the *rav's* income with *G-Z-E-I-L-A-H!* That is, certain items could only be purchased from the Rebbitzin. "*Gimmel*" for *gazze* (kerosene), for their lamps; "*Zayin*" for zaltz — salt, a staple in every home; "*Yud*" for *yayin* — wine; "*Lamed*" for *licht* — Shabbos candles; "*Hey*" for *heivin* — yeast, a must for home-baking. For centuries, no one ever dared to invade this franchise. Different communities selected different items to reserve for the Rav. For instance in Tiktin, only yeast was franchised to the Rav. Most *Rebbitzins* would subrent their monopoly to one or two grocery stores for a fee.

Hence the popular joke: "A Rav lives from *g'zeilah* (literally, 'robbery')."

⋅§ Recent Events: World War One

□ *And where was Dinah? Yaakov hid her in a chest ... lest Eisav cast his eyes upon her — Rashi to Bereishis 32:23.*

During wartime, when cities and villages often changed hands, Jewish girls would hide in their attics or basements. Not until the fighting front-line-troops passed or martial law was established would a Jewish girl dare to show her face in the streets. Because of this guarded behavior, many an army suspected the Jewish community of being hostile.

During World War I, my grandfather Reb Shmuel Leib — called *Panie* (Sir) Shmulke by the non-Jews — was *Rosh Hakahal*. The Czar's general mobilized civilians to dig trenches, so my grandfather pleaded with the Commanding General to free the Jews from digging on Shabbos, offering Sunday instead. The arrogant Russian officer had him arrested at once, for interfering with the war effort, to be tried by the military. His many Polish and Russian friends organized a delegation to assure the general of his patriotism, honesty and religious devotion, and thus saved their "beloved Shmulke."

The Russian army retreated and Germans occupied the town. In those days, the Germans were better educated and considered more humane than Russians or Poles. However, they had two major problems, communication and provisions, and these drove them to extremes. The further East they penetrated, the less they could communicate with the local population, except for the Jews who were able to make do with Yiddish. As for food supplies, Germany imported food during peacetime; during the war the army was all the more dependent on local sources.

When the Germans occupied Tiktin, the first order was to rebuild the bridges over the Narew River, destroyed by the retreating Russians. Again *Zeide*, who spoke German fairly well, went to the German commandant to plead for the Jews that Sunday be substituted for Shabbos. He even offered a number of Jews to serve as translators on Shabbos, but not to labor. The German officer, although polite and less arrogant than the Russian general, had refused the exchange and ordered *Zeide* arrested. No charges were specified, but he spent two days and nights in a military prison. No one was left to intervene, so the Jews resorted to their last line of defense and said *Tehillim*. While the heart-rending sound of the prayers poured through the open windows of the *shul*, two German Jewish officers passed by and inquired as to the cause. Then they went to the commandant who had Grandfather released.

A few days later, the German Commandant summoned *Zeide* into his office, demanding that the Jewish community supply food for his men. *Zeide* explained that city-folk do not grow food. Farmers no longer gave them credit because the currency was worthless; as a result supplies diminished, and the people themselves went hungry. When the German nodded his head, *Zeide* thought the case closed, only to discover otherwise the following day — Friday.

An elderly Jew was arrested while checking the *eruv* (a wire enclosing the city to make carrying permissible on Shabbos), charged with espionage: supplying the enemy information through the *eruv* wires! The Commandant set the hour of execution for 10 a.m. Saturday. The town was in shock, the ridiculous charge was obviously trumped up to pressure the community into delivering food supplies to the army — but how could they do so?

Again *Zeide* appealed to the Commandant: "You *will kill* an innocent man and food will still not be forthcoming. That deaf old man is as much a spy as I am!" *Zeide* then asked permission to leave.

The German, realizing the Jews would be more responsive if the life of their leader were in danger, turned to *Zeide* in anger: "You have just confessed to spying! You are under arrest!" He then sent the old prisoner home, and advised him to let the family of "Herren Shapiro" know that he'd be shot the next morning at ten. The whole town was in a turmoil, and again people gathered in every *shul* to say *Tehillim*.

My grandmother, known variously as "Feigel the business-woman" or "Faigel the *tzaddeikes*," had her own special methods of reaching Heaven in an emergency. There was no time at all for niceties, for she had to act swiftly.

She entered the big *bais hamidrash*, shocking the men saying *Tehillim*. She took *Zeide's Gemara* and placed it inside the *aron hakodesh*. Then, burying her face in the *sefer Torah*, she sobbingly prayed that in the *zechus* of his learning Torah, of his *gemilas chessed*, and of his children and grandchildren who studied Torah, her plan would succeed.

Without a word to anyone she marched off to the Commandant's office where, as the wife of the prisoner, she was admitted. Casually she explained that she had a house full of hungry children, and that when she had been on the way to her favorite farmer-friend to get some supplies, she heard of her husband's arrest, so she came immediately. Her pained heart sent off a prayer to Heaven that the officer should swallow her bait. He turned to her with a conniving smile: "*Ach so, Frau Shapiro*, you have hungry children to care for. You must not wait. Go at once. When you will return home, your husband will be there waiting for you."

She walked out pretending to be unaware that she was being followed, all the while praying and saying *Tehillim*, until she reached the house of Jan Syzmanski in the outskirts of Tiktin. Mr. Szymanski, the most vicious Jew-hater in town, who prided himself that no Jew ever crossed the threshold of his house, owned a big farm and a large house. *Bobbe* Faigel walked up to his front gate, opened it halfway, and then turned around suddenly. "Discovering" the sergeant and the two armed soldiers, she quickly closed the gate and continued along the dusty farm road. A deep sigh went up to Heaven that they, too, should swallow her bait — and they did. They would not be misled by that stupid old Jewess who did not want them to know who her supplier was. Running through the fields and side streets, she made it home where she found *Zeide* waiting for her.

No one ever knew the amount of food confiscated from Szymanski, but for the next six months he was in bed recuperating from the terrible beating from the German soldiers. When he finally appeared in the streets, supported by two crutches, the Jewish citizens could not suppress their smiles. And my grandmother gained yet another title — "Faigel the *Chachamah* (the wise woman)."

◆§ Rosh Hakahal and Mayor

Since Tiktin was 75% Jewish, it could have elected a Jewish mayor. But the anti-Semitic Polish Government gerrymandered the districts in Tiktin to include neighboring villages, ensuring that a Pole always be elected. In my time, however, the vice-mayor was Jewish — Reb Yisroel Cohn, a *talmid chacham* and a well-to-do businessman who also was a great *anav* (humble person). Everyone called him "Srolki Kadishes" since his father's name was Kadish. No sooner was Srolki elected *Rosh Hakahal*, but the Polish Mayor became ill and died and Srolki Kadishes succeeded him as Mayor; and he wore both crowns with characteristic humility and dignity. One might expect the two independent positions to overlap or conflict, but he kept them independent of each other, as the following incident illustrates:

One summer, on the way home from Baranovitch (where I was studying in Rabbi Elchanan Wasserman's Yeshiva), I stopped off at Tiktin to see my uncle Reb Shlomo Pines who was a *parnes* in the *kehillah*. Uncle Shlomo was on the way to a meeting of the *Kehilla board* in the *bais din shtub* and he invited me to come along "so you could talk to the Rav, Rabbi Kalmanowitz." When I had been learning in the yeshiva in Tiktin, the entire class would report to the Rav for oral examination. The Rav would begin by asking a few questions, then the *Rosh Yeshiva* in him would take over and the *bechinah* (exam) would turn into a *shiur* (lecture). But now I was all by myself, and petrified.

While the meeting was taking place in the *bais din shtub*, I was in the next room, preparing myself. After the meeting adjourned, the Rav entered my room in all his splendor: tall, erect in a colorful silk house coat. His pointy *yarmulka*, plus the knee-high boots shining to a glow, with the pants tucked in them, all

added to his height. Combing his long gray beard with his fing
he said: "Chaim'ke come here! You're learning *Tagrei Lud* (a very
complicated subject), eh?" He then inquired about Reb Elchanan
Wasserman, my father, and the family. Before closing the door,
he called out to the *shamash*, "Go to the *Magistrat* (City Hall) and
tell the mayor that if he doesn't send in the rent by Friday, I shall
have the community school evicted."[4] The *Rebbitzen* called out
from the next room, "Srolki Kadishes was just here. The Rav
couldn't tell him that in person?"

With authority in his voice, the Rav replied, "When Reb
Yisroel Cohn is in my *bais din shtub*, or in the *bais hamidrash*, or
in the streets of Tiktin, he is the *Rosh Hakahal*. Only when he is
in the *Magistrat* is he the mayor."

◆§ "Yachsonim" and "Vertlach"

Many cities in Poland had nicknames, which give a fairly accurate reflection of its inhabitants. Here are a few examples: Warsaw's *"Varshever Ganovim,"*[5] Lomza's *"Lomzer Balonim,"*
"Kolner Peklach," "Bialystoker Kuchns" ... and Tiktin's
"Tiktiner Yachsonim," for almost every one in Tiktin considered
himself a *yachson* (of an aristocratic lineage). Yet they seldom in-
termarried, for they knew too well the other's *yichus* and it was
always below theirs.... When asked after an out-of-town marriage how they managed to assess an outsider's *yichus*, they
would reply: "The Jews made the Golden Calf — why? Because
they presumed Moshe to be dead. So what? They could still have
chosen a leader like Aharon, Chur or Koleiv. Why settle for a
calf? But they felt — let it be a calf as long as it comes from
the outside."

◆§ Getting Married in Tiktin

In Tiktin, every *chupah* took place on Friday in the backyard
of the *shul*. After the *chupah*, the procession would dance to
music through the streets to the house of my Uncle Shlomo. His
living room was the largest in the entire town and was always

---

4. In Poland, elementary local education was obligatory (grades 1 to 7, ages 7-14). The city
government was required to furnish a building and pay for the teachers. In Tiktin, the
Jewish children would not attend school together with non-Jewish children. The *kehillah* owned a school building, for which city hall paid rent and teachers' salaries.

5. Warsaw was famous for its flim-flam operators and pick-pockets. A Lomzer was called
a *ba'alon* (shopper) because he was always interested in buying anything. The round,
flat *kuchens* called "bialys," so popular in New York's Lower East Side, originated in
Bialystok.

available for the reception-*kiddush*. Big receptions and large dinners were strictly forbidden. On Shabbos morning, the *chassan* and *kallah* walked to *shul* together, and then after *davening*, followed by a dancing crowd, they went to the *kallah's* parents for *kiddush*. Once a poor widow sold her last pillow in order to cover the costs of the morning *kiddush*. When the Rav heard about this, he enforced a new *takana* (ordinance): only the immediate family members were permitted to participate in that *kiddush*. Such *takanos* were strictly upheld. Thus, much to the amazement of visitors, the parents of the *kallah* stood in the doorway greeting all well-wishers, responding to their *Mazel Tov's* with an invitation: "Come in, you are one of the family." Yet, no one would enter.

◄§ Chevros

A boundless love for one another thrived among the Jews in Tiktin. This found expression in both personal relationships and institutional life. Thus, there were numerous charitable *chevros*, where besides paying dues, the members donated their services. In addition, a special *Shabbos* every year was dedicated in all *shuls* to appeals for funds for each *chevrah*. *Someich Noflim* (Support for the Fallen), the fund which secretly aided families in need, had their *Shabbos* when *Behar* was read, which included the passage: "And when your brother falls...you shall surely help him" (*Vayikra*: 25:35). *Linas Hatzedek* and *Bikkur Cholim* (Helping the Sick) had *Beshalach*, which includes: "I am the L-rd your Healer" (*Shemos* 17:25). The functions of these two were clearly defined: *Linas Hatzedek* would provide all types of medical equipment and drugs. In those days of primitive medicine, ice was a major cure. It would be placed on the ill person continuously, until the crisis was over and the temperature dropped. The members would volunteer in winters to cut the river ice, which was stored in specially equipped cellars for the entire year. The members of *Bikkur Cholim* volunteered to care for the sick overnight while the family rested, cooked for the family, and fed the children.

In addition, there were *Shabbosos* for the Talmud Torah, the yeshiva, Bais Yaakov, *Hachnosas Orchim* (Traveler's Aid), *Hachnasas Kallah* (Financial Aid for the Poor Brides), and of course, *Hekdesh*. The *Hekdesh* served as a shelter for the indigent, the elderly, and the incurably ill.

One should bear in mind that Tiktin's Jews supported all

these charities in the days when the term "tax deductible" was not yet known.

❧ Personalities

Telling of Tiktin without mentioning some of her outstanding personalities would be a sin, indeed! Each one was an institution, and besides being of interest on their own, shed light on Tiktin as a whole. Among them were:

□ Srolki Kadishes (whom we have met earlier), a successful business man and *talmid chacham* who had studied in the Yeshiva of Volozhin. He had served as both *Rosh Hakahal* and Mayor. When the Chofetz Chaim visited Tiktin and urged everyone, especially the *Kohanim*, to study *Kadashim* (the section of Talmud which deals with sacrificial order) in anticipation of *Mashiach's* coming, Srolki Cohn and my *Zeide* (both *Kohanim*) convened a daily two-hour session before *davening*, dedicated to studying *Kadashim*. Srolki always carried large sums of money with him, stopping boys at random, asking: "Show me your *tzitzis*," or "What is the *Omer* count today?" A positive reply would earn a handsome cash reward.

□ Reb Yanke'le Levinsohn, a *tzaddik* and *ba'al mofes* (miracle worker), had undertaken to support Torah students and scholars in need. Once Reb Yanke'le approached two childless well-to-do families in Tiktin. "Last night I dreamed about a baby in a cradle. Give me one thousand rubles (a fortune in those days) for the yeshiva, and I guarantee that you shall have a child." One family rejected the offer, the other accepted. Exactly one year later a boy was born to the second family.

□ Rabbi Yerucham Barash was the town wine maker, but no one knew when he made the wine, for most of the time he was in the *bais hamidrash* with two fingers stuck in his ears so as not to be distracted from his studies. When the government declared a monopoly on all alcoholic beverages, he was arrested and convicted to a one-year prison sentence. In jail he went through *Shas* twice. After his release, he commented, "Every Jew must serve in jail once in his life. One year is not enough — at least, two, preferably three ..."

□ In a town full of *yachsonim*, my grandfather Reb Shmuel Leib Shapiro was the *yachson* of them all. He spelled his name with a *shva* under the *Shin*, not a *pasach* — which, according to tradition, was a sign of a true *Kohen*. He studied in the Chofetz Chaim's *Kollel Kadashim* and knew *Kadashim* by heart. As a successful businessman, he would often return to Tiktin from a trip late at night, never going home, but straight to the *bais hamidrash* to study until *Shacharis*, the next morning. While the Jews referred to him as "the *Pike'ach*," for he was extremely wise, the non-Jews called him "*Panie* (Sir) *Shmulke*," for he knew the civil and criminal law as well as their own judges. Before standing trial, they would often come to him for advice.

He was frequently involved in court cases with Polish land owners, hardly ever losing a case. As the District Court was located in Lomza, he was a frequent visitor in our house. Rabbi Yechiel Mordechai Gordon, Rosh Yeshiva in Lomza, once told me, "When your *Zeide* arrived in town, I knew he was occupied in court. Yet he always found time to come and visit me and ask a few *kushyos* that would take me a month to answer."

Rabbi Ravich of the Tel Aviv *bais din* told me, "Your *Zeide's* place of study was behind the *bima*. Once when he walked away for a few minutes, some pranksters turned his *Gemara* upside-down. When he returned, he continued studying out loud for three hours without straightening the *Gemara*. We then realized that he had become blind in his old age."

☐ The last *Rosh Hakahal* of Tiktin, my uncle Reb Shlomo Pines,[6] was a *talmid chacham*, businessman and a *Lavnik* (member of the executive of the city council) — a most honest man, trusted by Jew and Gentile alike. When the Jewish merchants opened their first commercial bank, they did not have a safe to store the cash on hand, so it was delivered daily to Reb Shlomo. Every merchant eagerly awaited Friday, the market day. Reb Shlomo, however, donated his living room for every wedding reception, which usually took place on Friday. Neglecting his own business, he personally welcomed the wedding party to his home. When the Tiktiner Societies of New York and Chicago sent funds for the poor twice yearly (*ma'os chittim* before Pesach, and money to buy firewood and potatoes for the winter, before Succos), the checks

6. His youngest daughter, Menucha, wanted desperately to enter the Seminary in Cracow, but she was only twelve and the minimum acceptance age was fourteen. When he refused to falsify her age and told her to wait two more years, she complained to our *Zeide*. *Zeide* went down to City Hall, ordered a new "birth certificate" written to specification, and she was accepted. When she graduated, Sara Sheneirer sent her to Frampol (near Lublin) to open a Bais Yaakov school. How could a mere fifteen year old impress a community and its Rav, and win its children? A tall girl, she put on heels and fixed her hair in a mature fashion, and succeeded. She was then dispatched to Chelm to strengthen the Bais Yaakov there, and later to Sokolov. She returned to the Seminary every summer for more courses, given by Dr. Deutschlander. In 1940, she escaped to Jerusalem where she taught in Bais Yaakov.

were addressed to him and made out in his name.

□ Zir'l Lisansky, the midwife who delivered all babies, also the *gabbai'te* of the local *Chevrah Kaddisha* (burial society). People said: "She brings them to this world and she returns them." A midwife possessed special status in town — since the time the author of the *Sefer Ma'aros Hatzovos* served as Rav in Tiktin. When he had found an increase in the number of halachic queries in *she'eilos nashim* especially after confinement, he dismissed the midwife serving Tiktin and imported a replacement from Germany. Ever since, a midwife in Tiktin was professionally trained and skilled, and no obstetrician could ever get established in Tiktin.

□ Beile Dvora Shulman was the wife of Reb Simcha Shmuel Shulman, who had received *semichah* (ordination) from the *Aruch HaShulchan* (Rabbi Yechiel Michel Epstein), beginning with the words: שמחה במעונו ושמואל בקוראי שמו. Yet he refused to accept a rabbinical position, and became a manufacturer. After he died at forty, his young widow dedicated the rest of her life to raising her eight sons and one daughter to a life of Torah. In spite of all sorts of difficulties, she realized her goal: Some learned in the Lomza Yeshiva (they ate Shabbos and *Yom Tov* meals in our house for years), some in Slobodke, some in Kamenetz. One of them, Reb Mordechai, married the daughter of Rabbi Isaac Sher of Slobodka, and became Rosh Yeshiva in the Yeshiva Slobodka in Bnai Brak, Israel.

□ My grandmother Faigel was a millionaire in *mitzvos*. Every morning, she was ever consulting the clock, for she knew the exact minute when she could catch a *Kedusha* in the *Chevra Chumash Bais Hamidrash*, a *Borchu* in *Chevrah Mishnayos*, an *Omein-Yehei Shmei Rabbah* in *Chevrah Tehillim*. By the time she opened her store at 8 AM, she already had a stock of *mitzvos* that would take someone else a month to accumulate. She ran the business to permit *Zeide* to spend more time in the *bais hamidrash*. While she was active in all charities, her pet project was the *Hekdesh*, where she was *gabbai'te*.

She had strange kabbalistic ways for meeting all emergencies. When my father was a little boy, he became very ill and the doctors gave up on him; yet, she knew exactly what to do. First, she went to the cemetery and measured the entire length of its fence. She donated the same length of linen to the *Hekdesh*, which she made into sheets and pillow cases. *Shuls* and *yeshivos* recited *Tehillim* on his behalf, and he was given the additional name of "Alter" to signify that he should live to a ripe, old age. She vowed to give a year's supply of meat for Shabbos and *Yom Tov* to the *Hekdesh* in his merit ... To the shock of the local doctors, the boy recuperated. Previously, the boy was considered to have a *grobbe kop* (to be thick-headed), for his *Rebbe* could scarcely teach him the *Aleph-Bais*, but after his illness he developed into a near-genius. He went on to study in Radin, then to Slobodke where he learned *be'chavrusa* (in partnership) with Rabbi Reuvain Grozovsky. He became a *talmid* of the *Alter* of Slobodka who sent him later with Reb Reuvain and eight others to save the yeshiva in Mir. There he became a *talmid muvhok* (prime disciple) of Reb Yerucham Levovitz.

Rabbi Avraham Kalmanowitz in his *hesped* (eulogy) on Tiktin writes ... "When I arrived in Tiktin I met *ba'alei battim* (laymen) who knew a number of *mesechtos* in *Shas* literally by heart. Just to mention a few: Reb Shmuel Leib Shapiro, his son Alter, and all his sons-in-law; Reb Berl Glickman, a relative of the *Sfas Emes*; and Reb Naftoli, my father-in-law ... "

The True Lomza

remembering Lomza, Poland before its destruction in World War II — and a commemorative volume that violates the truth

The Last Rav of Lomza
Rabbi Moshe Shatzkes זצ״ל

THE *ZOHAR* says that even a *Sefer Torah* must have *mazal* — in some we read often, in others only on *Simchas Torah*. It should be no surprise, then, that European communities also fared according to their individual *mazal*. Some will never be remembered, while others will find their way into the awareness of posterity as Jewish centers of Europe, if they are memorialized in a *Yizkor Book*. Over 500 such books have already been published. Most are in Yiddish, others in Hebrew or a combination of both; some even include English in their text.

They usually begin with a historical background: when, where and how the city was founded; when and why Jews settled there; followed by chapters about the rabbis who served there through the years: their biographies, their greatness in Torah (that chapter, it seems, is the pride of every town, and the book lingers over every detail). Then follow institutions of learning, the spiritual centers of the town — the *batei midrashim*, associations, charity societies. On to the economic pictures — types of work, political parties, vignettes about personalities, groups, or a profile of the entire city. The final chapter is always the same: the destruction of the Jewish community, and stories of survivors.

The purpose of all these books is certainly not for the survivors; rather it is for posterity, for future historians that they are written. So we ask: do these books really give us a true picture of their cities? Or do the editors sometimes bend the truth in order to grind their own ideological axes? Churchill once said, "History will be good to me, because I will write it." — Are these histories only good to their historians? I can not evaluate a book dedicated to a city I have never even visited. But there are three books that I can discuss with some knowledge; they immortalize my two hometowns, Tiktin and Lomza. *Sefer Tiktin* published in Hebrew (Tel Aviv, 1959), *Sefer Zikaron Lekehillas Lomza* in Hebrew (Tel Aviv, 1952), and *Lomza* in Yiddish (N.Y. 1957).

◄§ The Lomza Distinction

Sefer Tiktin (606 pages) is the pride of my library. To my great sorrow, I can not say the same about the two books on Lomza. Neither the 371 double pages of the one nor the 377 pages of the other give a true picture of my town.

Certainly credit is due to the editor, Dr. Yom Tov Levinski, for a superior technical job. The detail and organization of historical material in Yiddish, Hebrew, and Polish shows painstaking research, with limited materials available.

Everything, indeed, did seem faithful to my Lomza until I came to page 120, where suddenly the truth took an unexpected twist. After an excellent description of the last and most beloved rabbi of Lomza, the Gaon Rabbi Moshe Shatzkes (later Rosh Yeshiva in Yeshivas Rabbi Yitzchak Elchonon in New York), the editor adds the following comments: "With the outbreak of the Second World War, the Rabbi forsook his flock and escaped to Vilna, his birthplace ... His escape in such hard times was a great blow to the Jewish community. Often they complained 'We have no rabbi; no leader; we are lost!' "

A few paragraphs later: "When Rabbi Shatzkes left Lomza, the community was left like sheep without a shepherd. With a heartbreaking sigh, they would tell of Rabbi Yehuda Leib Gordon who risked his life many times under the Czars. They remembered their Rabbi, Elya Chaim Meisels, who was constantly concerned that no Jew be drafted into the Czar's army. Now there is no one to help."

Now let us look at the facts: In 1939, the Germans (far more deadly than any of the Czars!) bombarded Lomza mercilessly because it was the first major city near the East Prussian border.

The inhabitants left town and spread out through the surrounding villages and fields. When the German army came, they found all the Jews in the fields. They placed machine guns around a field full of people and shouted orders to keep their faces to the ground. Then they started shooting over their heads. Several people raised their heads only inches, and were killed. Then the Germans tied the rabbi to a tree, and aimed a machine gun straight at him. A Jewish refugee who had been an officer in the Kaiser's army pleaded with the German officer to spare the rabbi's life. The German officer pulled out half of the rabbi's beard, relishing his painful screams, and then he released him.

With the Stalin-Hitler pact on the division of Poland, no one expected Lomza to be transferred into Russian hands, since it was so close to the East Prussian border. Yet on *Hoshana Rabbah*, the Soviet tanks rolled into town. The first worry on everyone's mind was the welfare of the Rav. A spellbinding orator, he had often condemned the Communists from the pulpit. The older generation knew the Bolshevik's policy of keeping records on every personality — with their men in every town and village, it was no difficult feat for them.[1] So the community leaders pleaded with Rabbi Shatzkes to hide, or if possible to escape, before he would be arrested ... And these "historians" have the audacity to criticize him!

◁§ Saved from Bombardment

In the heavy bombardment, three quarters of the city was destroyed, including our home and business, but the impressive buildings housing the Yeshiva and the Talmud Torah were unharmed. The Rosh Yeshiva's house, located next to the Yeshiva and across from the Talmud Torah, was also undamaged. So my family and those of my two uncles moved in. (The Rosh Yeshiva, Rabbi Yechiel Michel Gordon, was in New York at that time.) The Talmud Torah housed ten grades, 500 children learning *Aleph-Bais* on up to those studying *Gemara* independently. The entire third floor was assigned by the *kehillah* to the Rabbi for his personal use: a *bais din shtub* (rabbinical court and receiving room), library, and a spacious apartment for his family.

The Bolsheviks immediately confiscated the building for use

---

1. When the Rosh Yeshiva of Kamenitz, Rabbi Reuvain Grozovsky applied for an exit visa in Vilna, the Bolsheviks showed him their dossier on him, listing all his activities since he left Minsk from the time of the Bolshevik revolution. The same with Rabbi Aharon Kotler.

as a public school. And we watched helplessly as the children were indoctrinated in Soviet ideology.

Once, a delegation of local dignitaries accompanied by the Commissar for Education of the White Russian Republic (from Minsk) visited the school. (Lomza was incorporated into White Russia; a Commissar is the counterpart of the Secretary of Education in the U.S.) In the class of my little brother Shimonke, then age ten, the Commissar took out a kaiser-roll[2] from a bag and presented it to my brother. The child hesitated for a moment but the Commissar insisted *"Vozme sinnok, pokushay"* ("Take it child, eat"). The boy took the roll, put on his cap, and said the *brachah* in front of the Bolshevik delegation, and half the class answered *Omein*.

The principal and the teacher turned white; the Commissar turned red. He grabbed the roll out of the child's mouth and screamed: "What did you say? What language was it? Not Yiddish?" The boy replied. "It's a blessing in Hebrew: Jews give thanks to G-d before they eat anything."

The Commissar shouted further: "Stalin sent you that roll, not G-d! Did you ever see G-d? *Chapukha!* (nonsense) There is no G-d! Stalin,the father of all labor people, the sunshine of the world — he gave you that roll!"

He then turned to the faculty: "Is that how you raise Soviet children? Religion instead of Marxism, Leninism and Stalinism? Whose hand is involved in this? Tell me and I'll cut it right off!"

The principal replied, "We know whose hand is involved in it — that cleric who used to live upstairs. If we could only get hold of him, we would take care of him ourselves, but he escaped to Vilna."

That same day, my father — fearing arrest — took off for Bialystok until things would blow over. As the news hit town, every Jew raised his eyes to Heaven: "Thank G-d our beloved rabbi is in Vilna!" And now these learned men, safe and secure in Tel Aviv and New York, criticize our beloved rabbi for forsaking his flock!

◆§ The Party Paragraphs

I turn more pages ... So many familiar faces, photos and names — apt descriptions of places and events I knew — it breaks

---

2. In poverty-stricken USSR, white bread or rolls was eaten only on holidays. In Poland, we would eat white bread and rolls every day, and *challah* every Shabbos. But to a Commissar in those days, a kaiser-roll was a big prize.

my heart. So many institutions of learning and charity. Only 12,000 Jews out of a general population of 30,000, and look at what they had accomplished in spite of being surrounded by anti-Semites! In spite of meager means, they accomplished more than the Poles did, in every field of community life — an achievement unrivaled by any other people.

I read the chapter on *chinuch* and education, and not a word on the Bais Yaakov school for girls (organized by my aunt Chana Shapiro).

I reached the chapter titled *"Miflagot"* (p. 215: political parties; in the Yiddish edition — *"Partayen"* p. 145). Living — rather, existing — in a hostile environment is difficult. The government made it official policy to shut out Jews from every source of livelihood, telling them to emigrate. But where to? Palestine was closed by the British; America had a quota system and a waiting list of years; and the rest of the world, totally closed. Government jobs were closed to Jews. There was not one single Jewish mailman, policeman, or janitor in all of Poland. There was indeed one way to obtain a government job — by converting to Roman Catholicism. In spite of poverty, there were no applicants.

In response, a variety of political parties was born within the Jewish community, each with its own program of how to help the people. The party-spectrum ranged as follows: (1) Agudath Israel, (2) Mizrachi (Religious Zionists), (3) General Zionists (Chaim Weizmann's group — in Israel today, they form part of the Likud); (4) Zionist-Revisionists (Jabotinsky's party, which gave birth to the Irgun — Jabotinsky's best known disciple is Menachem Begin); (5) Poalei Zion (Labor Zionists who combine Zionism with Socialism — their Israeli counterpart is the Mapam); (6) The Bund (anti-religious, anti-Zionist — they wanted to build a better society with pure socialism, uniting with proletarians of all nations. As for the Jews, they naively sought to build a Jewish autonomous society, based on Yiddish language and Yiddish culture — such as the tales of Sholom Aleichem and the history of Shimon Dubnow); (7) Communists (dialectical-Marxists, split into two factions: Trotskyites and Stalinists. As for the Jews, they envisioned a Jewish socialist culture where they would assimilate into the local population and live happily ever after. They hated religion as "the opiate of the masses," and Zionism as a fascist-nationalism for Jews). The Communist party made strides among the naive youth. They represented the USSR, as a heaven for Jews: no discrimination, neither rich nor poor classes, free education; heaven, indeed, in comparison to the bitter reality of anti-Semitic Poland.

Now let us examine how the party spectrum is recorded for posterity and history in *Lomza:* Agudath Israel fared with exactly twenty and one half lines; 162 words (in the Hebrew text, 29 lines). The Mizrachi did a little better with three-quarters of a page, plus six photos of its youth organization, Hashomer Hadati, forerunner of Bnei Akiva. General Zionists got eight pages plus fourteen photos. Zionist-Revisionists — twenty-three lines plus one picture. Poalei Zion (Labor Zionists) — fifteen pages plus twenty pictures. Bund — twelve pages plus fifteen photos (in the Yiddish book, twenty pages plus the pictures). The Communists got four pages and three pictures.

Is this my hometown? I don't recognize it! Was this deliberate falsification or simply lack of material? And look who writes an article on the Socialist Zionists: a familiar face — how can I forget him? He was a part-time geography teacher in Talmud Torah. Then one day he didn't show up for class. Rumors had it that he skipped town, charged with a crime unheard of among Jews, namely, sexual assault. Somehow he made it to *Eretz Yisrael* — and now his photo is decorating this book!

⇜§ The Lomza Party Structure — As It Was

The Jewish community was organized in a *kehillah,* which supervised every phase of communal life and represented the Jews before their neighbors and the government. The board was elected in democratic, secret-ballot elections. The thirteen members of the board (each one was called a *Dozor* or *Parnes)* elected a president called the *Rosh Hakahal.* The Agudah and Mizrachi always formed a united religious block for the election, winning a majority with ten members.[3] By agreement, the two would alternate the presidency. At no time ever was there a *Rosh Hakahal* from any other party. In fact, the very last *Rosh Hakahal* was Reb Mendl Kalinski (Agudah) — a soap maufacturer, a Gerrer Chassid who dressed in Chassidic cap, beard, and *kapota.*

And Agudath Israel was recorded in the book with twenty lines!

Before the Germans organized a *Judenrat,* the *kehillah* still

---

3. In one term the board included: my father; my uncle, Reb Yechiel Kamchi; Reb Y. Boruch Mishkovsky (the son of the Stavisker Tzaddik and brother of the Krinker Rav); and Reb Nechemia Rabinovitz (secretary of the Lomza Yeshiva and son of Rabbi Akiva Rabinowitz, Rav of Poltave and publisher of *Hapelles);* also Reb Zvi Mark (see later).

represented the Jews. The Nazi commandant once requested fifty Jews from the *kehillah* for one week, to do various jobs for the German authorities. The *kehillah* obliged. Next week he came for another fifty Jews, even though the previous group had never returned. Only two members of the board, Mizrachi leaders, were in the *kehillah* office. They demanded to know the whereabouts of the previous fifty Jews.

"It's none of your business," the Nazi replied, and went on to warn them, "If you don't supply me with another fifty you will be shot immediately."

The two refused and with proud heads held high, Reb Yaakov Tablicki and Reb Yankl Gelcinski הי״ד marched off to their death. And no Jews were given.

Mizrachi did not even rate one full page in the book!

⋙ The Bund and the "Tregers"

The Bund and the other parties claimed to represent the working class — the proletarians. The symbol of the proletarians in Lomza were the *tregers* — the stevedores who unloaded and carried anything and everything on their strong backs. (They used to say "the heavier the load, the easier it is to carry.") Without a trade, they were the lowest on the pay scale — "*Amcho.*" Let us examine how close they were to the Bund, the Communists, or other Socialist parties ... And who knows more about the *tregers* than I? I was practically raised on their knees.[4]

Their base was located in front of our store, which was in the center of town (across the street from the *Magistrat*-City Hall). While waiting for a job, they would sit on the front steps of our store. We made two benches for them, to keep the entrance to the store free. ... Looking at the photo, I see the first one from the left on the bench — the *Meshugene Dveire*, as he was known. He hated children, but he had to tolerate us four Shapiro boys. One summer day (I must have been nine or ten), I stepped inside the Chevrah Tehillim to daven *Minchah.*[5] There he was, sitting and saying *Tehillim* (Psalms). He motioned to me, and hesitantly I approached him. He placed his huge arm around me and asked me to say *Tehillim* together with him. He must have just unloaded a

4. The local ruffians knew that to lay a hand on the Shapiro boys meant the *tregers* would twist their arms off.

5. In Chevrah Tehillim (a *Polush* from the big *shul*, located one block from the City Hall), *minyanim* would *daven* from sunrise until midnight. The beggars there were called "millionaires," for in one day, they would acquire *Omein's, Borchu's* and *Kedushah's* worth a million. In between *minyanim*, people would say *Tehillim.*

The "Tregers": "Meshugene Dveire" at extreme left, "Moshiach" third from left, with Reb Yude to his left.

wagon of flour because he was white all over, and the dust got onto my clothes. When I got home, my mother was ready for me: "What have you done to your clothes?" I had the best excuse; "You won't believe it! The Meshugene Dveire put his arm around me and made me say *Tehillim.*"

"You mean Reb Shloime said *Tehillim* with you!" (That's how they were called — always "Reb" in front of their names.)

The fourth from the left is Reb Yehuda. His wife and daughter visited us almost every Shabbos, for tea and cake. His son, Meir, became the business agent of the *tregers.* Each morning, he would walk up to his father in front of everybody and roll up his sleeve to prove that he had put on *tefillin.*

The third from the left was called "*Moshiach.*" He was their king — the tallest (close to seven feet), the strongest, and the biggest mouth of them all. Moshiach had six sons and three daughters, all tall and strong. Some followed him in the trade. When the *muzinik'l*[6] was born, Moshiach decided that he should be a rabbi. He sent him to Talmud Torah through all ten grades. He was my brother Lazar's classmate, and both graduated with honors. Together they were admitted to the Lomzer Yeshiva and they became *shutfim.*[7] The pride would glow from Moshiach when he talked about his Yude'le. With esteem, he would address

6. A *muzinik'l* means the youngest of the children, or a *ben z'kunim.*
7. In Lomza, a *chavrusa* (study companion) was called a *shutef* (literally "partner").

my father ever so often: "Reb Alter, your Lazer'ke and my Yude'le are *shutfim*. Please test him to see how he's doing in the *Gemara*." He would constantly boast, "My *muzinik'l* is a *chaver* (colleague) of the Kolaker's[8] *einik'l*, can you believe it?"

Then one summer day, the two boys (age fifteen), both excellent swimmers, went swimming in the Narew River. They had rented a row boat, and out on the river it ran into a high current and turned over. My brother made it to the shore but "little Moshiach" (as we called him) did not. What a tragedy! What a funeral! My brother knew that Yude'le had been copying the *Rebbe's shiurim*. He also wrote Torah of his own. My brother found Yude'le's notebook in his *shtender*. He didn't have the heart to deliver it personally, so he sent it to the parents with me. With love, Moshiach pressed the notebook to his heart, telling his wife, "This is our Yude'le's Torah."

Then the Rosh Yeshiva, Reb Y. Zelig Ruch, came with some of the directors of the yeshiva to offer their condolences. The moment the Rosh Yeshiva opened the door, the giant man fell to the floor, grabbed the Rosh Yeshiva's both feet, and between sobs said, "*Rabbi, ich bin an erlicher Yid. Farvos hob ich nisht zoche geven tzu zen a zun a Rav?*" (Rabbi, I'm a sincere Jew. Why did I not merit seeing my son become a rabbi?)

The *tregers* had their own *shul* called *Poalei Tzeddek*. A Rabbi taught them *Chayei Odom (halachah)* and *Ein Yaakov (agaddah)*. Moshiach made sure that their Rav was paid every week from the *treger's* meager income: "We carry on our backs and we want to get paid. The Rabbi carries the Torah in his head and tries to teach us *grobbe kep* (lunkheads). Why shouldn't he get paid?" No one dared contradict him.

Are these the revolutionaries, the socialists, the antireligionists, the Bundists, the Communists, the Zionist-Socialists, that these historians talk about?

In 1935, the first Jewish port opened in Tel Aviv (Jaffa was

---

8. A "*poretz*" (pl. *pritzim*) was a big land owner. Under the Czars, there were many Jewish *pritzim*. My grandfather, Rabbi Chaim Velvl Szeniak, was one of them. He was a *talmid chacham* who had a daily *shiur* in *Rambam*. He was the owner of an entire village called Kolaki (located between Lomza and Zembrove). When the peasants began their uprising against the land owners, the first to be attacked, naturally, were the Jewish ones. *Zeide* realized this, and moved his family to Lomza just in time. He bought property and established a big business. There he became known as "the Kolaker", and we the "Kolaker's *einiklach*" (grandchildren of the Kolaker). Interesting to note, in 1965 a report came through London that the city government of Zembrove unveiled a monument for 5000 Jews killed by the Nazis, in the village of Kolaki. Little do they know that legally this is *my* land, for I'm the only survivor. I'm even named after my *Zeide*.

an Arab port). The Jewish stevedores of Salonika[9] came to help in the operation of the new port. The *tregers* of Lomza immediately sent off a telegram: "We are just as strong and willing as the stevedores of Salonika."

Are these anti-Israel Bundists?

◄§ The Mark of Falsification

I keep on turning the pages: four pages for the Communists. — What a travesty of justice! — What a lie! *Wait, here is a familiar face; what do you know, Berl Mark!*

Reb Zvi Mark lived in the third house from us. He was my father's friend. They once served together on the *kehilla* board. He used to *daven* and learn in *Chevrah Magen Avraham*. He was a *gabbai* in the *Hashgochas Yesoimim*[10] and a member of Mizrachi. Reb Zvi somehow became a *maskil*. This eventually rubbed off on his two intellectual sons and both secretly became Communists (the Communist Party was illegal in Poland).

After the war, I found out that his son Berl was still alive. He had spent the war years in Moscow, a leader of the Polish Communist Party. He was a prominent member of the committee that organized the new Polish Army in the USSR. And when the Communist regime was finally established in Warsaw, he returned, together with the other leaders. He could have gotten any position with the government, but chose to be the head of the "Jewish Historical Institute" of Warsaw, because he was a Yiddish writer before the war (perhaps he was too "Jewish" for the Poles).

In those days, no one was able to emigrate from the USSR except Polish citizens, who could return to Communist Poland. I needed some help on behalf of a relative who was not permitted to leave Russia for Poland. I then wrote to Berl at the Historical Institute. My name alone evoked his memories, and he promised to do his best, as he had excellent connections in the Polish Embassy in Moscow. A deadline was established for the returnees by an agreement of the governments of USSR and Poland. Yet there was no action on my case even though the final day was approaching.

In the meantime, the Polish foreign minister arrived in Washington. According to the newspapers, he invited a Baltimore

---

9. The port in Salonika, Greece, was closed on Shabbos, for all the stevedores were *Shomrei Shabbos*.

10. An orphanage for boys. There was a *Kinderheim* and a separate orphanage for girls.

industrialist — the late Jacob Blaustein (vice president of Amoco, and Standard Oil of Indiana) — for a meeting about oil business in Poland.

With great difficulty I got an appointment with the multi-millionaire and he promised me to take up the case with the Foreign Minister. The Pole tried to butter up the oil man: "Mr. Blaustein, you are a member of the US delegation to the United Nations. You are a national and international personality. Why do you get involved in private cases of this kind?"

But Mr. Blaustein did not fall for the flattery. "Your excellency," he replied, "this is a democracy. Every individual counts and free movement of people, free emigration is basic to democracy." While the result was nil, it did have some repercussions in Warsaw, for I soon received a letter from Berl Mark: "Please do me a favor. Stop writing to me." Such a request from behind the Iron Curtain means the person's career or life is at stake, so I stopped writing.

Then my *landsman* became *Professor* Berl Mark, and he began publishing books like *Uprising in the Warsaw Ghetto*, *Uprising in the Bialystok Ghetto*; all kinds of pamphlets and "scientific papers" — all following the party line: The Communists and their fellow travelers organized all the uprisings, helped by the Communist "People's Army" and Soviet partisans ... while all other parties within the Jewish community were cooperating with the Nazis.

I knew that the Poles[11] falsified history to fit their line of propaganda; that's *their* business. But falsifying *Jewish* history as head of a Historical Institute hurts. So I sent off a letter to him, against his wishes. And if it would hurt him, so be it: "I don't know where your father is buried — Is he together with my father[12] and uncle Reb Yechiel Kamchi, and our old *dayan* Reb Avrohom Yoseph Cynowicz in the Felciner forest? If so, Reb Zvi Mark is ashamed before his life-long friends because of the lies his son is writing about the religious parties of which your father was a member. — Did he die in Auschwitz? Then his ashes must be twisting and turning in the wind, in shame of the falsifications

11. The Soviet encyclopedia and the history of the USSR and the Bolshevik party is rewritten every so often. What was true in one encyclopedia becomes false in the next. The current official Polish history is totally false, doctored to fit the Party line.

12. Before there was even a ghetto, the Germans arrested 150 prominent people. Among them were my father, my uncle and the old *dayan*. Later they claimed that someone had committed sabotage by cutting the telephone wires. All 150 were taken out to the Felcine forest near the city and shot.

his son is trying to establish as historical facts."

And Professor Berl Mark — photograph, writings and all — graces the pages of the *Lomza Yizkor* book!

ᒫᗧ From Prison to the Book

I keep on reading: there is a photo of Hershel Smoliar. Who is he? It turns out that, actually, he is not from Lomza, but from Zembrove (15.5 miles from Lomza — 25 klm), but he spent a number of years in the famous Lomza prison for Communist activities. I guess that makes him a Lomzer.

But that's not all. There is more to his "*Yichus.*" The party and the government of the Polish People's Republic appointed him as head of all the Jews in Poland. And in that capacity, like a faithful dog, he followed the party line to the letter, above and beyond the letter. The Arabs were "progressive elements" to him, Israel and its Jews a gang of Fascists. His campaign against *Yiddishkeit* and against Israel was the most vicious in all of Poland. He did all he could to stop Jews from leaving Poland. He threatened the few remaining Jews into staying to build the new Socialist fatherland. But no decent Jew would want to build a new life on a cemetery. (And what was Poland, if not a huge Jewish cemetery?) So they found a way out, in spite of Smoliar.

Most interesting: when things got too hot for the Jewish Communists in Poland, Hershel Smoliar forsook his "Socialist fatherland" and escaped to — of all places — his "Fascist" motherland — namely, Israel. And Mother Zion opened her arms to welcome her renegade sons, who had spit in her face for so long. All those Communists who were rejected by the party only because they were born Jewish, found refuge in Israel — including the widow of Berl Mark.

ᒫᗧ The Alef Encounters

The book carries more names of "Communist leaders" who are still building the "Socialist fatherland" to this very day. Names I never head of. *But wait! there is one I do know: Colonel Gershon Alef. How could I forget him!*

It was right after the war. My tank battalion was stationed in Osoviec, near the town Novi Dvor, close to Warsaw. At every opportunity, I would go to Warsaw to look for fellow Jews. I could not tell this to my Russian colonel, so I used to go without a pass and spoke and saluted only Russian style even though in Polish uniform (with full hand, as opposed to the Polish two-fingered salute). The Soviet MPs thought I was a Russian officer attached to the Polish army, while the Polish MPs did not dare question me, thinking I was a Russian officer.

One day, while still in working uniform and tank helmet, I hitched a ride with a Russian military truck and got off on a Warsaw street, full of the debris of the war's destruction. I noticed a ship-shape Polish colonel at the other end of the street — a pencil pusher, in shiny boots. Normally, I would have totally ignored him, for men of battle resent desk officers; but I was without my medals and battle insignia, and I did not want to start an argument. I gave him the Soviet salute, and to my surprise he returned it, identically! Our eyes met for a split second, and after we passed one another, we both turned around. He was a Jew from back home — Alef, whose parents lived at the other end of our street! Military protocol demanded that I wait for him to speak first, for I was outranked — but how could I? It was my very first "regards" from home. Just to be sure, I said in Polish, *"Panie Pulkowniku, zdaje mi sie, ze Pan pochodzi z Lomzy"* ("Sir colonel, it seems to me that you are from Lomza). He smiled and replied, *"Pewnie Panie Poruczniku"* (Certainly, Sir Lieutenant). Overwhelmed, I was sure now that it was indeed Alef. I dropped all formalities, stretched out my hand and showered him with questions in Yiddish:

Shalom Aleichem, Alef, Recognize me? Have you been in a ghetto or in Russia? Thank G-d, you are alive! The first Jew from home I have ever met!

He shook my hand and said in Polish, *"Bardzo przepraszam ja sie spiesze"* (I'm very sorry, I'm in a hurry). He saluted and marched off.

I was mortified. The first Jew I met from home and he won't even speak to me! I sat down on the heaps of rubble. If not for my shame of people passing by, I would have cried. *Why didn't he speak to me? Was it my speaking Yiddish in public? Does the name of G-d irritate him? Why didn't I chase after him?*

I never saw him again, but I heard and read a lot about him. He served with the Partisans, under the name "Bolek" or Bolkoviak, where apparently he earned his rank of Colonel. He was later appointed Polish Military Attache in Washington. No military expert, he served as the eyes and ears of Stalin. That was later obvious, for as soon as Tito began his revolt against Stalin, Col. Bodek was transferred to Belgrade. As soon as Marshal Tito made his final break with Moscow, the first one to be expelled from Yugoslavia was the Polish Military Attache, my *landsman* Colonel Bolkoviak.

He married a non-Jewish woman, and while most Jewish Communists left Poland, he remained there to build the Socialist Peoples Republic, to this very day. *And that infidel is in the pages of Lomza!*

Every nation is entitled to its share of renegades and traitors. We Jews, because of our circumstances, are perhaps entitled to a larger share. But do we have to enshrine them for posterity?

◄§ A Yom Tov for Our Enemies

When I read the Lomza book for the first time, I was so enraged that I sent off a letter of protest to the editor, Dr. Yom Tov Levinski. He replied that he understood my anger, but let's face it; because of the economic conditions in Poland, the Communists did make strides among the youth. Besides, he said, "In a way I was forced." His last words puzzled me. Who forced him? Berl Mark may have been forced to follow the party line. Or perhaps he felt he was preserving documents in the only way he could hope to save them — by publishing them before the Poles destroyed them. But who could force an editor in Tel Aviv?

I had a second look at the publishers and editors of *Tiktin* and compared them to the publishers of *Lomza*. In *Tiktin*, I found Reb Yosef Pines (my uncle's brother), who left his fortune for the establishment of a *kollel*; Rabbi Shulman (now a chaplain in the IDF), an alumnus of Baranovitz and Kamenitz; Rabbi Ravitz (member of the *Bais Din* of Tel Aviv); Rabbi Pinie Levinsohn, Brooklyn.

On the other hand, most of the members of the *Lomza* publication committee are unknown to me. They probably arrived in America before I was born. However, I do know the editor, H. Sobotko. He was a leader in the Bund back home, and in America, he was an executive member of the Forward Association, which is the local fortress of the Bund.[13]

Could that be the answer to my puzzle? The final analysis seems to indicate: On reading a *Yizkor* Book, first check the ideology of the editors and writers. You can be sure that they will

13. Until recently, the *Forward* was still decorating its mast-head with the slogan "Proletarians of all nations unite!" Nowadays, in tune with the sentiments of its religious readership, it has changed its slogan to: "Freedom for all people," "Freedom for Jews to lead a Jewish life," "A secure *Medinas Yisrael*," and "A free labor movement." Gone is the hatred of Zion, gone is the hatred of religion. It even quotes from the *Parshah* of the week and the *Daf Yomi*!

twist the facts to their fancy, to suit their ideology. How can you check further? If the editors or writers personally write in detail about the leftist parties, you know for sure that the book is not a true mirror of the town. Those who never were in Europe will never understand. So don't try to become an "expert" by reading one or two *Yizkor* Books ... After all is said and done, it may be best to stay away from the subject completely.

❧ Rabbonim, Gaonim and Tzaddikim

Men of stature
too great to be described
by the position they held

The "Chofetz Chaim"

the man within
the legend

Rabbi Yisrael Meir HaKohen Kagan זצ״ל
5899/1839-5693/1933

I. A Scholar for All Times

A LITTLE more than one hundred years ago, an unknown author was arranging for the publication of an anonymous work on a much-ignored topic. Reb Yisrael Meir Kagan of Radin, Lithuania, had spent two winters, 5630 and 5631 (1870 and 1871), writing *Chofetz Chaim*, a compilation of the laws regarding slander and defamation. During 5632, he was engaged in getting pre-publication orders from the general public and securing testimonials from outstanding rabbinic authorities. In those days, when he was a young man in his thirties, Reb Yisrael Meir still thought he could retain his anonymity. He introduced himself as the publisher, rather than the author, of the novel *Shulchan Aruch*. In this guise he succeeded in evading recognition by the masses, but the spiritual giants of the age — men like Rabbi Yisrael Lipkin (Salanter) — saw that they were dealing with one of those rare figures who would leave his imprint on a nation. More than sixty tireless years, twenty-four additional volumes, and countless public letters and appeals lay ahead of the young "publisher," but the pattern of his long and busy life was already apparent when he was still unknown by circumstance as much as by choice.

A major reason for the enormous influence and acceptance won by the Chofetz Chaim was his utter and complete integrity. Statements and actions that would have seemed unctuously pretentious in ordinary humans were natural and unaffected coming from him. A case in point is the very topic of his *"Chofetz Chaim"* — gossip and witty character assassination are not twentieth century phenomena; human tongues have always been loose and hard to control. The Talmud says, "Most people are guilty of dishonesty, few of vice, but *all* of *lashon hara"(Baba Basra 165).* Anyone presenting a book codifying the sins of slander could expect to be greeted with much scorn — private if not public. Yet, when Reb Yisrael Meir mounted pulpits in town after town to discuss the forthcoming *Chofetz Chaim,* he was listened to with respect. The people sensed that he was no salesman hawking a product, but one of those rare finds — an honest man whose love for his fellow Jews was expressed by trying to bring them closer to Torah, and who truly believed in the ability and obligation of people to pursue perfection. They were convinced that he wrote *Chofetz Chaim* not for recognition and for library shelves, but — as advertised — because he expected working men as well as scholars to form study groups to learn and put into practice what he had gleaned and compiled, and what was forged into his personality.

Many of the rabbis whom he approached for endorsements were skeptical of the first person to so systematically attack a sin that the Talmud considers universal. To avoid bringing ridicule not only upon himself but upon his stated purpose — and thus, paradoxically, provide yet another topic for gossip mongering — the personal credentials of the author as one who "withholds his tongue from evil" had to be unimpeachable. Some went so far as to assign students or colleagues to engage Reb Yisrael Meir in conversation to try to trap him into *lashon hara,* thus revealing him as no less mortal than the next man. The ruses invariably revealed the greatness of the author, and the endorsements were forthcoming.

No one knows for sure what prompted Reb Yisrael Meir to write *Chofetz Chaim,* but it was certainly not his finding an unexplored, fertile field for research, for the Chofetz Chaim never took pen in hand, except in response to a concrete need. To reveal his reason for compiling his *Shulchan Aruch* on *lashon hara* would have involved dredging up sordid stories of the very type he was trying to still. His son, Reb Aryeh Leib, conjectured that his father's first masterpiece grew out of a bitter controversy in the town of Radin during his youth. Acrimony had swirled about the town and all efforts to bring peace had failed. The town became divided into factions and its rabbi was forced to leave. He died after a few years in a new position and many blamed his early death on the anguish he suffered during Radin's little war. Reb Yisrael Meir, then a young man, had seen his fellow townspeople turn their tongues into ugly lethal weapons. As long as he lived, he never discussed the dispute, saying simply, "I have a self-imposed restriction against speaking of it," but it may very well be that the *Chofetz Chaim* was his response in the form of an appeal that there be no more such incidents in Radin — or elsewhere.

◆§ A New Need / A New Book

Whenever he wrote, it was to answer a need. Russia's conscription policies forced many Jewish boys into the army for periods of at least six years, cutting them off from religious teaching and influence. They needed encouragement and answers to basic questions of halachah in layman's language. The result was *Machneh Yisrael,* a book that became the link to Judaism for many a Jewish soldier.

□ Heartbreaking tales of the breakdown of religion among Jewish immigrants to America led to his *Nidchei Yisrael.* In providing practical answers to the halachic problems peculiar to the immigrant, Reb Yisrael Meir often rendered lenient decisions that took into account the emergency conditions of the immigrants, but which were inappropriate to the thriving religious life of Eastern Europe. Because of this, he had hoped that *Nidchei Yisrael* would not be distributed in Eastern Europe, but inevitably some copies were seen. This led to criticism of the Chofetz Chaim — something he regretted, but considered unimportant in view of his primary goal of aiding the uprooted Jews in America.

□ Reb Yisrael Meir felt that the practical laws of kindness and charity were too often ignored. His reaction was to do for *gemilas chessed* what he had done for *shmiras halashon* (guarding one's tongue) — codify its laws, and actively campaign for Jews to join study groups to learn and to act upon them. As a result of his slim classic *Ahavas Chessed,* literally hundreds of free loan societies, shelters for the homeless, and *bikur cholim* societies sprang into being. Many of them sent requests to the Chofetz Chaim for letters of greeting and blessing that would be bound as the first page of a new organization's ledger book.

☐ Weakening of adherence to the laws of family purity and of personal modesty led to pamphlets in both Hebrew and Yiddish addressed to Jewish women.

☐ There were booklets in both languages urging men to pursue Torah study in their homes ... and the list goes on and on.

The personal attention Reb Yisrael Meir devoted to the publication of his ethical works did not end when the volumes were printed and distributed. He did not write his books to be purchased; he wrote them to be used. His frequent lecture tours in behalf of one or another of his *sefarim* were devoted primarily to encouraging people to set up groups for the study of the *sefer*. In later years, when he was too old or too busy to go on personal tours, he hired "field representatives" to carry on his work. But they were firmly instructed that they must sell the message of the books by personal example and persuasive lectures.

Fire-and-brimstone preaching was not his approach; he was a firm believer in the superior efficacy of a spoonful of honey to a gallon of vinegar. Once a traveling preacher complained to him that no matter how much he thundered and reprimanded his audiences, they seemed to ignore his calls to repent. The Chofetz Chaim replied, "Who told you that the way to perform the *mitzvah* of correcting sinners is by shouting and storming? Putting on *tefillin* is also a *mitzvah* — do you holler and shout when you perform that *mitzvah?*"

◆§ An Imminent Need / A New Syllabus

In addition to salvaging neglected *mitzvos*, the Chofetz Chaim assumed responsibility for reviving interest in a long neglected area of the Torah. For centuries, *Kadoshim*, the section of the Talmud dealing with the laws of the Sanctuary and sacrificial offerings, had been virtually excluded from the curricula of major Torah centers. Rare were the scholars who had more than a passing familiarity with its intricacies. Reb Yisrael Meir saw this as a far more serious matter than a lack of knowledge among Torah intelligentsia. With the deceptive simplicity that masked his penetrating insight, he would ask, "We believe that *Mashiach* can arrive today. If he does, are we ready to bring our offerings to the *Bais Hamikdosh*? Do the

Kohanim know the laws of sacrifices? Do the scholars know enough to train the *Kohanim?*"

Obviously, the answer to all these questions was a shameful "No."

"Then are we not somewhat lacking in our prayers, hopes, and beliefs in the imminent coming of *Mashiach?*" The solution was simple: organize groups to study *Kadashim.* Thus was born a trend that continues to this day. Far from being neglected, the study of *Kadashim* is now a mark of prestige; the endeavor of the most advanced group in nearly all yeshivos.

Typically, the Chofetz Chaim showed the way by practical example as well as by exhortation. He published *Toras Kohanim,* a compilation of the Tannaitic interpretations of *Chumash Vayikra,* with an amended, completely accurate text; and an original commentary that ranks as a model of conciseness and clarity. He also composed *Likutei Halachos* modeled after the *Alfasi,* which is a compilation of halachic sections of the Talmud dealing with *Kadashim* topics; and included an elucidating original commentary.

⮕§ Magnum Opus: "Mishnah Berurah"

Of all his literary efforts, his acknowledged masterpiece and the one which continues to have the greatest influence is *Mishnah Berurah,* a work that was twenty-five years in the making.

The Chofetz Chaim was concerned by a serious gap in halachic literature. There was no modern commentary on *Orach Chaim* (the section of the *Shulchan Aruch* dealing with daily and festival rituals) that summed up the centuries of comment and responsa, and rendered authoritative decisions in areas of dispute. Clearly such a work was much needed, but it could be undertaken only by a giant in Torah scholarship. The mantle was not sought by the Chofetz Chaim. He urged it upon others, but finding no one willing to assume the responsibility, he finally accepted it upon himself. The breadth, conciseness, clarity, and genius of *Mishnah Berurah* speak for themselves, as does the almost universal acceptance it has attained. This is the supreme testimonial to its author's stature as a sage.

He did not write the *Mishnah Berurah* simply because he wanted to, but because he saw it as a task that had to be done by someone, and his inability to find that someone left the responsibility at his doorstep. This is testimonial to his greatness as a person.

II. The Man of the Legends

THE Chofetz Chaim was surely a scholar's scholar. More than this, however, he was also a genuine folk-hero. Scholars respected him, but the common people loved him with a rare passion. The reasons are many and no doubt complex. But the most compelling one is simply that he considered himself as one with them and their problems. Even his books, despite the great scholarship they represent, were written to be used by ordinary men — and in many instances, by ordinary women, too. Sensing that he identified with them, people did not hesitate to seek his advice and assistance.

Although he never accepted the position of rabbi in Radin, he was in fact its spiritual and temporal leader. When some townspeople unfairly criticized and embarrassed their rabbi for the deficiencies of the town's *mikvah*, it was the Chofetz Chaim who guaranteed the funding and supervised the building of a new one. When Radin was devastated by fires that, in successive years, destroyed first one half and then the other half of the Jewish section, it was he who organized emergency relief, fund-raising, and the rebuilding of the town.

A poor workingman was not ashamed to ask him, as author of *Ahavas Chessed*, how a laborer living hand-to-mouth could be expected to perform the *mitzvah* of lending money to others. And he did not feel patronized when he was told to save a few pennies a week, eventually building it up to a fund of several rubles, for loaning to fellow workers short of pocket money. That was down-to-earth advice that was followed by thousands, and it was typical of the pragmatic idealism of a man who never took a penny offered to him by people who had the notion that his greatness entitled him to gifts.

The Chofetz Chaim's awesome care in maintaining the strictest possible standards in his financial dealings has become legendary. No doubt many of the stories attributed to him are apocryphal — but, for most of them, there is more than ample first-hand testimony ... He insisted that his son reprint hundreds of sections of *Mishnah Berurah* to replace originals where pages had inadvertently been put in the wrong order. ... The Chofetz Chaim himself once went dashing through the Jewish quarter of Warsaw shortly before Shabbos seeking to pay printers who had left work early without getting their pay for the week ... When a non-Jewish railroad employee put parcels of his books on board a train for free delivery, the Chofetz Chaim tore up an amount of postage stamps sufficient to defray the loss of revenue to the government ... In his first speaking tour on behalf of the book *Chofetz Chaim*, he accepted orders, but not deposits, because of the possibility that he might not be able to make delivery to some pre-paying customers, thus becoming guilty of improperly taking their money ... The stories are legion.

◄§ Saint and Pragmatist

It is commonplace for people to believe that the Chofetz Chaim, as a saintly personality, could not have been terribly practical and certainly could not have coped with the rough and tumble of the world — especially today when so many accept as axiomatic that "you cannot make an omelette without breaking a few eggs," and that "nice guys finish last." Nothing could be further from the truth. It was this same saint who once remarked that one fool can do more damage than ten villains. Men like Rabbi Chaim Ozer Grodzensky of Vilna greatly valued his wise counsel when searching for practical solutions to the knottiest of problems. Indeed, in the crisis-laden years following World War I, when Reb Chaim Ozer was the undisputed leader of Lithuanian Jewry, he and the Chofetz Chaim were in constant consultation on all major issues. Their names appeared side-by-side on scores of proclamations and appeals in behalf of all the major causes in Jewish life.

The Chofetz Chaim was one of the first to realize that Torah Jewry must up-date its tactics to counter the onslaught of its enemies. Organized activities for the Torah community and its educational needs could succeed where efforts on the individual scale could scarcely cope with the juggernauts of Haskalah and secularism. Thus he took the lead in organizing and supporting Agudath Israel as the international organizational arm of traditional Jewry. As usual, he saw this as more than a matter of strategy, but as a religious obligation: "In a time when our values are under attack as never before, even small acts in defense of Torah are multiplied many times over in the Divine scales for ultimate reward."

Though he was the senior of the two by nearly thirty years, the Chofetz Chaim considered Reb Chaim Ozer to be the *gadol hador* and deferred to his authority as a matter of course, despite the fact that Reb Chaim Ozer held him in awe. During the 1920's, pressure was brought to bear on Reb Chaim Ozer to travel to America to raise money for the European yeshivos, which were on the brink of financial ruin. He was told that only his own presence in America could assure contributions in the millions. Reb Chaim Ozer answered that his health was too precarious to permit such a trip. Though the other Torah luminaries at the meeting continued to exert pressure upon him, the Chofetz Chaim ended the debate by saying very simply, "The well-being of Reb Chaim Ozer is synonymous with that of *Klal Yisrael*. We dare not jeopardize it."

৵§ Storm Over Vilna

The prestige of Reb Chaim Ozer was responsible for an unheard-of departure by the Chofetz Chaim — an open attack upon adversaries of Torah Judaism. His general policy had been always to avoid engaging Torah's enemies in debate. To reply to the virulent attacks made by *maskillim, yevsekes* (Jewish Communists) and others, he felt, would be self-defeating because it would grant them unearned recognition, and merely provide them with fuel for vituperation and ridicule. Better to isolate them from the mainstream of religious life, while devoting the available talent and resources to the more productive course of strengthening Judaism by upgrading education and observance within yeshivos and communities. Then came the storm over the Vilna rabbinate.

The government required that Vilna have a Chief Rabbi. Although Reb Chaim Ozer was a recognized leader of religious European Jewry, Vilna's official Chief Rabbi was to be elected by the entire Jewish population, which included a large secular contingent. Agudath Israel doubted that Reb Chaim Ozer would be able to command a majority of the total votes, so they joined a coalition of the Mizrachi, Socialists, and Reformers to "elect" a Rabbi Rubinstein as a pro-forma head of the Jewish Community, with the understanding that he would not assert any authority without Reb Chaim Ozer's approval. After his election, Rabbi Rubinstein's secularist supporters used this consensus as a pretext for treating him as the actual Chief Rabbi of Vilna, and Reb Chaim Ozer, the man who was revered the world over, found the ground cut out from under him in his own city. Strangely enough, the only important Torah figure whose serenity was not shattered was Reb Chaim Ozer himself. That did not prevent his adherents, led by the Chazon Ish and guided by the Chofetz

Chaim, from doing battle to defend the honor of Torah. The Chofetz Chaim published a blistering letter attacking the perpetrators of the coup as enemies of Torah. Though disciples of Reb Chaim Ozer attempted to negotiate a face-saving compromise, the Chofetz Chaim torpedoed these efforts as going against the inviolable principle of Torah supremacy.

The secularists' reaction to his bold position was one of those human spectacles that must be greeted with laughter or rage. The non-religious Jewish press in Vilna vilified the Chofetz Chaim for stooping to *lashon hara* against the liberal Jews! His reply was simple and to the point: "When Torah values are being destroyed, Torah Law permits their defense."

His deference to Reb Chaim Ozer, however, did not prevent the Chofetz Chaim from arguing his own causes in the humorous, self-deprecating manner that he used so effectively. In 1923, the Chofetz Chaim felt that the community must be organized to provide kosher meals for Jewish soldiers. He called his new project *Kessel Kosher* (Kosher Kettle) and, naturally, his first move was to travel to Vilna to secure the endorsement and support of Reb Chaim Ozer. The endorsement was not forthcoming. Reb Chaim Ozer replied that there were many overriding considerations making such a campaign inopportune at that time.

The Chofetz Chaim shrugged and replied, "What can I do? People consider me to be a God-fearing Jew. When I am called to the world-to-come, they will ask me why I did nothing to provide kosher food for Jewish conscripts. What will I say? Perhaps I'll tell them that I was not lazy or indifferent; I made the hard trip to Vilna even though I was weak and past eighty. But the Rabbi of Vilna was the *gadol hador* and he said I was wrong. Who knows better than the *gadol hador* what is right or wrong?"

Reb Chaim Ozer knew he had been bested. He called a public meeting in the central synagogue to be addressed by the Chofetz Chaim. At that meeting *Kessel Kosher* was born.

III. As the Chofetz Chaim Would Say ...

PRECISELY because he had such a keen feel for the pulse of the people and the needs of the time, it is fascinating — and useful — to wonder what the Chofetz Chaim would have said to today's problems. Indeed, we should go a step further and wonder how he would have defined the *real* problems of today. After all, *Chofetz Chaim* and *Ahavas Chessed* were effective replies to problems not even recognized by most. It would be a mistake to take the sizeable collection of his major and minor writings, apply them to each era, and assume that the Chofetz Chaim would have had nothing more to say.

How would he have diagnosed today's ills? This question should be answered by the few survivors of his era who knew him well, but perhaps we can hazard some guesses.

□ There is little doubt that he would be appalled at the sharp and shady business practices that are so much a part of modern life, Orthodoxy not excluded. We live in an age when ethics have not kept pace with sophistication, and Jews have not escaped contamination. How would he have prodded our conscience?

□ Picture the Chofetz Chaim entering a typical middle-class home today with its emphasis on "creature comforts," and recreational pursuits rather than a Torah atmosphere ... Would he have smiled tolerantly? Or would he have considered his surroundings more appropriate to the House of Romanoff than to the House of Israel, and told us so?

□ What would he say to the growing gap that divides yeshiva, rabbinate, and laity from one another?

□ And what about the organizational weakness of Orthodoxy? He was one of the founders of Agudath Israel, long aware that modern times required modern tactics — and organizational unity was one of them. Surely he would work to end today's factionalism.

□ In this time of turbulence when the values of centuries are being discarded, we may be certain that the Chofetz Chaim would have found our attitude wanting and far too complacent. We are content to condemn the drug culture, but are ill prepared for our own acid test. Indicative of this is a memoir of one his students, Rabbi Avrohom Hillel Goldberg, later rabbi of Kfar Pinnes in Israel:

> It was near the end of his life and the Chofetz Chaim was in a summer cottage near Radin. He was heart-broken over the persecutions of Jews in Russia. He saw their situation as the severing of an entire limb of the Jewish body from its life-sources of Torah and mitzvos. "There is only one real hope," he said — "Mashiach must come soon. The Final Redemption must come sooner or later, but it is up to us to hasten its arrival. We must demonstrate our overpowering desire for Mashiach. How many of us religious Jews who say

'Ani Maamin' every day truly long for his coming? Why don't we cry out to Hashem to help us? This is no time for silence!

"Even in the Egyptian exile the Torah says that only when B'nei Yisrael cried out for help — then did their outcry go up to Hashem. We must do the same now! I must go to Vilna to Reb Chaim Ozer — without him nothing can be done!"

His family and students were aghast. He was over ninety years old and he could scarcely leave his arm chair for the length of a day. He might not survive the difficult trip to Vilna. They pleaded with him to abandon his plan, but he would not be dissuaded. The goal was worthy of even mesiras nefesh. They told him that Reb Chaim Ozer was a man of halachah and action; such ideas as the Chofetz Chaim's were out of his domain. He smiled as if to say, What do you know of Reb Chaim Ozer?

To his deep regret, the journey to Reb Chaim Ozer never took place. Had they met, who knows?

The Chofetz Chaim Comes to Vienna

✦ The Grand Assembly: Postponed —

THE CHOFETZ CHAIM was 75 years old in 1913, no youngster by any standard. But in that year he joined most of the Torah luminaries of his period in launching a new organization, issuing a proclamation calling for the First Knessia Gedolah (Great Congress) of the new-born Agudath Israel to be held the following summer in Kattowitz. But the conference never took place, for the world was otherwise involved — World War I broke out, bringing four years of strife, slaughter, and exile.

Even during his difficult war years, while leading the remnants of the Radin Yeshiva from town to town in Russia, the Chofetz Chaim never lost sight of his goal of unifying traditional Jewry under the banner of an international Torah organization. In 1917 he issued a public proclamation urging Russian Jews to join Agudath Israel. But with the success of the Bolshevik Revolution, that country became closed to all public religious activity. Nonetheless, the Chofetz Chaim continued to view Agudath Israel as an urgent stratagem in the battle for Torah life; the emergence of the new Leninist regime would merely shift Agudah's center of gravity from Russia to Poland.

✦ Until 1923

It was not until 1923 that post-war Jewry had stabilized to the point where the first Knessia Gedolah, nine years postponed, could finally be called. It was to be held in Vienna. By then, the Chofetz Chaim was 85, but he resolved to demonstrate his own continuing allegiance to the Agudath Israel concept by making the long, uncomfortable trip from Radin to Vienna.

The Knessia Gedolah had all the markings of a great event. Its five hundred delegates included nearly all of the great rabbis, *admorim,* and *roshei yeshiva* of the day; thousands of spectators would attend to hear and see the greatest single assemblage of Torah leadership in many centuries; and millions of Jews would follow the proceedings with interest and allegiance, or dread and disdain, depending upon their political and religious orientation. No matter what part of the Jewish spectrum one occupied, the Knessia Gedolah was an important event.

As the most beloved and universally respected Jewish figure, the Chofetz Chaim's position toward Agudath Israel was the object of intense speculation. True, he had been one of its original and warmest supporters, but he was also "above politics." Perhaps, said many, he merely favored Agudath Israel in the abstract, as an expression of organized Jewish unity under the banner of Torah; but he probably would not join in the practical workings of an organization that would descend from the ascetic ivory tower and become involved in the sometimes unpleasant battle for souls. The Chofetz Chaim, after all, was one of those rare men who, in his lifetime, had won the adulation of all circles and was claimed by them all. The non-religious Jewish press, therefore, attempted to portray him as being less than enthusiastic about the goals and methods of Agudath Israel's more vocal partisans.

◆§ "The Chofetz Chaim Local"

For tens of thousands of Jews along the rail route through Lithuania and Poland, the center of interest was a train schedule. The train carrying many of the greatest Torah figures of the day would be passing through, and every railroad station was mobbed with Jews seeking to shake the hand or catch a glimpse of their revered leaders.

On the same train rode the Chofetz Chaim, the Gerrer Rebbe, the Sokolover Rebbe, Rabbi Meir Dan Plotzki of Sokolov, and many others, with their entourages. The Chofetz Chaim followed his usual practice of traveling third class. As an unusual token of deference to the venerable sage, Rabbi Plotzki accompanied the Chofetz Chaim on the journey.

At one of the stations in Poland, a large crowd stood and clamored for an appearance by the Chofetz Chaim, to no avail. A committee of local rabbis and lay leaders boarded the train to plead that he show himself. Still he refused. Reb Meir Dan, his traveling companion, asked why he was so adamant.

The Chofetz Chaim explained, "All my life I fled from

honor. How can you ask me to seek it now? Glory is a risky undertaking. Rabbi Yehuda HaChassid said that a person's share in the World-to-Come is not diminished by material rewards in this world. But honor is different; it is a spiritual thing and when it is granted in this world, it is subtracted from his share of the World-to-Come."

Rabbi Plotzki replied, "First of all, I think it is worthwhile to give up a bit of *Olam Haba* to satisfy the request of so many Jews. Secondly, I doubt that this type of honor can cost you a portion of the next —"

The Chofetz Chaim interrupted, "Enough. Your first argument is sufficient." And the Chofetz Chaim rose and walked over to the coach window. When the crowd saw him, it began pushing and shoving to shake his hand. For the aged and frail sage, this represented considerable physical danger. He raised his hand, waving to them, motioning to them to stop: "Shalom Aleichem, fellow Jews. The *pasuk* says, 'Shalom, Shalom larachok v'lakarov — Peace, peace to far and near.' The verse seems to say that one can give *Shalom* from afar. It isn't necessary to shake hands."

When the train pulled into Chenstochav, he was exhausted and he decided that he would not greet the crowds. He asked that the door and windows be closed so that he could rest. Suddenly, the conductor rushed in and ordered that the coach be evacuated; an axle was on fire. To which the Chofetz Chaim characteristically remarked, "Such is the power of a *tzibbur* (multitude). Try as we might avoid it, we have no choice but to come out."

◆§ Vienna: "The Chofetz Chaim is Coming!"

Finally they arrived at Vienna and, despite the presence of many other foremost Torah personalities, the tiny, frail, old man from Radin was the center of attraction. Why? Self-deprecatingly he found his own answer when he reluctantly acceded to the request that he be the first speaker at the Knessia Gedolah — he was chosen not for his Torah or good deeds, he insisted; he had precious little of those. He was chosen because he was the oldest delegate and a *Kohen*. Priesthood and seniority are gifts of G-d, and by their virtue it would not be presumptuous of him to bless the assemblage.

That was his version. It is doubtful that anyone else agreed. The public pulse, both within and without the Knessia hall, was better tapped by Gedalia Bublik — distinguished editor of *Tageblatt*, a leading Yiddish daily in New York — who wrote that

Agudath Israel's greatest triumph in arranging the Knessia Gedolah was in achieving the presence of the Chofetz Chaim.

"There is no person now living who has so hallowed himself and is so universally acknowledged as a holy person as the Chofetz Chaim. The public considers him the leading *tzaddik* of the generation, even more than it considers him a Torah genius ...

"When the call is heard, 'The Chofetz Chaim is coming!' — a panic breaks out in the hall. Everyone jumps from his seat and cranes his neck to see him ..."

(The general public may have considered the Chofetz Chaim, as Bublik reported, more *tzaddik* than *gaon*. One of the greatest Torah figures of the previous generation disagreed. When the Chofetz Chaim's classic halachah masterpiece, *Mishnah Berurah,* was published, Rabbi Chaim Soloveitchik of Brisk said of its author, "His greatness as a *tzaddik* obscures his even greater statute as a Torah genius.")

✎§ Speeches: Frequent and Deceptively Simple

He spoke often at the Knessia in his deceptively simple manner. Like so many of his works, his brief speeches could be understood on many levels; the simplest layman and most learned scholar could feel that the delicate, indomitable saint from Radin was talking to *him* — talking not up, not down, but directly *to* him. And what is more, there was a total lack of affectation about him, a sincerity that made it possible for him to make demands upon the conscience of his listeners that would have been infuriating had they come from a lesser man. Thus, he could call upon the efforts of the leaders insisting that they dedicate themselves to spreading Torah, and not content themselves with personal achievement:

"*Havu laHashem kavod va'oz* — Ascribe to G-d glory and might. Give to the Master of the Universe the glory that is his due. When a mortal king visits a province, the custom is that the governor and all his retinue greet and honor the king. When he enters a town, the mayor greets him and assumes responsibility for his honor and safety. Wherever he goes, the leader of the district is ready to do his duty toward the monarch. The constable of the smallest side street is as responsible in his little realm as is the mighty governor in his.

"So it is with the King of Kings, the Holy One, Blessed be He. He first appeared to our ancestors Abraham, Isaac, and Jacob — and they honored Him. They revealed His glory to the whole world. Then, He revealed Himself to the prophets and they announced His glory and greatness to humanity. Then came the *Tannaim*, the *Amoraim*; later the *gaonim*, the *rishonim*, and *tzaddikim* of succeeding generations. Each in turn fulfilled the obligation of safeguarding and proclaiming His greatness and glory. We, in our generation, are like the simple constable compared to the great men of generations ago. Our duty to safeguard the Heavenly Glory, however, is no less an obligation than that of earlier, greater generations."

Not many people like being lectured to; most resent it. But, these words were spoken by the Chofetz Chaim, and they were natural, telling, irrefutable, and well-received.

⋓§ A Secularist's-Eye-View

It is informative to see how journalists of the period described the Chofetz Chaim's impact on the Vienna Knessia. Religious journalists might well have had a prior point of view, so it will best serve our purpose to look to a secular correspondent.* Following is a dispatch filed by H. Mauskopf in the September 23, 1923 edition of the New York *Forward*, a Yiddish daily noted for its socialist policies and its rabid anti-religious attitudes. It was the *Daily Forward*, in fact, that achieved notoriety early in the century as the sponsor of the infamous Yom Kippur Balls on the Lower East Side. Here is Mr. Mauskopf's report:

> *The Sokolover Rebbe, who is in the midst of speaking, is suddenly silent, his hand remaining outstretched as though frozen. The audience, the presidium, the journalists, and the guests in the galleries all stand up. Rabbis, tzaddikim, and religious Jews arise from their places. There is a silent, restrained movement, a rustle of awe and respect, stern outcries are heard from the ushers — Make room! Make an aisle! The crowd makes way. People push atop one another, with bated breath, with a shudder in their hearts. They step back momentarily and form two rows of people in the center of the hall: two rows of rabbinical delegates in shining satin coats with long white beards and, between the two rows, several rabbis escort — why do I say escort? — they virtually carry a tiny, frail, old man; a venerable, hunched little man with a small white beard and a simple, poor black coat, a plain black scarf around his neck ...*

* The Viennese German newspapers also wrote many enraptured articles about the Chofetz Chaim.

When you first see the little ninety-year old man, he makes a strange impression on you — you feel a shudder of awe and love, an enormous respect and regard which is boundless. When you look more closely, you see the face of an angel, of a servant of G-d. The Divine Presence rests on that face and you must close your eyes because of the brilliance that shines from the small, gray, wise eyes. When he stands at the rostrum and speaks, two rabbis flank him and support him by the arms. The entire assemblage listens standing. His voice is weak, but clear. He calls Jews to unity, to peace, to goodness, to piety, to love, and to action. His small, bent frame shakes as he speaks. His small white beard glows from the distance like freshly fallen snow. From the eyes, glows an entire world of wisdom and goodness...

This is how I imagine Hillel the Elder must have appeared.

Out of the hall he goes between rows of standing rabbis. He walks quickly, energetically, with the white head bent toward the ground ...

And when he is lifted and helped into the car, the whole street is black with people. They push "head upon head" to see the Chofetz Chaim. Christians remove their hats out of respect. Jews clamber onto the automobile, on the wheels, on the hood. Everyone wants to see the Chofetz Chaim, to touch the hem of his poor long coat. Those closest extend trembling hands into the car. The Chofetz Chaim gives "Shalom," his frail, thin fingers ... touching the thick, trembling hand: Shalom. It is chaotic ... the police are powerless. They can't bring order. They, too, push and look captivated and respectfully at the strange, small old man with the satin cap on the white head ... the Chofetz Chaim.

◄§ House Guest: One Man and a Continent

During his stay in Vienna, the Chofetz Chaim was the guest of Rabbi Akiva Schreiber, a grandson of the Chasam Sofer. The honor did not come to Mr. Schreiber easily, however. Before his distinguished guest accepted the invitation, Mr. Schreiber had to agree to allow him to either eat his own food or pay for his meals and other expenses. As would be expected, the Schreiber home became public property during the stay of its distinguished guest. It seemed as though everyone in town wanted to visit, consult, or just feast his eyes on the *tzaddik* from the once unheard of little town that he had turned into a household word.

One of those who came to the Schreiber home failed to achieve his goal ... and yet he succeeded. He was Abraham Pinchas Landau of London and he needed the Chofetz Chaim's advice on a pressing personal problem. Mr. Landau was a businessman who was one of the most community-minded Orthodox Jews of London. He was *gabbai* of *Machzikei Hadas*, leader of a *Talmud Torah* and other institutions. His business, however, had suffered as of late and he had been hearing about it from his family. *What right had he to spend so much time and energy on his community work at the expense of his business? How dare he allow privation to overtake his family in a quixotic attempt to save the world?* Mr. Landau sought the guidance of Torah leaders in Vienna, and one of those he attempted to consult was the Chofetz Chaim. Pushing his way into the Schreiber home, Landau looked around and gave up on any hopes of a private audience; the house was mobbed. Still, it was a rare privilege to spend some time in the same room as the Chofetz Chaim, in close enough proximity to hear him talk. It was an opportunity afforded few spectators at the Knessia Gedolah in the pre-microphone era when the old sage's remarks could never be heard beyond the first few rows. So Landau stood and waited.

His meal over, the Chofetz Chaim began talking, making the apparently random remarks and comments that always brought people flocking to him. He always concluded his meal with a Torah thought before *Bircas Hamazon.*

"*Ach tov vochessed yirdefuni kol yemei chayai* — Only goodness and kindness shall pursue me all the days of my life. A remarkable thing! People sometimes suffer for performing deeds of goodness and kindness. The truth is that every human being suffers some sort of tribulations in life. And if he must suffer, it is far better to suffer for good deeds than for evil ones. That is what King David meant: if I *must* be 'pursued' in my lifetime, then please, G-d, let it be for deeds of goodness and kindness!"

Abraham Pinchas Landau trembled. "How could he know what I wanted to ask him? He was talking to me!" Did the Chofetz Chaim know? Perhaps not. But he *was* talking to Abraham Pinchas Landau. And to hundreds of thousands of others. As he always did. As the whole world learned in Vienna.

The Chazon Ish

a towering
personality as
revealed in his
personal
correspondence

Rabbi Avrohom Yeshaya Karelitz זצ״ל
5639/1878-5714/1953

THERE is ever so much that one can learn from a close
association with great men. Our *Chazal* tell us that one can
benefit greatly from absorbing their teachings, but one can gain
even more from observing them in their day-to-day activities.
How edifying would it have been, then, to have been granted the
privilege of spending days, or even hours, in the presence of a
Chofetz Chaim, a Lubliner Rav, or a Chazon Ish!

While the opportunity for such first-hand associations has
been the privilege of only a select few, some knowledge of the
personal habits and the private thoughts of great personalities is
still available — long after their passing — through their writings.
The Chazon Ish, of blessed memory, is very much revealed as a
distinct individual of commanding countenance through his
talmudic commentaries and discussions, his halachic work, his
philosophic discourses, and his personal correspondence. They all
unite to reveal him with an immediacy that cuts through befog-
ging distances and changing times.

Most striking about the Chazon Ish is the immense scope and volume of the works he produced. They range over every area of the Talmud. They cover all subjects with a profound depth and a mastery of the intricacies that can only amaze anyone studying them. Still, his clarity of style made many neglected areas of the Talmud accessible to the novice in these topics. For hundreds of years, few people ventured into *Kadashim* and *Taharos*, which discuss sacrificial laws and ritual purity. His works deal with every single *Mishnah* in these sections. In addition, upon his arrival in *Eretz Yisrael* in 1933, he devoted vast amounts of time and energy to *Seder Zeraim*, which deals mainly with laws pertaining to the land, to answer the many halachic problems inherent to a life in the Holy Land consistent with Torah.

His thousands of pages of writings are the product of decades of study with an unimaginable diligence and toil. He taxed his mental and physical faculties to their utmost in his pursuit of Torah knowledge — his primary goal in life. Here he experienced a supreme joy that he often attempted to convey to others:

> Sweet experiences can impart a sense of pleasure to a person's body and to all his limbs in a limited way; but this pleasure can never compete with the noble pleasures of toiling for wisdom, in which the soul of man is lifted above the atmosphere of this world to the heavens above, where it absorbs pleasure from the glow of elevated wisdom (Collected Letters, Volume I, 9).

Or as he writes another aquaintance:

> I must take you to task for I see that you are not evaluating yourself properly, and without thought you are becoming irreverent toward the goal of knowing Torah. Take note of the person who has the good fortune of absorbing a knowledge of Torah; that is, his intellect strikes root into his being — akin to a seed planted into soil — uniting the man and his wisdom. He may walk among men and appear to be a mere person. But in truth he is an angel that lives among mortals. And he lives a life of nobility above and beyond all blessings and praises... (Vol. I, 13).

> What then is good — to eat? to drink? If but this, then what advantage has man over beast? Shame on the insen-

sitivity of your heart, that after your successes in your sacred endeavors — teaching Torah to Jewish children — you fail to recognize the good fortune that is yours! (Vol. I, 18).

⋖§ Man of Torah and Science

To the Chazon Ish, knowledge of Torah required a knowledge of the physical world as well. In his person one saw a synthesis of the two in a manner that made general knowledge virtually a part of Torah. His mastery of the Jewish calendar entailed an exhaustive knowledge of astronomy, and for his command of the Laws of *Eruvin* he developed skills in related fields of mathematics.

When he was presented with the problems of *Shmittah*, he was not content with merely issuing decisions when asked. He also compiled a *sefer* that contained both *halachos* and practical advice for the farmers, and in it he displayed a keen understanding of the science of agronomy.

⋖§ Man of the Shulchan Aruch

The Chazon Ish was a man of the *Shulchan Aruch* — and this was reflected in his writings as well as in his every move. In many respects, he was considered the *posek acharon*—the final halachic authority of his time.

In his writings, the Chazon Ish departed from the norm of the yeshiva movement in that he was not content to work on the theoretical level alone—concentrating on analysis of the *Gemara* without consideration to its further, practical application. Instead, he developed every subject from its source in the Talmud through pertinent commentaries, to the *halachah* as recorded in the *Shulchan Aruch*. He then united theory with its practical application by explaining the *Gemara* in a manner that reflected the *halachah*.

In a sense, he was considered a *machmir* — one who takes a stringent approach to *halachah* — but as he writes,

I have been physically broken all my days and I never savored any of the [earthly] pleasures of life....The only pleasure for me is to do the bidding of my L-rd. I could suffer no greater hurt than to be ensnared by a sin. My teachers taught me that before any move, one must consult the Shulchan Aruch. And I am not at liberty to do anything without consulting those laws relating to the matter at hand. That is all I have in this world (Vol. I, 153).

His life, however, was not dry, nor was it bitter. As he admonished a young man:

Ever bend your heart toward happiness, for from happiness one can receive an abundance of wisdom from on high (Vol. II, 9).

Man's main vitality stems from self control. The righteous are in control of their desires, rather than finding themselves being governed by their desires. It is the sweetest of pleasures, the greatest of joys to rule over one's animal instincts. It means constant happiness, and it restores one's soul (Vol. II, 13).

He went to great pains to see that mitzvos should be done with the utmost care, as one can see in this letter to the Brisker Rav:

I am happy to inform you that I succeeded in finding someone who is willing to let me process the skins for the tefillin *straps according to our wishes. I myself placed the leather in the first bath and said* 'leshem retzuos shel tefillin'... [He continued the letter with a detailed description of the entire process] (Vol. II, 134).

ᴐᴈ Communal Leadership

This deep immersion in Torah study, however, was only one aspect of his great personality. The other facets of his greatness did not fully emerge until he immigrated to Eretz Yisrael.

In Europe, where he lived until 1933, he rarely stepped out of the four cubits of Torah study. In a sense he lived underground. Although Reb Chaim Ozer Grodzensky of Vilna consulted him on many difficult matters, he refused to become openly involved in general problems. This was perhaps due to his deference to others who were able to carry the burdens of the community, whereas he saw it as his own duty (as he later taught his disciples) to grow as much as possible in Torah, as an investment in later years of leadership. He thus devoted every spare minute and every ounce of strength to his studies and his writings.

When he arrived in *Eretz Yisrael*, however, a complete change took place. Here, in his concern over the future of Torah in the new *Yishuv* (settlement), he assumed the responsibility of leadership. He became involved in the construction of *mikva'os* —

In the northern part of Tel Aviv we are building

mikva'os to be a pride and glory. We have already invested tens of thousands of pounds in the buildings, and many of our religious brethren are involved... (Vol. II, 21).

He affixed *mezuzos* on new apartments in Tel Aviv. Concerned with the sanctity of *Shabbos*, he created a furor until he succeeded in having the farmers milk their cows on the Sabbath in a manner consistent with *halachah*. He worked toward the complete, unequivocal observance of *Shmittah*, and he succeeded in turning the tide, which would have made it a relic of the past. He was firmly opposed to the selling of the land to non-Jews as a method of circumventing the Sabbatical restrictions of farming the land during the *Shmittah* year. Although many authorities endorsed this practice, he viewed the *Shmittah* as an opportunity for living within G-d's command that should be sought, rather than as a problem that should be avoided. (Vol. II, 69 — a delightful letter records his own successful experiment in *Shmittah* restrictions.)

Above all, he worked to build Torah. Upon his arrival in *Eretz Yisrael*, he was determined to create a center of Torah in the new *Yishuv* — and that was to be in Bnei Brak. Through his encouragement and financial support, he had a hand in building almost every Torah institution in Bnei Brak.

He also worked for political power for the religious populace, even under the Mandate. He urged one of his disciples to return to his home in time for the elections in order to vote:

"It is my opinion that many important aspects of Torah and the existence of Yiddishkeit are dependent on...[the election's] outcome" (Vol. I, 102).

Eventually, the Chazon Ish became recognized as a clear voice of Torah authority on countless issues. He spoke out most strongly against the conscription of girls into the Israeli Army, as well as on other topics, and it was out of recognition of the Chazon Ish in the role of perhaps supreme spokesman for the religious *Yishuv* that David Ben-Gurion paid his famous visit to him in his humble home in Bnei Brak.

⋖§ Advisor and Mentor

It is remarkable that despite all of this communal pressure and his own great devotion to Torah that did not permit him to waste a minute, the Chazon Ish never lost sight of the individual and he always made time for him. His two-room dwelling was open to all. People from all parts of *Eretz Yisrael* came to him with their personal problems. He worried and cared for countless yeshiva students and often intervened on their behalf. Many of the sick came to him for *brachos* and for the expert advice he was able to offer. (He had a very detailed knowledge of medicine and surgery.) Others came for comfort, and still others for him to settle their disputes. He took many orphaned boys into his home and personally cared for them for many years. Today many of them head yeshivos in their own right.

The following letters are but a small sampling of the many published and unpublished letters that portray his deep concern for the individual and his understanding of the human personality in all its complexities. The variations in style and nuance of expression reveal the different approaches he applied to each person and each situation.

In a letter advising someone to recommend a youngster to a yeshiva:

> *He possesses a gifted mind and is personable. He is also distracted by his inclinations — as are many bright fellows. He therefore needs constant guidance. But these are the ones who are destined for greatness. Therefore first tell the administration the brighter part, so they will accept him. Then it might be prudent to reveal the rest... (Vol. I, 75).*

> *Just recently a young father passed away leaving a widow and two small children. They are extremely poor. The widow wants to place the children in an orphanage run in accordance with Torah. Please see if you can assist... (Vol. II, 56).*

He was constantly concerned about the health and welfare of yeshiva students:

> *I arranged for...to take a vacation at the home of...as his health is wanting (Vol. II, 67-d).*

> *Perhaps you can arrange to go to a resort for a month for recuperation. Ask your soul to be kind to your body (Vol. II, 2).*

> *Please let me know of your health. What of the health of ...? I heard he was suffering intestinal distress...I wish him a complete recovery and a happy Yom Tov... (Vol. II, 103).*

> *It is sometime now that I have not heard how you are faring, and it is that that my soul yearns to hear. My preoccupations have prevented me from inquiring, but when I*

think, I find it difficult not to know....I eagerly await your letter... (Vol. II, 121).

A student by the name of ... came to me with his bitter story. Due to family problems, he cannot remain in Jerusalem. Therefore he turned to your yeshiva. But it is already a week that he is wandering about in your yeshiva. I understand that, according to the administration, he cannot be accepted, and he has no place there. I cannot possibly give him the positive answer he expects from me; that is for your administration to do. And for me to tell him that matters are outside of my realm — this response was long ago disqualified, as has been said: 'Is that a way to answer a bitter soul?' I therefore told him that I would try [to gain him admission], but could not guarantee anything definite. I am keeping my word to him with this letter, and because the situation of this student is such a difficult one — especially in our days when those attending yeshivos are so few...If you can answer affirmatively please do not keep the good news from me (Vol. II, 53)

In our days, the saving of a boy for a Torah training is no less urgent than saving him from drowning. Because of his age ... can be developed and elevated to the level of a scholar in a very short time, but he needs special attention. Perhaps private tutoring can be arranged mornings and evenings. This could be handled by one of the older boys (Vol. II, 57).

I have received your letter. There are no words with which to console you. But there is nothing to prevent the One who can comfort you from bringing you good on this world, to console your lonely soul. Towards this end I send my blessings... (Vol. II, 117).

You are missing the experience of sharing the pain of another. The way to achieve this is by trying to help him and shelter him from suffering. The actions will then affect the heart. Also attempt to pray on behalf of the next one, even though you do not yet fully feel his anguish (Vol. II, 123).

❀ ❀ ❀

A full appreciation of the Chazon Ish's personality can best be gained by studying his own writings. There is a most fitting tribute that can be applied to him, however, that was written some twenty centuries ago by Rebbe Meir:

"Whoever occupies himself with the study of Torah for its own sake merits many things; and not only that, but the entire world is worthwhile because of him. He is called friend, beloved, one who loves G-d, one who loves mankind. He brings joy to G-d and joy to mankind .... [The Torah] clothes him with humility and reverence ... People enjoy from him the benefit of counsel and sound wisdom, understanding and strength ... To him are revealed the mysteries of Torah, and he becomes as an ever-flowing fountain and as a river that never runs dry ..." (*Avos*, 6:1).

A Daughter Recalls a Great Father

"Moreinu" to the world — "Father" at home

Moreinu Yaakov Rosenheim ז״צל
5631/1870—5726/1965

I SEE my father seated with his *Gemara* in our book-lined study where he spent almost every waking moment he could spare from his other duties of the day. This was his sanctuary, and of a quiet evening — with the younger children asleep — my mother would join him with her sewing. Occasionally she would look up and smile and exchange a word with him.

This was the family harmony that permeated our home, as I remember it. Father was the dominating, quiet focus of our life, with our mother the ever-present smiling buffer between the lively activities and noise of nine children with their problems and varying activities. Our father's deep *yiras shamayim* and love of Torah were the guideposts of much of our development.

He was ever available to us. The three meals each day were family gatherings where we aired views and exchanged news, with our father listening, smiling and advising. Ours was a lively family — no limits were put on our conversation until a hint of *lashon hara* would reach his ears. With a word or a look he was able to put an end to any expressions which bordered an *lashon hara* or *r'chilus*. And so we were early taught by example the trait of *guarding one's speech.*

Seated at the head of the table, we anticipated his needs, for in all his life, father never *requested* anything at his own table. Unless it was provided, he would go without food; he often said to us: "Never ask for anything, unless it be given to you voluntarily."

Shabbos and *Yom Tov* were focal points of our lives. How I longingly recall the Friday evenings when our father — in our beautiful large dining room — presided over the long table with gleaming silverware, the children ranged by age along the table. His high melodious voice rang out at *Shalom Aleichem* when we stood, with our mother at his side, each child grasping one finger of his hand, as a tree with the branches springing from its roots. Each blessing with his hand resting on one's head was given with such warmth and feeling that his words permeated our whole being and created in us — even at a very young age — the Shabbos spirit which *we* in turn have tried to impart to our children. No Shabbos meal was complete in our home without two or three guests. They came from far and wide whether it was a *yeshiva bachur*, or a famous rav from the East. A procession of fascinating travellers, scholars, writers and rabbis graced the Rosenheim table each Shabbos.

I recall our excitement and interest when an outstanding *rebbe* would be our Shabbos guest. His *shtreimel* or *talis* or coat would be in our keeping until after Shabbos, so once or twice we could not resist snipping off a small piece or thread of a garment as a memento of an unforgettable visit. From East or West — every guest in our home was a king in his right — the Shabbos at the Rosenheim's was an experience not easily forgotten.

In his earlier years and in my earlier recollection, father often travelled away from home in connection with his work for *Klal Yisrael*. He would always return home in time for Shabbos. In our possession today is — as we called it — "father's *sefarim* suitcase." It is a small object and battered, proof of frequent use. On one occasion, at least, this suitcase had to be left at home, much to our father's chagrin. Prior to a trip to Poland, he was informed of a border restriction which did not permit foreign language books into Poland. Our father recalled with a smile and relish how his essential two or three *sefarim* — without which he would not travel — were smuggled into that country. A kind lady, sharing his train compartment, spirited them across the border — at his request — *in her personal hatbox*.

Forever mindful of his family and the importance and impact

of a *Yom Tov* celebration, our father introduced and continued a *minhag* for each of the *Shalosh Regalim*. Each family member — the servants included — received a personally selected *sefer*, appropriate to his age and interest. All his children own many books of lasting value, each with his loving personal inscription, ranging from children's stories by M. Lehmann to newly published rare *sefarim*. His satisfaction and contentment at our expressions of joy are part of our warmest memory.

It is well known that the *gedolei Yisrael* honored our father with the unusual title of *Moreinu*. It is, however, not known that no one in his home was ever permitted to discuss or even mention this honor. Some time after this memorable *Knessia Gedolah* we found the folded parchment document hidden carefully in the *far back* recesses of one of his bookcases.

My mother, always his companion and confidante, often was torn between her great pride in him and the humility he wanted everyone to show concerning any honors or tributes he was awarded. On the many occasions of an address, lecture or *shiur* to large audiences, we, his family, were always seated in the rear row of the hall or room. This was an unspoken rule in our family — never requested by our father, but showing him our understanding of *his* and therefore, *our* concept of living, forever shunning pride or ostentatious behavior.

Our father was known as an outstanding orator. His speeches were masterworks of organized thought which held his audiences spell-bound for as long as an hour or even two. And yet, after such an address, we would find a small white 2"x2" card in his pocket with perhaps four or five points arranged by number, pencilled in his beautiful Germanic script.

We left Germany in 1935 after two years of living under the Hitler regime. Nothing has ever been told of the actual circumstances of our flight or of our father's difficulties prior to his departure.

Father was greatly respected by the city government and police authorities of our native city Frankfurt-on-Main. As publisher of a German-language weekly newspaper he had frequent and cordial contacts with the authorities. At one point, early in the Hitler regime, he published an editorial expressing his dissatisfaction with an order to all Jews (as well as all citizens) to fly the German flag in celebration of some Nazi anniversary. This resulted in a peremptory summons on Shabbos morning to police headquarters — a walk of three quarters of an hour. I accompanied father on this walk on an icy cold winter Shabbos. We had spared my mother any knowledge of this, and set out on what may well have been the road to a prison or concentration camp. I will never forget our conversation, warm and yet casual on my personal problems, on my school studies as well as the *Parshah* of the week. He was calm as always, exuding faith as always. As we were about to enter the imposing Police building, he turned to me: "Wait for me here, if I have not returned within thirty minutes, you will know where I am. Return home and be of good cheer." The Almighty was with us and we returned home together after he was issued a "warning" to "temper" his editorials.

Our actual departure from Germany was caused by a set of circumstances, known to few people. We had returned on a Friday morning from a trip to Holland. We were told of the shocking morning edition of the *Voelkischer Beobachter*, the leading Nazi-newspaper, which had splashed across the front page our father's name and that of two other Agudah leaders (one already out of the country, another passed on). They were accused of being traitors to the Third Reich and of having plotted behind the scenes against the Nazi regime. It was almost Shabbos. Uncertain of the consequences, our father left his home again for a small town nearby to avoid possible arrest and yet not to desecrate the Shabbos. After Shabbos he continued his journey to Berlin where he learned the origin of the newspaper attack.

In early 1933, our father — with other Agudath Israel leaders — had an audience with the Pope in the Vatican to discuss a possible Nazi victory and to try to forestall utter disaster. One of the printed reports of this meeting issued to top Agudah leaders was lost in a hotel room in Berlin and found by a member of the Nazi party. Two years later the report was sold to the highest bidder — the infamous *Voelkischer Beobachter*.

Father returned home and quietly continued his work untouched by the fear of those around him, his deep faith unshaken as ever. He had friends amongst notorious Nazis and the local government. Guided by their old past friendship and their deepseated respect, the "powers to be" issued their "last warning" and thus *Moreinu* Rosenheim was put on the infamous Nazi "blacklist." Two months later, we were on our way to England and thus, the new Agudah World Headquarters were established in London.

The "Ba'al Seride Esh"

*his Torah
scholarship was
a bridge
between East
and West*

Rabbi Yechiel Yaacov Weinberg זצ״ל
5638/1878—5726/1966

THE PASSING of the renowned Gaon Yechiel Yaacov
Weinberg, זכר צדיק לברכה, stirs up memories of a remarkable
epoch in the recent history of Jewry on the Continent. It was
characterized by two outstanding personalities of genius, who
created a bridge between East and West and had an extraordinary
influence on the German-Jewish intelligentsia and especially two
Orthodox rabbis who grew up between the two World Wars:
Avraham Eliyah Kaplan, זצ״ל, and Yechiel Yaacov Weinberg,
זצ״ל.

These two great men had much in common. They both came
from Lithuania and were renowned Talmudists, writers and followers of the Mussar movement; both had found their way to the
Jewish outlook of Samson Raphael Hirsch, and both were connected with the Orthodox Rabbinical Seminary in Berlin. Their
aim was the same: to bring about a great revival of Talmud study
in Western and particularly in German Jewry by a combination of
what was best in the heritage of Lithuanian and German Jewry
and especially by a synthesis of the cognate religious philosophies
of Rabbi Yisrael Salanter and Rabbi Samson Raphael Hirsch.
However, while Rabbi Avraham Eliyah Kaplan died in the prime

of his life in 1924 and was thus spared the tragic catastrophe of European Jewry, Rabbi Weinberg personally experienced and survived the great *Churban*, broken in health but unbroken in spirit, and productive to his last day. When he died at the age of 88, he was universally recognized as one of the greatest authorities on Jewish law; a unique phenomenon in the world of scholarship, combining Talmudical authority of world fame with an equal mastery of modern secular knowledge. Unfortunately, most of Rabbi Weinberg's manuscripts were lost when he was arrested by the Nazis in 1938. However, what was saved by the thoughtfulness and courage of one of his disciples, Rabbi Eliezer Berkovits, is sufficient to secure for Rabbi Weinberg an outstanding place in the history of Jewish halachic and philosophical literature. In the years 1961, 1962 and 1966 (shortly before his death), three bulky volumes of his responsa were published by the Mossad Harav Kook in Jerusalem under the characteristic title of *Seride Esh*, i.e., "Remnants of the Fire." They deal with halachic questions addressed to Rabbi Weinberg from all over the world concerning the great problems of modern life — technological, social and personal. These three volumes have already become classics in the world of halachic literature. Like all great responsa works, they are — apart from their intrinsic halachic value — a faithful mirror of the time in which they were written and no doubt will become a fertile source for the research of future Jewish historians and sociologists. There seems little doubt that it is this monumental responsa work by which Rabbi Weinberg will be known and immortalized in Jewish history: as the *Gaon Ba'al Seride Esh*.

No less classical than his responsa are Rabbi Weinberg's studies on Talmudical methodology published under the title *Mechkarim beTalmud* in 1938 while Rabbi Weinberg was principal (rector) of the Orthodox Rabbinical Seminary in Berlin. This publication laid the foundation for Rabbi Weinberg's responsa work *Seride Esh*. It contains not only a great number of *sugyos*, explained in a novel manner by Rabbi Weinberg, but may be considered a handbook on Talmudic methodology. In *Mechkarim beTalmud*, the traditional Lithuanian *derech halimud* and the modern scientific approach to the study of Talmud became an organic unity. As for the typical Lithuanian method of Talmudical study which reached its zenith in Reb Chaim Brisker, Rabbi Weinberg had already described it in a series of essays which appeared in Wohlgemuth's *Jeschurun* as far back as 1916, in the following manner:

> "The first step in the task of reaching the deepest content of a halachah is to collect its details and then to unify them into an overall conceptual picture. Only then can one grasp the fundamental idea that underlies the details of a halachah and finally reach a logical definition of the halachic principle and thought-category. This combination of what is called in logic the inductive and deductive method infused new life and productivity into the Talmudic studies of the Lithuanian yeshivos."

◦§ His "Derech Halimud"

Rabbi Weinberg always remained loyal to the Lithuanian *derech halimud*. But he added to it, or rather organically combined with it, the modern scientific approach to Talmudic studies which is mainly concerned with the history, structure, and textual integrity of Mishnah and Gemara and uses the historical and philological method in Talmudic research. This method had been applied before Rabbi Weinberg, with great benefit, by such great Orthodox scholars as David Hoffmann and Hanoch HaKohen Ehrentreu. Of special interest in the work *Mechkarim beTalmud* are the chapters which deal with the *derech halimud* of the *rishonim* and with the justification of the traditional explanation in *Mishnah* and *Gemara* of *Exodus* 22:4, against a rendering in a fragment of the Palestinian Targum which was found in the Cairo Geniza and published in 1930. Among the many other important essays which Rabbi Weinberg wrote on the problem of Talmudic methodology are *Mechkarim beMishnah ubeTalmud* in *HaMeayen* (Jerusalem, Tishrei 5715) and *Mechkarim al Parshanut HaTalmudit leMishnah* in *Talpiot* (New York, Iyar 5715).

Rabbi Weinberg's philosophical writings dealing with *hashkafa* (Jewish outlook on life) were equally important and are on a par with his Talmudic writings. His Jewish religious philosophy was a synthesis of the philosophies of Reb Yisrael Salanter and Rabbi Samson Raphael Hirsch. These two great men moulded his Jewish outlook on life and he dealt with their *hashkafa* in a great number of outstanding Hebrew and German essays written over a period of more than fifty years. Rabbi Weinberg's essays on the great Jewish ethical revivalist movement known as Mussar first appeared in Wohlgemuth's famous journal *Jeschurun* during the years 1918-1921 and have been republished in a revised form and in an English translation in Dr. Leo Jung's anthology entitled *Men of the Spirit* (New York, 1964). There exists in Jewish literature no work which is comparable to Rabbi Weinberg's essays on the Mussar movement as far as the penetrating, psychological insight into Jewish moral philosophy, the soul of the Lithuanian Jew and the world of the Lithuanian Yeshiva are concerned. These essays bear the imprint of a genius of the first order. Equally distinguished by their understanding of the great problems of our time are the essays contained in his work *Volk der Religion* (Geneva, 1949). They deal with such themes as "Jewish Traditional Loyalty and Creative Freedom", "Faith and Modern Science", "The Physical Survival and the Spiritual Salvation of the Modern Jew" and "Judaism and World Civilization". The latter essay deals mainly with the religious philosophy of Samson Raphael Hirsch. Although Polish-born and Lithuanian-trained, Rabbi Weinberg had developed an extremely beautiful German prose style which was matched only by his mastery of modern Hebrew. As an appendix to the work *Volk der Religion* there was published the moving essay on "Religion and State in Israel." It was obviously written under the first impact of the creation of the State of Israel in 1948. Although he never identified himself formally with the Zionist movement, Rabbi Weinberg considered the re-emergence of the State of Israel as a visible manifestation of the Divine Providence in Jewish history. "I firmly believe," he used to say, "that the souls of our 6,000,000 martyrs gathered around the Throne of the Almighty and urged Him to show a visible sign of His loving care for His people and of the beginning of the Redemption of Israel." Nevertheless, he was very concerned about the religious position in the young Jewish state and movingly pleaded with the workers and heroes of Israel not to betray our religious and national heritage. The same concern and urgent pleading is evident in his reply to Ben-Gurion's well-known question "Who is a Jew?"

◆§ Influence of Rabbi Yisrael Salanter

There is hardly an Orthodox Hebrew journal of note, whether published in Israel or in the Diaspora, which does not contain a halachic or philosophical essay written by Rabbi Weinberg during the last 20 years of his life. All these essays have their roots in his Hebrew work *Lifrakim* (Warsaw, 5696-1936) which deals with *hashkafah* in the *Aggados* of the Talmud and their useful application in sermons, lectures and homiletical addresses. Influenced by the views of Reb Yisrael Salanter, Rabbi Weinberg laid great stress on the importance of the *drashah* as a means of popular education and inspiration and he often repeated the complaint of the founder of the Mussar Movement that the *lamdanim* had neglected the *drashah* at the expense of traditional Judaism. It is known that Reb Yisrael Salanter was not only a gaon in Talmudic learning, but a first-class orator and master of the *drashah*. Here too Rabbi Weinberg strove to emulate the example of his master. To anyone who studies the work *Lifrakim* it also becomes evident how greatly Hirsch's writings had influenced Rabbi Weinberg's Jewish philosophy, and that Rabbi Weinberg constantly tried to show the similarity between the views of Rabbis Hirsch and Salanter. (On the famous meeting between Hirsch and Salanter see *Three Generations*, London, 1958, p. 41.)

The extraordinary life story of Rabbi Yechiel Yaacov Weinberg — briefly described in the introduction to *Seride Esh* — led him from Lithuania to Berlin, from there to the Warsaw Ghetto and other concentration camps, and finally, after his liberation, to the calm resort of Montreux, Switzerland, where he spent the last 20 years of his life — secluded, but in constant correspondence with Jewish religious leaders throughout the world. The influence of the *Gaon of Montreux* — as he became known in later years — on the religious, halachic, and intellectual life of contemporary Jewry was enormous, though not outwardly apparent, because he shunned all publicity. His life and work awaits the description of future Jewish historians. It will be an uplifting task to write the story of the *Illuy of Czechanowic*, the brilliant *bachur* of the *mussar* yeshivos of Slobodka and Mir, the Rav of Pilwischki, the university lecturer of Giessen, the rector of the Hildesheimer Rabbinical Seminary in Berlin, the war-time president of the Agudas HaRabbanim of Warsaw who completed the cycle of his life in a remote Swiss townlet, having left all his titles and official positions behind him and yet wielding more influence than ever in the realm of the Jewish spirit by the sheer force of his personality and the stupendous range of his Torah scholarship and encyclopedic knowledge. It is a story full of grandeur though also of national and personal tragedy.

Perhaps I may be permitted to conclude this short sketch with a few personal reminiscences. As a young student I attended Rabbi Weinberg's lectures at the University of Ciessen. His lectures were always crowded. Not only students of theology and oriental languages, but also students of other faculties and even university professors sat at his feet, impressed by the depth of his thought and enchanted by the slow and deliberate manner of his lecturing and his deep sonorous speaking voice. I can never forget his brilliant strictures against Bible criticism and his convincing arguments in favor of the authenticity of Jewish tradition. Few were able to combine Talmudic and Biblical scholarship as Rabbi Weinberg did. With his sharp dialectical mind and his wide range of knowledge, this proud Lithuanian Jew did not find it difficult to impart, even to non-Jewish listeners, a deep respect for Jewish traditional values.

◆§ The Stamp of Greatness

When I saw Rabbi Weinberg last in Montreux a few years before his passing he had lost nothing of his intellectual brilliance, his moral stature and his open-mindedness to the great problems of our generation. A universal genius and of a deeply religious mind, he bore the genuine stamp of greatness; simplicity. Although he gave an occasional *shiur* to the students of the Montreux Yeshiva, he mainly kept to himself and was surrounded only by a few selected students and personal friends. And yet his little room in Montreux was the religious and intellectual nerve center of an ever-widening circle of religious leaders, writers, thinkers and men of affairs in contemporary Jewish life. He *davened* in a little *minyan* and those who were privileged to listen to his talks on Shabbos afternoons can never forget the lucid and simple way in which that great man was able to deal with the deepest problems of the human mind. He could truly say of himself: *nil humani mihi alienum est* (nothing human is strange to me). Judaism was for him ennobled humanism and the Torah the formative power of Jewish life. The essence of Judaism he saw in the fact that it elevates all human activities into the sphere of the religious, and a *tzaddik* to him was a hero in the sanctification of life. The mitzvos he considered as the natural, functional expression of the living Jewish soul. He objected to religious observance turning into no more than routine habit instead of arising out of an inner need, bursting from the depths of the soul and becoming a dynamic force controlling the whole human being.

Rabbi Weinberg was deeply fond of nature. To accompany him on a walk along the shores of the lake of Montreux, surrounded by the majestic Swiss mountains, and to listen to his words of wisdom, meant to experience a living demonstration of the synthesis of soul, intellect, natural beauty and, above all, the beauty of holiness. But then, he was not only a great Sage, but also a great *ba'al mussar*.

Rabbi Yechiel Yaacov Weinberg was one of the rare great ones who succeeded in embracing in the course of a single life a whole period of Eastern and Western Jewish history and in telescoping these two worlds into a single unit. In Rabbi Weinberg's genius East and West met in a rare cross-fertilization, the fruits of which will only be recognized in the future. Many years will pass until his true position in the history of Jewish life and thought will really be understood.

In one of his essays on Samson Raphael Hirsch, Rabbi Weinberg wrote: "His whole life was a single cry from the depth of an aching heart — a cry which is echoed in the words of the poet: התנערי מעפר קומי לבשי בגדי תפארתך עמי "Shake Thyself from the dust, arise, put on the garments of thy glory, O my people!" With these words it seems to me, Yechiel Yaacov Weinberg wrote his own epipath.

Dayan Dr. I. Grunfeld wrote this article shortly after his retirement from the London Beth Din (Court of the Chief Rabbi), the Central Beth Din of the United Hebrew Congregations of the British Commonwealth, which he served since 1938. Dayan Grunfeld enjoyed an international reputation for his original works on Orthodox Judaism in the English language, and especially for his translations and interpretations of the works of Rabbi Samson Raphael Hirsch. The above is an extract from a work by Dayan Grunfeld on the Life and Work of Rabbi Yechiel Yaacov Weinberg, who himself was an exponent of the Hirschian philosophy.

The Or Same'ach

*the light that
shone from
Dvinsk*

Rabbi Meir Simcha HaKohen זצ״ל
5603/1843—5686/1926

◆§ Dvinsk — City of Gaonim

LIKE a woman who has been forced into many unwanted
marriages, the city has been known by many names. Yet, no
one speaks of Daugavpils today; Dunaburg is mentioned only
momentarily when one relates a *vort* from Reb Reuvele
Dinaburger's *Rosh LaReuvaini.* Even the larger area of Latgale is
forgotten, and Latvia herself lies silently anonymous in the belly
of the great Russian bear.

But *Dvinsk* lives on. For as long as Jews study the
monumental works of Reb Yoseif Rosen, the Gaon of Rogatchov, and Reb Meir Simcha HaKohen, the name of Dvinsk will
be spoken with respect and a touch of awe! Indeed, in the century
and a half of the existence of the Jewish community in Dvinsk,
two of the Torah giants of all ages flourished there, in the same
period: From 1888, when the Rogatchover assumed the position
of Rabbi of the Chassidic community of the city, until Reb Meir
Simcha's death in 1926, Dvinsk was a dual Torah center for the
world.

Despite differences in approach to halachic problems, in personal temperament and in deportment, Reb Meir Simcha's and the Rogatchover's "constituency" was the same: *Klal Yisrael.* Letters from around the globe poured into Dvinsk seeking Torah guidance. It is no wonder that Reb Meir Dan Plotski, author of the *Klei Chemdah,* declared with unabashed admiration upon leaving the city: "I am envious of the city of Dvinsk for having merited the presence of two such great *gaonim.*"[1]

◂§ The Two Half-Rabbis

The phenomenon of two rabbis in a Lithuanian city was a common one, for almost every city contained two distinct communities, the Sephardic — here referring to Chassidim — and the Ashkenazic, also known as the Misnagdim. In the case of Dvinsk, the distinction was somewhat blurred because all factions of world Jewry claimed each of the two Torah giants as their own. Reb Meir Simcha had joked good-naturedly about the dichotomy.

□ *Two rabbis who had come to visit Reb Meir Simcha were waiting in his study for him to rise from a nap. The Rebbetzin notified Reb Meir Simcha that two rabbis were waiting for him, but when he glanced through the door and saw who they were, he corrected her, "No, there is only one rabbi. Like me, each of them is only a half a rabbi; thus only one is waiting."*[2]

The two "half-rabbis" of Dvinsk maintained a unique relationship, testing each other upon the most esoteric and abstruse Talmudic questions,[3] and each humorously commenting upon the other's Torah knowledge and greatness:

□ *Someone once commented in front of Reb Meir Simcha that the Rogatchover had a phenomenal memory. "Nonsense," replied Reb Meir Simcha, "he hasn't any memory at all. A person with an extraordinary memory is one who many years later remembers something he studied long ago with the same freshness. Reb Yoseif reviews the entire Talmud daily and is always in the midst of every portion of the Gemara. Is this memory?"*[4]

On another occasion, Reb Meir Simcha characterized the Rogatchover's myriad references to any Talmudic question in the following way:

□ *When the Rogatchover cites ten places in the Talmud to elucidate a difficult question, one of them is a perfect reference which exactly fits the question as if the Rashba had*

◦§ A Reb Meir Simcha Sampler

Upon even the most preliminary study of the Meshech Chochmah, *one's first and continuing impression must be one of wonder at Reb Meir Simcha's absolute mastery of so many disciplines, styles and approaches, each brought into play precisely where it is needed and where it does the most to elucidate that particular passage.*

The examples in this sampler were selected in an attempt to convey the incredible eclecticism of the Meshech Chochmah. *Within his commentary upon five passages, one may find a halachic interpretation of what seems to be merely a narrative; a deep philosophical essay; a profound discourse traversing all of Jewish history and relating the* pasuk *to contemporary problems; an eloquent call to morals and ethics worthy of great* ba'alei mussar; *an excursion into the abstruse world of* Kabbalah; *a light, almost humorous touch.*

For the sake of brevity, we have selected only short commentaries.

Bereishis 12:16 — "And [Abraham] had sheep and oxen and male donkeys, and men-servants and maid-servants and female donkeys and camels." One reason for this detailed list is to note that Abraham never intended to settle permanently in Egypt: he had not purchased horses. The Egyptians did not permit the export of horses (see *Ramban* on *Devarim 18:16*) and since Abraham would soon have to sell them, he did not buy any to begin with.

Bereishis 13:4 — "To the place of the altar he had built earlier." The Talmud *(Menachos 10a)* states concerning another matter that whenever the expression "the place of..." is used, the subject (of ...) is no longer in existence. Here, too, the place where Abraham had built his altar had been made into a center for idol worship. Therefore *(Avodah Zara 52b)*, the altar itself lost all holiness and, indeed, became a forbidden object. However, the ministrations of the idol-worshiper could not defile the place itself (in accordance with *Avodah Zara 45a*), which retained its holiness.

Tehillim 26:8 — "L-rd, I love the dwelling of Your house and *the place* of Your Holy Sanctuary." As in the above passage, even in the absence of the Holy Ark and the Sanctuary, the *place* itself is holy.

been speaking. However, the Rogatchover himself does not know which one.[5]

The Rogatchover, too, would comment upon Reb Meir Simcha in a similar vein, saying, "Reb Meir Simcha claims that he has no knowledge of *achronim* (later Torah authorities), but I know for a fact that he is an absolute master of every word in the *Shach*."[6]

Of course, the witty exchanges between the two Torah giants were merely reflections of a deep inner mutual respect and affection. The Rogatchover Gaon paid Reb Meir Simcha the ultimate compliment when he sent all those who came to him for a blessing to Reb Meir Simcha. "Go to the *Kohen*," he used to tell all. And Reb Meir Simcha would often refer questions requiring great amounts of research and erudition to the Rogatchover. "I will have to toil all night over this," he would say, "but step in to the Rogatchover and he will answer you on the spot."[8]

◆§ The Enlightening "Light"

Today, with the aid of a half century of evaluation, we can easily say that both the Rogatchover's *Tzofnas Paane'ach* and Reb Meir Simcha's *Or Same'ach* are true Torah classics. Yet, time has also shown that while the Rogatchover's *sefarim* remain the domain of a select few who have become accustomed to his terminology based on the *Rambam's Moreh* and the myriad references to every point, the *Or Same'ach* is the cherished treasure of many a *ben Torah*. Terse, to the point, often resplendently brilliant in its original interpretations, the *Or Same'ach* is a "must" in countless *batei midrash*.

Torah classics do not achieve their status easily. There is no weekly best-seller list, and no published book review can grant instant status to a new *sefer*. Perhaps no other type of publication in the world receives as careful scrutiny as volumes of Torah *chiddushim*. Experts in the field examine every thought and idea again and again, generation after generation. Talmudic discussions are not studied in moments of light reading, but from total immersion in one minute area of thought. Very few have survived such scrutiny and maintained their lofty status.

The names are engraved in our minds and hearts — the *K'tzos* and *Nesivos*, Reb Akiva Eiger ... and the *Chazon Ish*, *Chiddushei Reb Chaim*, and the *Achi Ezer* in many communities ... and the *Or Same'ach* on the *Rambam*. A *talmid chacham* maintains a unique relationship with each of these classics. As he

begins a paragraph, there is a picture in his mind's eye of a *gadol
baTorah*, one of the *tzaddikim* of the generation, a man whose
Torah opinions have become integrated into the eternal Torah
heritage.

And yet, as one examines a new *sevara* — a new concept — by
one of these *gedolim*, the relationship is an intellectual one.
Nothing is taken for granted, no explanation is accepted *because*
Reb Meir Simcha has written it, or *because* Reb Chaim has said it
must be so. Every word is reevaluated afresh, every concept dis-
sected, every interpretation critically analyzed.

It is under these incredibly exacting conditions that the *Or
Same'ach* is today considered an indispensable Torah classic.

◆§ The Tenth Man

Only once during the period from 1887 to 1926 did Dvinsk
have but one rabbi. When World War I broke out, in 1914, the
Russian Commander, Grand Duke Nikolai Nikolayevitch (uncle
of Czar Nikolai II) ordered the expulsion of the Jews from along
the Russo-German Front. Dvinsk became dangerous for Jews,
with famine and disease wreaking havoc. All who could fled the
city. Even the Rogatchover was prevailed upon by his followers
to escape.

But Reb Meir Simcha would not go. Neither the entreaties of
his friends and students nor letters from *gedolim* around the
world could persuade him to abandon his post. "As long as there
are nine other Jews in that city, I will be the tenth for a *minyan*,"
he declared, and so infused hope and courage into his brethren.
When he was reminded of the constant danger, Reb Meir Simcha
declared, "Every bullet has a designated address and none will
reach where there has been no Heavenly decree that it do so."[9]

□ *One stormy October during this difficult period, terrifying news quickly spread through Dvinsk: "They're taking the Rav!" Everyone ran into the street and beheld the shattering sight of Reb Meir Simcha surrounded by burly Cossacks carrying drawn revolvers. Only the serene visage and calm demeanor of Reb Meir Simcha saved the horrified crowd from hysteria.*

Despite the obvious dangers of doing so, thousands of Jews and Gentiles signed petitions attesting to the nobility of the Rav's character and his vital importance to the well-being of all members of that city. That very day, Reb Meir Simcha was freed and was never molested again.[10]

✺§ The Respect of the Gentiles

The above incident illustrates one of Reb Meir Simcha's more unique qualities: his relationship with the non-Jews of Dvinsk. A *Gaon* following the most ancient of traditions — spending virtually all of his time studying and teaching Torah — Reb Meir Simcha developed a reputation as a Holy Man among the Gentiles of the city. Indeed it is said that when Reb Meir Simcha was incarcerated by the authorities, a certain Christian tanner presented himself in the *Rav's* place, imploring, "Please do not harass this holy man. For the good of the city, let him go."

Reb Meir Simcha's reputation was so widespread that even non-Jews sought him to settle their quarrels. Some say his acceptability began with the case of the Jew and the gypsy.

□ *A Jew and a gypsy had been business partners when a major conflict of interests developed between them. Not being able to come to an agreement themselves, the gypsy suggested they go to Reb Meir Simcha for a decision. The Jewish man agreed and they presented their case to the Rav. Reb Meir Simcha listened with particularly careful attention and proceeded with his own independent investigation. After satisfying himself about the facts, Reb Meir Simcha decided in favor of the gypsy. From that day forward, the word of Reb Meir Simcha's justice and objectivity spread throughout all of Dvinsk and indeed Latvia.*[12]

Reb Meir Simcha was known to joke about this phenomenon and with a smile would say, "A Chassidic Rebbe often has many types of Chassidim, but I draw *all* types of followers."[13]

Another aspect of the singular esteem in which Reb Meir Simcha was held was the widespread belief in his ability to literal-

✑ A Reb Meir Simcha Sampler

Bereishis 15:8 — "How shall I know that I will truly inherit
the land?" The understanding of Abraham's question
lies in the knowledge that only a promise made by G-d
through a prophet cannot be revoked (see *Rambam, Hilchos
Yesodei Hatorah* 10:4 and *Introduction to Mishna);* a promise
made to an individual can be rescinded due to that person's
sins. Therefore, although Abraham knew that his children
were secure because they would hear G-d's promise through
Abraham *the prophet,* he was worried that his own sins could
exclude *him* from participation in the promise.

ly bring about miracles. A resident of Dvinsk relates the following:

□ *I remember when the Dvina overflowed its banks and
threatened to flood the city. Gentiles and Jews alike swore by
all that was holy to them that they saw Reb Meir Simcha
mount the embankment, gaze at the swirling waters for a
moment, murmur something very quietly and — the waters
withdrew and the danger passed.*[13]

Another such story was often related by an important
member of the Dvinsk *Koholisher Shul,* where Reb Meir Simcha
prayed.

□ *Once, on my way to catch a train which was scheduled to
leave shortly, I stopped in to say goodbye to the Rav and to
notify him of my trip. Departing from character, the Rav
began to ask me questions about this and that, seemingly unaware of my great rush. Every time I protested that I would
miss my train, the Rav brushed aside my complaints and
brought up another subject. Out of respect for the Rav, I
could not simply leave, and I missed the train. Later, I found
out that the train had derailed causing many deaths and
casualties.*[15]

✑ The Wise Judge

Despite his reputation for powers bordering on the miraculous, Reb Meir Simcha's primary traits were his incredible
wisdom, his genuine concern for people, and the eloquence and
beauty of every phrase.

□ *In a* din Torah *brought before Reb Meir Simcha, both litigants claimed a piece of land. The Rav attempted to bring the two men to an acceptable compromise, but both stood their ground stubbornly. Suddenly the Rabbi announced that he wished to see the plot of land under dispute. When they were all standing on the contested ground, Reb Meir Simcha planted his walking stick into the ground and announced: "Here are two people, each has a valid claim and each declares, 'This ground is mine.' And here is the ground which declares,* 'you are both mine.' "

The words made a deep impression on both men and eventually they were able to compromise.[16]

In addition to his mastery of the technical details of halachah, Reb Meir Simcha had an amazingly accurate ear for discerning truth and falsity. This trait stood him in good stead during the Russian occupation of Dvinsk in 1919, when the Bolsheviks prohibited rabbis from adjudicating disputes according to the laws of the Torah. They were only allowed to act as arbitrators following secular guidelines.

□ *Two butchers had submitted a dispute to Reb Meir Simcha for binding arbitration. During their presentations, Reb Meir Simcha discerned that one of them was presenting false evidence. Immediately, the Rabbi stood up and declared to the man in awesome and measured tones: "No doubt you are brazen enough to present your false claims because you know that my capacity here is merely that of arbitrator. But I am sure, that were I to tell you that as Rabbi of the city, I hereby administer to you a Biblical oath to tell the truth, you would not persist in your lies."*

Reb Meir Simcha's powerful words, imposing stature, and flaming eyes completely disarmed the butcher and he admitted that his claims had been false all along.[17]

On another occasion, Reb Meir Simcha's keen insight into human nature rescued an innocent young man from a terrible fate:

□ *The son of the rabbi of one of the villages in Latgale maintained a small grocery store, not far from the local church. A young servant-girl, who worked for the priest, regularly bought supplies from this store. One day, it became known that the girl had succumbed, and that she had imputed the act to the Jewish merchant. A paternity suit was swiftly brought against the young man and he was*

Bereishis 24:7 — The fact that Abraham did not *command* Isaac to refrain from marrying a Canaanite woman is proof of the *Maharik's* position (167; *Rama, Yoreh Deah* 240:25) that a son is not required to listen to his father concerning the woman he wishes to marry.

scheduled for trial the following week. Distraught and panic-stricken, the young man followed his father's advice and went to Reb Meir Simcha for counsel. After listening to the sorry tale, Reb Meir Simcha advised, "Announce before the judges that you are indeed the father of the child and are prepared to accept full responsibility for his upbringing as a Jewish child."

The Rabbi's advice left the pious young man thunderstruck, but he accepted the words as if they were written in the Torah itself.

The courthouse was packed and in the front row sat the accusing servant-girl and near her, the priest. When the young man stood up and announced his acceptance of paternity and his intention to bring up the child in Jewish tradition, the simple peasant-girl let out a cry, "Oh no, holy spirit, I cannot allow the son of such a man to be brought up as a Jew!"

The priest's face turned crimson and the truth of the child's paternity emerged.[18]

His Special Way With Words

In seeking to define the special quality of Reb Meir Simcha which allowed him to influence so deeply the members of his community, we may follow his own example in discovering the *uniqueness* of many *gedolim* who had preceded him. For instance, he would single out the *Nodah B'Yehuda* for the clarity of his explanations, the *Tumim* for his intellect, the Vilna *Gaon* for the comprehensiveness of his erudition, the *N'sivos* for his profundity and Rabbi Akiva Eiger for his methodology.

A thorough examination of Reb Meir Simcha's Talmudic novellae in his *magnum opus* the *Or Same'ach* is beyond the scope of both this writer and this biographical sketch. But a clue to Reb Meir Simcha's success in human relations lies in a line from his monumental posthumously published work on Chumash, the *Meshech Chochmah*.

□ *In* Vayikra *(5:20) Reb Meir Simcha explains a passage using the principle, "One of the characteristics of the Torah is that statements are arranged in accordance with the beauty of the language."*

This concern with not only the content of what is said, but with the aesthetics of the framing of a statement, was a prime factor in Reb Meir Simcha's use of the spoken and written word. His every utterance radiated an elegance and refinement which granted every word he used a special and definitive meaning. Just as he believed every bullet had an address, he understood that every word had to speed directly to its target, else something infinitely precious would be wasted. Thus, in his dealings with transgressors of any kind, his words were not meant to hurt or destroy, but to nurse the spiritual wound and rebuild the ravaged soul.

□ *One Shabbos, on his way to* shul, *Reb Meir Simcha met the son of one of the city's trustees as the young man was lighting his cigar. The disconcerted fellow stood riveted to the spot, the color quickly rising to his ears, as he was too frozen even to remove the cigar from his mouth.*

"A gutten Shabbos, Meirel," said the Rabbi serenely, "you've no doubt forgotten it's Shabbos. Yes, of course, 'Remember the day of Shabbos to keep it holy,' " and the Rabbi proceeded on his way as if nothing had happened.

The young man was later to say it was a lesson he would remember for the rest of his life.[19]

◄§ The Fruits of a Torah Life

Reb Meir Simcha's acumen in judging human beings was not simply a personal wisdom, developed through scientific methods, enhanced by the fortune of an excellent brain. Reb Meir Simcha's sagacity was *pure Torah.* He knew no other source of knowledge, and indeed he neither sought nor needed it. By the time he was seven, the *Tanach* was on his fingertips; by nine, he knew one-sixth of the Talmud thoroughly; by ten, he was teaching himself, for there was no longer a *rebbe* in Baltrimantz capable of teaching him Torah.[21]

By the time he was in his teens, Reb Meir Simcha had become — totally and completely — a vessel for Torah knowledge.

Vayikra 1:1 — Our early sages are in dispute concerning the reason for the commandment to bring sacrifices. The *Rambam*, in *Moreh Nevuchim*, states that sacrifices are meant to prevent the Jewish people from becoming lured into idolatry by the enticement of following their natural inclination toward sacrifice. The *Ramban*, strongly objecting, states that sacrifices accomplish results of far-reaching universal significance, beyond the furthest reach of the human mind. A meeting point of these two views may be found in the understanding that only the permission to sacrifice upon a *bamah* (private altar) was granted to avoid Jewish enticement to idolatrous practices. In the *Bais HaMikdash*, however, the purpose of the *korbanos* was always to perform those esoteric functions of the cosmos, which only the Creator totally understands.

His speech reflected statements in the Talmud, and indeed even in writings he never intended to publish, the cadences of *Chazal* are audible in every line.

An example may be found in a gloss written by Reb Meir Simcha in his youth upon a page of the Responsa of the *Chasam Sofer*. It was his custom to fill almost every *sefer* in which he studied with comments on the subject at hand.

In this particular responsum, the *Chasam Sofer* had strongly criticized a Talmudic discourse written by the author of the *K'tzos Hachoshen*, who was a *Kohen*. Reb Meir Simcha prefaces his remarks in defense of the *K'tzos* with the words: "A *Kohen* comes to the aid of a *Kohen*."

If we did not know otherwise, we might dismiss such a line as a mere curiosity, or perhaps a young would-be scholar amusing himself. But we are speaking of Reb Meir Simcha HaKohen, the future *Or Same'ach*, to whom each word is precious, and indeed, Torah. Thus, not surprisingly, the *Gemara (Eruvin* 105a and *Chulin* 49a) records that sages of the Talmud, also *Kohanim*, "came to the aid" of their brother *Kohanim* with appropriate interpretations of Scripture.[22]

Especially noteworthy, Reb Meir Simcha wrote his comment on an old volume in the *bais hamidrash* of Baltrimantz, never dreaming that the glosses would one day be published. Why then abstruse references to obscure statements in the Talmud which are not even relevant to the subject at hand? Because even then Reb Meir Simcha *thought* in terms of the words of the Talmud. Reb Meir Simcha's *sichas chulin* (ordinary talk) literally came from *Mesechta Chulin*, as well as all the other Talmudic tractates.

Reb Meir Simcha in his teens was already a living embodiment of Torah — breathing, walking, and personally reflecting every line of the Talmud. What did he do then? *He sat down for twenty-seven uninterrupted years to learn Torah.*[24]

When Rabbi Lipele Halpern, author of the famed *Oneg Yom Tov*, passed away, the youthful Reb Meir Simcha was offered the vacated position of *Rav* of Bialystok. But Reb Meir Simcha felt he had to learn more, to delve deeper, to gain perfection, to become ... a *gadol*.

◆§ Three Generations: A Chain of Fiery Holiness

An example of this ability to stand back and view himself objectively, to remain steadfast and "not enter to see the holy place" may be seen in an incident which occurred during Reb Meir Simcha's period of study in Bialystok.

□ *A terrible canard had been circulated about Rabbi Yehoshua Leib Diskin, the Brisker Rav, and he was being brought to the capital city of Horodna for judgment. On the way to Horodna, the carriage carrying Reb Yehoshua Leib passed through Bialystok and all the Jewish townspeople went out to give honor to the great Rav of Brisk and to demonstrate their support. Reb Meir Simcha had wished to get close enough to Reb Yehoshua Leib to say "Shalom Aleichem," but upon nearing the carriage, Reb Meir Simcha gazed upon the holy visage of Reb Yehoshua Leib, who appeared to be more of heaven than earth, and ventured no closer.*

□ *Several years later Reb Yehoshua Leib conducted himself in a similar manner in relation to the Kosel Ma'aravi. Reb Yehoshua Leib lived within walking distance of the Kosel. He did not agree with those who maintain that it is forbidden to walk in the Kosel vicinity, yet, he never went. His close students relate that he was afraid that if he actually stood upon that holy spot, he would virtually faint from awe over the majesty of the place. On the one occasion that he did* almost reach the Kosel, *his entire body shook with uncontrollable tremors and he was literally in danger for his life.*[25]

As if to complete the "triple braided chain which cannot be broken," it is told that when Reb Baruch Ber Leibowitz, Rosh Yeshiva of Knesses Bais Yitzchok in Slobodka, heard that Reb Meir Simcha was coming to Kovna, he put on his Shabbos clothing and went to meet him. However, when he reached the house where Reb Meir Simcha was staying, he could not bring himself to enter.

"How can I approach him?" Reb Boruch Ber said. "The Rebbe, Reb Chaim Soloveitchik, called him the prince of the Torah." And he turned and went back to Slobodka.

Thus we have three consecutive generations of *gedolim* who were so humble in their self-perception that they could not bring themselves to approach what they perceived as unattainable holiness ... What shall *we* say?

◆§ Beyond Time and Space

Despite Reb Meir Simcha's acute awareness of the decline of Torah greatness from generation to generation, when he was deeply immersed in learning Torah time and space were totally irrelevant. Since he would often pace while pondering Talmudic problems, Reb Meir Simcha occasionally found himself far from home, *Gemara* in hand, when he emerged from his reverie. A contemporary *gadol* relates that his cousin was present when Reb Meir Simcha climbed a ladder to reach a *sefer* on an upper shelf. Opening the *sefer* while still high on the ladder, he soon became engrossed in its contents and *did not realize his position until morning.*[26]

Thus we may observe in Reb Meir Simcha's work, and indeed in his life, a wonderful paradox. Living most of the day and night in the timeless universe of the Torah, Reb Meir Simcha was nevertheless one of the keenest observers and critics of the contemporary scene. His haunting prediction of the Holocaust and events leading up to it — "They will think that Berlin is Jerusalem" — is now famous and an integral part of any Torah-oriented syllabus of Holocaust studies.[27] In his comments on *Megillas Esther*, Reb Meir Simcha discusses the then-current situation in Morocco and Romania.

One of Reb Meir Simcha's most provocative statements in his *Meshech Chochmah* concerns the deterioration of values in each new Diaspora, leading ultimately to the next one:

When they enter a strange land, they will undoubtedly be on a low spiritual level, a result of years of wandering and anguish. However, soon their inner, more noble and holy instincts will propel them to return, to learn, to advance, until their Torah knowledge and observance is on its highest achievable level.

Eventually, a new generation will have nothing to add in matters spiritual and sacred. They will slowly seek other areas in which to excel and to add to what their fathers have accomplished ... leading to denial of the value of their ancestral heritage ... [and] a storm of destruction follows.

(Interestingly, a theory on literary criticism that has gained prominence recently seems to echo this very same theme explicated by Reb Meir Simcha several generations ago.[29])

❧ The Last Days

In the summer of 1926, Reb Meir Simcha became critically ill and telegrams were sent from Dvinsk to *gedolim* all over the world to pray for their *Rav.* Reb Meir Simcha was staying at the Metropol Hotel in Riga, where he was being treated, and many *gedolim* visited him there. Rabbi Elchonon Wasserman later recalled that upon his suggestion that telegrams be sent to all yeshivos to say *Tehillim* in his behalf, Reb Meir Simcha responded characteristically with a statement from the *Zohar* that He Who cares for all of Israel will watch over this one of His sons also.

One of Reb Meir Simcha's students, Rabbi Chaim Horash, relates (in his memoirs *Simchas Chaim*) of his visit to Reb Meir Simcha's bedside on 2 Elul, 1926, two days before Reb Meir Simcha's passing:

It was eleven o'clock at night and the Rav was laying in bed, his lips constantly moving. As I moved closer, I was able to hear that he was studying Taharos by heart. When he perceived someone's presence, Reb Meir Simcha looked up and said, "Is that you, my son? Sit, my son, sit." Then he said in profoundly moving tones, "Oh Hashem, my suffering is great. I cannot study Torah properly." And then his lips continued to move with the words of Mishnayos Taharos.

❧ The Final Tribute

His funeral was well attended, but the greatest tribute was not the formal speeches.

□ *The* Chofetz Chaim, *then the acknowledged elder sage of world Jewry, sat on the steps outside the* bais hamidrash *where the eulogies were being conducted (a* Kohen, *he could not enter) and was heard to lament, after reciting the names of* gedolim *who had recently passed on, "And now Reb Meir Simcha is also gone...who has remained to guide us?"*

Even the Rogatchover Gaon, who dismissed the greatest scholars of his age with a word or phrase, paid Reb Meir Simcha the greatest posthumous compliment.

□ *Going to Reb Meir Simcha's cherished spot in the* bais hamidrash, *where he spent days and nights for almost half a century, the Rogatchover ordered that Reb Meir Simcha's* shtender *(lectern) be interred in the grave with him. The tradition of doing so is an ancient one but it is only performed where there is secure knowledge that the inanimate wood could testify in a Heavenly Court to its master's total dedication to Torah.*[30]

In Reb Meir Simcha's case, both the shtender *and the Rogatchover Gaon were thoroughly knowledgeable of the true extent of his dedication to Torah.*

It is scarcely half a century ago, and yet ... we no longer live in Reb Meir Simcha's world, nor perhaps even understand it. But we can yearn.

FOOTNOTES

1. Rabbi Zev A. Rabiner, *Rabbeinu Meir Simcha HaKohen, Tel Aviv,* 1967, p. 192.

2. Rabiner, p. 174.   3. See article on the Rogatchover Gaon that follows.

4,5,6. Rabiner, p. 193.   7. ibid., p. 43.

8. S. Levenberg, *The Jews in Latvia,* Tel Aviv, 1971, pp. 225-227.

9. Rabbi S. Y. Zevin, *Ishim V'shitos,* Tel Aviv, 1966, p. 159.   10,11. Rabiner, p. 48.

12. ibid., p. 38.   13. ibid., p. 173.   14. *Jews in Latvia,* p. 266.   15. Rabiner, p. 186.

16,17. ibid., p. 35.   18. ibid., p. 187.   19,20. ibid., p. 173.   21. ibid., p. 17.

22. For a detailed explanation of this concept, see Rabbi Reuven Margolies, מחקרים בדרכי התלמוד וחידותיו, Jerusalem, 1967, pp. 89-90.   23. Rabiner, p. 204.

24. Chronology: born: 1843; married: 1860 (17 years old); became Rav of Dvinsk: 1867; passed away: 1926.

25. Rabbi Moshe Sternbuch, *Moadim Uzemanim,* Jerusalem, 1970, v. 222, note 2.

26. Heard from Rabbi Yaakov Yitzchok Ruderman שליט״א, Rosh Yeshiva, Ner Israel-Baltimore.

27. *Mesech Chochmah* on *B'chukosei* 26:44.   28. ibid.

29. Harold Bloom in *The Anxiety of Influence and A Map of Misreading.*

30. For more on this custom, see Rabbi Shlomo Ashkenazi, *Doros B'Yisroel,* Tel Aviv, 1975, p. 309.

The Rogatchover Gaon

*genius in a
generation of
giants*

Rabbi Yoseif Rosen זצ"ל
5618/1858—5696/1936

*The obviously weary young woman tremulously
entered the room. She had already been to all the "experts" — doctors, wet-nurses — even to Chassidic Rebbes
for a* brachah. *All to no avail. Her infant son, premature
and underweight, strangely refused to nurse on Shabbos
and Yom Tov. Formula was out of the question for the impoverished family, and the long Succos holiday was approaching. Her neighbors terrified her with old wives'
tales, and well-meaning relatives thrust assorted amulets
open her. Nothing seemed to help and this was her last
desperate hope.*

*The imposing-looking rabbi, with the head that
seemed too massive for his frail body, looked up from his
Gemara and listened patiently to the bizarre problem.
Without a moment's hesitation, he counseled her: "Wear
your weekday clothing when you nurse the infant on
Shabbos and Yom Tov." A few days later, the woman's
husband came back beaming: "Rabbi, you're a prophet,
you have ruach hakodesh! Your advice worked!" he exclaimed.*

The rabbi seemed amused. "This matter is explicitly recorded in a Tosafos in Bava Kamma 37a," he explained. "The Mishnah states that an ox can be considered a mu'ad (needing extra guarding because he has gored a number of times) on Shabbos, but not on weekdays. Tosafos explains that on Shabbos an ox may not recognize those usually familiar to him because they are wearing different clothing. We see from Tosafos that intelligence at its simplest stages identifies people by outer factors such as color and shape. This poor woman had changed her garment in honor of Shabbos and her particularly sensitive infant mistook the change of clothing as a change of person."[1]

◆§ The Universe of Halacha

SUCH was the universe of Rabbi Yoseif Rosen — known as the Gaon of Rogatchov (his birthplace). A world where no phenomenon, no problem — cosmic or infinitesimal — is beyond the realm of the Torah. And not simply Torah, but *halachah*. It is far from unique in Jewish history to discover *gedolim* who found answers to all social, communal, and domestic problems in the Torah. Since Sinai, the only genuinely Jewish orientation has been אסתכל באורייתא וברא עלמא — the understanding that "the Torah is the blueprint for the world."[2] Yet, often that very Torah has been divided into ostensibly separate branches — *Halachah, Aggadah, Mussar, Kabbalah*, etc. The uniqueness of the Rogatchover was that he recognized no barriers within that G-d-given Torah. He perceived virtually everything that exists in terms of the living imperatives of *halachah* — the legal aspects of Torah.

Thus, in his commentary on *Chumash*, no "story" is interpreted simply in humanistic or even moral terms. Every sentence, word, and letter in the Torah is related to the eternal verities of *halachah*... The fate of Sodom and Amorah is understood in the light of the laws of *Ir Hanidachas*[3] (the totally corrupt city that earns destruction) ... the serpent's curse of being the eternal enemy of mankind is reflected in the *halachah* that a snake can be put to death without a *bais din*, a formal court proceeding, unlike other animals[4] ... Jacob set up stones to sleep because he was legally laying claim to the land; and in order to do so, it is not enough to simply sleep there, but one must "make the bed" as well.[5]

A universe of Torah and only Torah. For over seventy years, he virtually never stopped studying Torah. It is said that since early age he would not allow his hair to be cut for he could not stand the few moments he would be bare-headed, unable to learn. Over and over, he reviewed the familiar works of the Talmud he so revered. He rarely consulted works published later than the 17th century, never quoting anyone later than the *Rambam* (1135-1206). In the *Rambam*, he found his "*Rebbe*" and mentor, and he could often be seen pacing his room, copy of the *Rambam's Mishneh Torah* in hand, murmuring "dear, dear *Rebbe*."[6]

◄§ The Road to Dvinsk

How did the Rogatchover become *the* genius in a generation of giants? Undoubtedly, he was born with the makings of greatness. Born in the Latvian city of Rogatchov in 1858, he was fluent in a sixth of the entire Talmud by the time he was eight years old,[7] and by the time of his Bar Mitzvah, no one in his own city was qualified to teach him. Recognizing the young boy's potential for greatness, his father, Reb Fishel, sent him to Slutsk to the famed Rabbi Yoseif Dov Soloveitchik, author of the *Bais HaLevi*. There he studied with another future luminary, Reb Yoseif Ber's son, Reb Chaim, future Rav of Brisk. Eventually, he was also to study with the incisive Rabbi Yehoshua Leib Diskin, and drink deeply of the Chassidic founts of Ger and Chabad.

◄§ A Life Beyond Earthly Time

Even though he was blessed with genius, the Rogatchover's unique development could never have taken place without his almost superhuman diligence. The dates of his life (1858-1936) were fixed; his lifelong identification with Rogatchov and Dvinsk placed him within geographic boundaries; yet, he seemed unencumbered by conventional limitations of time and space. Time had meaning only in relation to *halachah* — *now is the time of Shacharis ... soon we will be blowing Shofar ... today is the 14th day of the Omer* etc. Space, too, was irrelevant unless it was related to the laws of *succah, eruv,* or the like. With the *Gemara* before him, his mind deeply engrossed in the world's *only* reality, even personal danger was not worthy of notice.

    ☐ The Rogatchover had been forced to leave Dvinsk because of pogroms sweeping the area. When he was staying in Minsk, word of a wandering anti-Semitic band reached the community. Major towns and villages had suffered great

> ### ⌐§ A Rogatchover Sampler
>
> *Bereishis* 19:20 — Lot's wife turned into a pillar of salt. Why
>   was she punished in so strange a way? Her sin was that
> she did not hearken to the edict of G-d as transmitted by His
> agent, the angel. The *Mishnah (Sanhedrin* 89a) tells that
> "Whoever disregards the word of the prophet...his death is in
> the hands of Heaven." Her punishment therefore had to be
> one that obviously came from G-d.

damage to life and property, and the local rabbis called a fast
day because of the dire situation. The entire Jewish community was evacuated and hid in the mountains. In the flur-
ry of activity, it was several hours before the Rogatchover's
absence was noticed. The two shelters were searched with no
trace of the rabbi. Finally two brave young men volunteered
to search the abandoned city for the Rav.

*Going directly to his modest lodgings, they found him
immersed deep in thought before the ever-present* Gemara
and Rambam. *When he noticed the young men, he laughed
and said: "Isn't it odd that the rabbis have declared a fast
day? Undoubtedly, they were thinking of the* Gemara *in*
Ta'anis ... *and the* Rambam ... *but, of course, you realize
that they forgot the* Yerushalmi *and* Tosefta..."

*The young men realized with a jolt that the Roga-
tchover was not thinking at all of his personal safety, but of
the* halachic *implications of the situation.*[9]

In the Rogatchover's tens of thousands of responsa to rabbis
and laymen all over the world, the Torah's power to transcend
time — even to control time — manifests itself in startling ways...
In a letter from the Rogatchover, virtually *every* facet of the
responsum is intimately involved with *halachah*, even the date.

   □ *A letter answering two difficult questions in different
parts of the Torah is dated the 11th of Tishrei. For other
letter-writers of the past twenty generations, the date — as a
simple mechanical device for recording the time — would be
sufficient. Not so for the Rogatchover. This date immediately conjures up for him the Mishnah in Krisus 25a: "It is said
that Bava ben Buta would offer an* asham taluy *(a con-
ditional sacrifice for a possible transgression) every day, ex-*

cept the day after Yom Kippur — the 11th of Tishrei." The Rogatchover then explains the unique status of this day as based on a statement in Me'ilah 14b that one need not worry about an unwitting transgression if only one day is involved. The 11th of Tishrei is but one day after the atonement of Yom Kippur, so no such sacrifice could be brought.[10]

The Rogatchover surely did not seek to impress his readers with his erudition, or look specifically for such recondite references. He *thought* of 11 Tishrei in terms of *Krisus* 25a, and he understood *Krisus* 25a in terms of Me'ilah 14b. Perhaps, like that of the *rishonim* or the *gaonim*, the Rogatchover's entire thought processes were attuned purely to Torah and therein found their entire sustenance.

❧ Torah: A Source of Worldly Knowledge

Total immersion in the universe of the Torah does not blind one to the physical aspects of the world. The Rogatchover, through his unique ability to view the entire world through the tele-microscopic lens of the Torah, saw everything in the world around him — and infinitely more, as well. Although he had never been to Israel, he impressed a visitor with his familiarity with every detail of the Holy Land's topography. When the visitor was relating the course of his travels through Israel, the Rogatchover stopped him and inquired why he had not taken a certain short-cut and saved an hour's travel time.[11]

A secular Jewish poet once acknowledged that "many Einsteins would never equal one Rogatchover" and the comparison gained much currency in both Torah and general intellectual circles. Interestingly, the Rogatchover deals with problems of time and relativity in their *halachic* context.[12] An example of the Rogatchover's philosophic concept of time is reflected in one of his references to the date of a responsum. Writing on Erev Rosh HaShanah 5687 (1927), he notes that the precise moment is rapidly arriving when two years meet each other in the stream of time. The Rogatchover notes that the *Yerushalmi* pointed out this phenomenon, referring to the microsecond as "the moment when two years kiss each other." He then closes with the wish for a befittingly smooth and happy entrance into the new year.[13]

Outside the stream of worldly time, the Rogatchover was totally involved in the river of *halachic* time. His every letter between Rosh Hashana and Yom Kippur reflected the awe of the season. A letter dated this period in 1927 responds to the query

Bereishis 22:6 — Before the *Akei'dah*, Abraham loaded the wood on Isaac, but not the knife, because there is a disagreement between the Talmud *Bavli* (Pesachim 66a) and the *Yerushalmi* (Pesachim 6:1) if it is permissible to lean the knife on the sacrifice once it has been sanctified. Abraham wanted to make sure that every detail of his precious *korban* was perfect, and was scrupulous to fulfill all halachic opinions.

whether one may wear glasses on *Shabbos* when one is not totally dependent on them. The letter begins with a short aside, "Tuesday, 8 Tishrei 5688, may we, G-d willing, merit receiving the Second Tablets this coming *Yom Kippur*" — not a unique expression in responsa literature. But then he launches into a deep exploration of the differences between the first and second *luchos* (Tablets of the Law given to Moshe) and sundry aspects of the giving of the Torah... Of a responsum of 38 lines, three are devoted to an answer to the question (if they help the *wearer* in walking, wearing them is permissible) and 35 to an exposition on the date.[14]

◆§ Moments of Amusement

Unusual? Definitely. Yet, the Rogatchover's unique style should not be dismissed as a simple curiosity. The torrential flow of Torah explanations, the apparent digressions and excursus grant us a glimpse into a world of greater purity where every phenomenon, every event, every concept reverberated loudly and clearly with Torah implications and halachic nuances. It is only a short 40 years ago, but it is already hard for us to conceive of a time when even *light* moments for "amusement" were amusements *in Torah.*

☐ *Once a year, on* Simchas Torah, *the two Chief Rabbis of Dvinsk, Reb Meir Simcha and the Rogatchover, would daven together. Watching the rejoicing with the Torah, Reb Meir Simcha would remark, "I have just completed a study and Rav [——] is mentioned in the Talmud but seven times." The Rogatchover would smile and answer, "You know, of course, that the sixth time, in Zevachim, is a mistaken text, and that you made up the seventh to test me."*

Such were the "light" moments of our sages of the last generation.[15]

⋙ The "Alarm" Telegram

Once the magnitude of a life completely immersed in Torah takes hold, many references in the Rogatchover's letters begin to be clear. In one letter, he writes that he cannot elucidate the problem in detail because of a bout with asthma, and instead, he writes the usual myriad of citations to passages throughout the Talmud which will answer the problem. When we carefully study the references, the first one — to *Bechoros* 44b — does not seem to make sense, having nothing to do with the subject at hand. Further examination, however, leads us to the Talmudic description of the devastating symptoms of asthma. When *we* think of an illness, we think of the latest known remedy, someone who has it, or sympathy for the sufferer. The Rogatchover's thought went immediately to *Chazal's* comments on the subject.

☐ *Immediately after the 1927 earthquake in Jerusalem, the Rogatchover sent a concerned telegram to the inhabitants. In a letter to his grandson, Tzvi Hirsh Citron, he explains the reason for the telegram: "I was very worried about the tremors in Jerusalem, but thank G-d I received a letter that in Petach Tikvah (where the boy's parents lived) all is well. I sent a telegram because the Yerushalmi states that the alarm is sounded because of earthquakes, and the Rambam explains that the reason for the alarm is that when adverse events befall a community, an alarm must be raised to notify all that adversity has come upon them because of their evil ways. Thus they will repent and the adversity will leave them. My telegram is in the way of an alarm."[16]*

⋙ His Sense of Humor

From his earliest youth, Rabbi Rosen exhibited a wit and sense of humor which also was channeled totally into the world of Torah. When ten years old, he was learning in Rabbi Yehoshua Leib Diskin's Yeshiva in Shklov. One of the older students once asked him, "How much of the Talmud do you know?"

The young genius answered with a twinkle, "Half of *Shas* (the Talmud)."

The elder responded with "Which half?" To which he replied, "Any half you ask me."[17]

This penchant for the witty reply later stood him in good

stead with the thousands of would-be "experts" who came to him
for *haskamos* — approval for their meager endeavors at Torah
publications.

□ *Once as he was reviewing a book brought to him for a*
haskamah, *he repeatedly murmured, "Amazing, wonderful."*

*The eager author could not contain himself and asked,
"What does the rabbi find so wonderful and amazing?"*

*The Rogatchover replied with a smile, "Wonderful ...
amazing ... I did not now that there was a publishing house
in Pyetrikof. Now I know."*[18]

His gentle yet caustic wit was often even felt by his friends.

□ *Once, a woman entered the study when a close friend and
famous rabbi in his own right was present. The woman
asked the Rogatchover to* bentch *(bless) her. As was his
wont, he refused, saying, "I am only a simple man; I* bentch
only after eating."

*The visiting rabbi then asked, "Why not bless her? The
Mishnah states that 'Even the blessing of a simple man
should not be light in one's eyes,' a* kal v'chomer *(all the
more so) your blessing, Rabbi."*

*The Rogatchover responded, "Why wait for me to
deliver the blessing with the aid of a* kal v'chomer? *You can
do it even without a* kal v'chomer."[19]

His wit was finely attuned to the least hint of avarice, even
"holy" avarice.

□ *An aged Jew once came to him and signed over his entire will to the Rogatchover, saying he had no heirs and that he was confident the rabbi would allocate the funds to the most needy and deserving charities. The man passed away, and before long the rabbi's house was full of people claiming to know the best way to use the funds. One proposal came from the* Chevrah Kadisha, *which was responsible for the upkeep of the cemetery: the cemetery needed a fence to keep stray dogs from wandering into the consecrated area. "I'm amazed," replied the rabbi, "at the dogs' keen sense of smell, perceiving that the money was in my trust."*[20]

Despite the bite of the Rabbi's rejoinders, no one left him feeling slighted or embarrassed. On the contrary, the penetrating sense of truth in his every utterance often solved otherwise irreconcilable differences and acrimonious disputes.

□ *A couple who had not been getting along with each other asked him if they should move to the Holy Land. The Rogatchover gave them a soul-piercing look and inquired, "Is there not enough controversy in the Holy Land?" The simple, razor-sharp words were just what the unfortunate couple needed at that moment.*[21]

◆§ The Gemara and the Contested Kvitentzia

There was a period in Czarist Russia when, for a large sum of money, one could be freed from military service. Upon receipt of the money, the government granted the purchaser a *kvitentzia*, which was transferable. The government eventually stopped this policy, but honored any *kvitentzia* still in circulation. The waiver then became a rare and expensive item, and its owner could obtain a fortune for it during times of maximum conscription.

□ *A wealthy man had purchased a* kvitentzia *and passed away. His will specified that the waiver go to his youngest son. The young man had a physical disability and decided to risk taking his physical. If freed because of his condition, so much the better. If not, he could always fall back on the* kvitentzia. *The boy was freed and when his brothers learned of this, they demanded a share of profits from the sale of the* kvitentzia. *They claimed that their father had only left him the waiver to protect him from conscription, but once that was no longer a threat, the document became part of the general family inheritance. The boy, on the other hand,*

When Yoseif visited his ailing father, Yaakov, he "took his
two sons with him" *(Bereishis* 48:1). The reason? There
are halachic opinions (see *She'iltos d'Rav Achai, Parshas
Acharei,* 93) that one should not visit the sick alone.

When Yoseif's brothers went to Egypt, the Torah *(Bereishis*
48:8) tells us that he recognized them but they did not
recognize him. *Rashi* explains that when they had separated
they already had had beards, but Yoseif did not. Another
reason might be that they did not gaze directly at his face
because the Talmud *(Chagigah* 16a) states that staring directly
at a monarch is damaging to the eyes.

claimed that their father had given it to him. It was no one's
business how he had been freed from the draft. All members
of the family agreed to consult the Rogatchover, and to abide
by his ruling.

After listening to the story, the Rogatchover called over
the young man and said kindly, "Come let us study a bit of
Gemara together."

The Rabbi opened the tractate Nazir to 24a and read:
"If a woman made a vow to become a nazir and had set apart
her cattle for the korban (offering) and her husband then
revoked her vow, if the cattle were his, then...if they were
hers, then..." He then showed him that the Gemara asks
upon this Mishnah, "What difference does it make if the
cattle had originally been hers or not? Even if they were her
husband's and he gave them to her, in the end, they belonged
to her." The Gemara answers, "He only gave her the cattle
for something she would need and since he revoked her vow,
she does not need the cattle. It is as if they were never hers."

"And so it is with you, my friend," the Rogatchover
continued: "Clearly, your father only designated the
kvitentzia for you because he feared for you should you be
drafted. Now that you are free without the kvitentzia, the
halachah views it as if it never belonged to you."

The decision seemed so logical and self-evident once the
Rogatchover had explained it, that the young man accepted
it with a glad heart and no remorse at all.[24]

The Gap Between Speech and Pen

The above incident illustrates a strange paradox in the Rogatchover's powers of explanation. When the Rogatchover spoke to elucidate the Torah, even the most esoteric explication seemed simple and inevitable. Thus, the young man who lost his rights to the *kvitentzia* left Dvinsk satisfied that justice had been done. Yet, in print the story was entirely different. For a number of reasons, the works of Rabbi Rosen read like those of no other *gadol*, except perhaps the Vilna Gaon.

Primarily, this difficulty is because the Rogatchover uses very few words. Citing pertinent Talmudic references, he felt, was sufficient. Unfortunately, not many others of the last few generations can approach a letter with as many as 2500 Talmudic references[23] as if reading an expository letter from a friend.

Another reason for the difficulty in understanding the Rogatchover's printed works is that he created a new halachic vocabulary to convey his profoundly original thoughts. His terminology is, interestingly enough, familiar to students of the Rambam's *Moreh Nevuchim (The Guide for the Perplexed)*, but largely unknown to Torah scholars of more conventional background. To the Rogatchover, the entire *Guide* is a key to *halachah*. The *Rambam* does not deal in mere philosophy or theology to convince those unsure of their religion. He has presented us with a map through the byways of the Talmud, and the Rogatchover uses that map to transverse the entire Torah.

To overcome these difficulties, Rabbi Menachem Mendel Kasher, with a group of Torah scholars, has unlocked the key to this great treasure. In his work, *Mefa'ane'ach Tzefunos*, Rabbi Kasher details each new term used by the Rogatchover and explains their philosophic meaning and halachic content.

Of Heroism and Kiddush Hashem

An immense debt of gratitude — so meager a word for so monumental a debt — is due for the incredible heroism of the Rogatchover's daughter, Rebbetzin Rochel Citron, and the Rogatchover's successor in Dvinsk and *talmid muvhak* (major disciple), Rabbi Yisroel Alter Safran-Fuchs. When the Rogatchover passed away on the 11th of Adar I, 5696 (1936), Reb Alter was chosen as his successor although he was only 25 and as yet unmarried. From the moment of his acceptance until the last day of his life, he spent every moment in dedication to the writings of his great Reb-

> ### ৵§ A Rogatchover Sampler
>
> In the prophet Yeshayahu's descriptions of the age of
>   Moshiach (Chapter 11), we find the passage, "And the
> wolf shall dwell with the lamb, and the leopard ... with the
> kid, and the calf with the young lion ... and *a little child shall
> lead them.*" These last words are often taken to reflect the
> state of utter docility which will prevail during the Messianic
> Era. Yet, there are no mere metaphors in the Torah. In truth,
> only "a little child" would be *allowed* to lead these *combina-
> tion* of animals, for their joining constitutes the prohibition of
> *k'layim* (forbidden combinations), and thus not even a child
> of educable age would be allowed to lead them, but only "a lit-
> tle child."[23]
>
> Why (in *Bircas Hamazon)* do we say מַגְדִיל during the week
>   and מִגְדוֹל on Shabbos and *Yom Tov?* The Gemara
> (*Shabbos* 116b) tells us that on Shabbos from *Minchah*
> onward we must not read from *Kesuvim* (Holy Writings), but
> we may read from *Nevi'im* (Prophets). Therefore, on Shabbos
> we make sure to say מִגְדוֹל, which is quoted from Prophets (II
> *Shmuel* 22:51), maintaining a distinction from the weekday
> version, which comes from Holy Writings (*Tehillim* 18:51),
> which may be recited any time during the week.[25]

be. Amazingly, during the most difficult of times, the war years
of 1940 and 1941, he managed to publish two volumes of
Responsa from the Rogatchover. During this desperate period,
the Rogatchover's daughter, Rebbetzin Citron — by then
widowed — left Palestine to help Rabbi Safran-Fuchs in his work
in Dvinsk.

But of course, times got worse. The end was coming closer
and the Nazis ימ"ש were nearing Dvinsk. Rabbi Safran-Fuchs
and Rebbetzin Citron had many opportunies to escape to America
where they had relatives, but they recognized an eternal purpose
in remaining in Dvinsk to save the writings of his Rebbe. Thus
began the great race against time. For two years, Reb Alter and
Rebbetzin Citron, against great and dangerous odds, made micro-
photographs of the Rogatchover's writings — the glosses on the
sides of his *Gemaros, Chumashim,* and other *sefarim* — and sent
them to his uncle in America. Every two weeks, he faithfully
mailed his precious cargo.

All in all, he miraculously managed to send one entire *Gemara (Makos* and *mesichtos ketanos)*, 2500 pages of Talmudical glosses, 1500 pages of commentary upon the *Rambam*, and 1200 more covering assorted parts of the Torah. The last package was sent *one week* before the Nazis entered Dvinsk; undoubtedly, by the time the invaluable package arrived in the United States, the young rabbi had already offered up his life to his Maker על קידוש השם.[26]

⋰§ The Treasure in Miniature

הכל תלוי במזל אפילו ספר תורה שבהיכל, *Even the Torah needs good fortune.* From June, 1941, when the last package of the Rogatchover's Torah writings was sent to America, until June, 1957, the tiny photographs lay abandoned and unread. Mrs. Yetta Leah Safran, in whose possession the writings have been entrusted, made a number of attempts to bring the manuscripts to the public attention. The organizations with whom she spoke were largely uninterested and claimed that, anyway, there was no way to sufficiently enlarge the miniscule prints. So the matter remained for sixteen years.

In 1957, the *hashgachah* — the Heavenly Hand — guided the confluence of a number of events to allow the Rogatchover's writings to finally emerge from obscurity. Rabbi Menachem M. Kasher found out about the manuscripts and, with the aid of several foundations, obtained the funds to initiate the *Tzofnas Pa'ane'ach Institute*, publishing the writings of the Rogatchover in understandable form. Also, an enlarger had been designed that could produce the pages of the Rogatchover's Talmud with sufficient clarity to allow faithful transcription of his words. Rebbetzin Citron and Rabbi Safran-Fuchs must know in Gan-Eden that their deaths were far from in vain, and that every letter of the Rogatchover's Torah studied throughout the world today is the direct result of their noble and heroic sacrifice.

⋰§ The Last Days

The Rogatchover, too, died a truly Torah death. He had been taken to Vienna for surgery, which proved unsuccessful, and he was in constant, agonizing pain. Yet, amazingly, when someone asked him a Torah question, the pain would seem to disappear and the old color and fervor returned. The Rebbetzin deliberately invited Torah scholars in to take the Gaon's mind off the excruciating pain, and the Gaon himself begged those in the room,

"Ask me questions about the Torah. Ask! Ask!"[27]

So it was that the holy soul that had spent its entire life on earth studying Torah was in the end soothed and quieted by the healing power of that Torah. And in a quiet moment, that great soul simply went from its earthly *Bais Hamidrash* to the *Mesivta D'Rakiya* — the Heavenly House of Study — perhaps more than an end, or even a new beginning, simply ... a continuation.

FOOTNOTES

1. Heard from Rabbis Shemaryahu Shulman and Tovia Preschel.

2. *Zohar*, Terumoh 161a and see the beginning of *Bereishis Rabba*.

3. See *Tzofnas Paane'ach* (herewith, *TP*) on *Bereishis* 18:21-24 and 19:1-20.

4. See *TP* on *Bereishis* 3:15. See also *Bava Kamma* 15b.

5. See *TP* on *Bereishis* 28:13. The *Gemara* in *Chulin* 91b is interpreted as saying that Yaakov was being *koneh* the land and *Tosafos* in *Bava Basra* 53b declares that it is not enough to sleep on a bed that is already prepared; the *koneh* must make the bed himself.

6. Quoted by Rabbi Chaim Sapir in *Hagaon Harogatchove V'Talmudo*, ed., Rabbi Moshe Shlomo Kasher, Jerusalem, 1958, p. 19.

7. Rabbi Shlomo Yosef Zevin, *Ishim V'shitos*. Tel Aviv, 1966, p. 91.

8. Quoted by Saul Silber, "The Gaon of Rogatchov," *Jewish Leaders*, ed. Leo Jung, New York, 1953, p. 397.

9. Heard from Rabbi Moshe Greenes who heard it from Reb Leib Furer, a *talmid muvhak* of the Rogatchover.

10. *Sha'alos Uteshuvos TP*, Jerusalem, 1968, 124 (page 96).

11. D.T. Pincus, quoted by Rabbi Zevin, p. 100, note 10.

12. See Rabbi Menachem Mendel Kasher's צפונות מפענח, especially pp. 87-113. This is a monumental work on the Rogatchover's unique terminology and provides some historical and philosophical background. See also Rabbi Moshe Grossberg's צפונות הרוגוצ'יבי, Jerusalem, 1958, pp. 1-25.

13. *Sha'alos Uteshuvos TP*, Jerusalem, II. 30 (p. 22). The *Yerushalmi* referred to is in the middle of the 15th Chapter of *Yevamos*.

The ancient and long-debated problem of the nature of Time involves the disciplines of philosophy, physics, mathematics, and, most recently, parapsychology (see J.B. Priestly, *Man and Time*, New York: Doubleday & Company, Inc., 1964, pp. 190-274). Therefore, even a cursory summary of the literature on the subject is beyond the scope of this biographical sketch. However, there are two related, but distinct periods, in the time of controversy concerning the nature of Time. Until the twentieth century, the question was if Time is one indivisible unit measurable in "units of time arbitrarily chosen" (Newton), or if it is composed of a myriad of "time atoms" (see Rambam, *Moreh Nevuchim*, I, 73). With the advent of Einstein's theory of relativity, the debate has centered around Einstein's assertion that "absolute time does not exist and ... its rate of flow, that is to say, the measure of time differences and increments, is not necessarily equal in different coordinate systems." In short, this means that the concept of simultaneity is relative. The chief opponents of Einstein in this field are Jacques Maritain and Henri Bergson who maintain that "two events that are simultaneous for one observer are necessarily simultaneous for all others."

The Torah implications of this controversy are discussed by Rabbi M.M. Kasher in *Talpiyos* Vol. V (1952). The Rogatchover's genius and uniqueness is that without concerning himself with the discussions of physicists, mathematicians, etc., he expounds in incredible detail upon these problems purely in the context of *halachah*. Two excellent chapters on the Rogatchover's views on the philosophy of time controversy may be found in Rabbi Kasher's *Mefa'aneach Tzefunos*, pp. 87-112, and

Rabbi Moshe Grossberg's *Tz'funos hoRogatschove'*, pp. 1-25. See, especially, Rabbi Kasher's note on page 73, where, without referring to Rabbi Grossberg by name, he disagrees totally with his interpretation of the Rogatchover's position concerning this matter.

14. Ibid., II. 33 (p. 24).
15. Heard from Tovia Preschel who heard it from a *talmid muvhak* of the Rogatchover, who was present at the time.
16. *Sha'alos Uteshuvos TP*, Jerusalem, 1965 (ed., Rabbi Kasher), 80, pp. 150-151.
17. Quoted by Rabbi Isser Frankel, *Yechidei Segulah*, Tel Aviv, 1956, p. 185.
18. ibid., p. 186.
19. Ibid., and Rabbi Zevin, p. 103.
20. Rabbi Frankel, p. 186.
21. ibid., p. 187.
22. Rabbi Zevin, pp. 97-98.
23. See Rabbi Zevin, p. 135.
24. See, for instance, the beginning of the *TP* on *Hilchos Terumos* and the new *sefer* by Rabbi Mordechai Savitsky of Boston (published in honor of the Rogatchover's 40th *Yahrtzteit*), consisting of Rabbi Savitsky's correspondence with the Rogatchover.
25. *Sha'alos U'teshuvos TP*, Yerushalaim II. 5 (pg. 6).
26. Hillel Seidman, *Ishim She'hikarti*.
27. Heard from Rabbi Dovid Cohen, Brooklyn.
28. *TP*, Yerusholaim, II. 5 (p. 6).

"Ish HaEshkolos"

*he led world
Jewry from
Vilna*

Rabbi Chaim Ozer Grodzensky זצ"ל
5623/1863-5700/1939

*In his hesped (eulogy) for the Chofetz Chaim, Reb
Elchanan Wasserman quoted the Dubner Maggid's hesped
for the Vilna Gaon: Our long history is a chain of tekufos —
distinct eras: That of Tanaim, Amoraim, Savroim, ...
Gaonim. What signals the end of one tekufa and the beginning of another one? The Dubner answered, Heaven dis-
patches a man who is so great in Torah that he lights up the
world with his knowledge and wisdom. We can sense that he
is not of our times, but rightfully belongs to earlier generations. When he passes away, a darkness, a void fills the
world. We can actually feel the precipitous fall in the world's
spiritual status: a heavenly signal that the end of a tekufa
has arrived. Just as Rav Hai Gaon, the greatest and the last of
the Gaonim closed his tekufa, so, too, did the Vilna Gaon,
who was of a greatness of earlier generations, end his era ...
and so, Reb Elchanan concluded, did the Chofetz Chaim
belong to earlier times — can't we already feel the darkness of
his absence?*

◆§ The Sense of Loss

SUCH were our feelings at the funeral of Reb Chaim Ozer. *The end of an era? We were witnessing the collapse of the entire world!* It was the third blow *Klal Yisrael* had suffered in ten months. (For nothing rivals the death of a *tzaddik* as a blow to the Jewish People — see *Devarim* 28:61.) On 9 Cheshvan, we had lost Reb Shimon Shkop — who had been Rosh Yeshiva in Telshe for 25 years, then in Brainsk and in Grodno. Our beloved Rosh Yeshiva, Reb Boruch Ber Levovitz of Kamenitz, died on 5 Kislev. And now the *Rav* of all *Rabbanim*, the leader of all yeshivos, supreme authority over the *poskim* — Reb Chaim Ozer Grodzensky had left us.

Each individual was personally wounded, as was evident as old men cried like children. One hundred thousand weeping people![1]

The political situation was dreadful: Nazi Germany to the West and the South, ready to annihilate us physically; the Soviet troops to the East and the North, poised to obliterate us spiritually. Who would protect the Jews? — the "mighty" Lithuanian bicycle Army?[2] On October 10, 1939 the Soviets had forced the Lithuanians to grant them bases in exchange for returning Vilna to them as their capital: thus the Jews of Vilna were added to the existing Lithuanian Jewish community. Then with the German attack on Poland in September 1939, Lithuania became swollen with the yeshiva students plus thousands of other refugees fleeing Poland. Exactly nine months later, on June 14, 1940, the Soviets delivered an ultimatum to the Lithuanian government, and on July 21 they annexed Lithuania as a Soviet Republic. And now the leader of our generation was snatched from among us. Is there any wonder that we felt the very earth crumble beneath our feet?

◆§ The Final Hours

For four years, only he and his immediate family knew that he had cancer. He showed no visible signs of his terrible suffer-

---

1. Vilna had close to 80,000 Jewish residents, plus 20,000 refugees. To this add the delegations from all over Lithuania.

2. Liberating their capital city Vilnius, the Lithuanian Army marched in, in full force: A dozen small tanks, followed by an army on bicycles, wearing white gloves, with rifles hanging from their shoulders. That was the extent of their "crack troops" — the motorized division.

ing; a smile was always on his face. He refused to enter a hospital, for he was ever aware of how world Jewry and the yeshivos in particular had rested on his shoulders for fifty-five years ... how could he possibly spare time for a hospital stay? When he finally did enter the hospital, his *klal* work went with him — including the burden of answering the steady stream of *sha'alos* (halachic queries) from all over the world.

On the last Thursday night of his life,[3] he issued orders regarding the dispersal of all the charity funds in his care. To the many visitors in his room he said, "Good night," then whispered, "Who can be *zocheh* to having a good night? Even so, I have no *taynes, chas veshalom* to the *Ribono Shel Olam* (no grievance to G-d)."

Friday, before noon, two men were at his bedside,[4] Rabbi Yechezkiel Mishkovsky and Rabbi Moshe Shatzkes (Lomza Rav) — whispering, not to disturb the sleeping *tzaddik*, not realizing that he had already passed on.

The hospital was three kilometers from the city, but as soon as the news of his passing reached Vilna the entire length of the road was filled with people. *B'nei Torah* were assigned to transport his remains on their shoulders until the city limits, then to place them on a wagon, fearing the reaction of Soviet authorities to any unusual demonstration. He was placed in the room where he had studied Torah, rendered decisions on *sha'alos*, dispensed *chessed* and *tzeddakah*, for fifty-five years. There, until Sunday, *b'nei Torah* said *Tehillim* (Psalms) and pored over his *sefarim* day and night.

◆§ The Funeral

Those responsible for arranging the funeral Sunday were haunted by an ugly experience with the Soviets at the funeral of Reb Lazer, Minsker *Gadol:* the Soviets arrested all the *maspidim* (eulogizers) as well as a number of mourners. Some suggested a quiet funeral for Reb Chaim Ozer, but that was rejected as impossible, for surely all of Vilna would come regardless of plans ... The authorities *should* be notified: but suppose they forbid a mass funeral? ... The decision: a public funeral would be held, without securing permission from the Soviets. Rabbi Yoseif Shuv, secretary to Reb Chaim Ozer, would take full responsibility

3. Most details are adapted from an article in *Hapardes*, 1940.

4. Reb Moshe Shatzkes was the stepson of Reb Itzele Blazer (Peterburger). Reb Yechezkiel Mishkovsky was Reb Itzele's son-in-law.

if the Soviets were to challenge the proceedings.

Sunday morning, Vilna's entire Jewish populace gathered, joined by the yeshiva students and the refugees to whom he had been father and sole contact with the outside world.

The first *hesped* was delivered at his house by the *Rosh Beis Din* (head of the rabbinical court), the aged Reb Henoch Eigesh. The procession then moved to the big *Shul*, where Rabbi Shatzkes and Rabbi Zalman Sorotzkin (Lutzker Rav) spoke. The procession continued, stopping every few blocks. A makeshift platform would be raised and a *Rav* would speak, adding up to a total of forty *hespeidim!* Instead of interfering, as feared, the Soviets dispatched a battalion of militiamen to preserve order.[5] No speakers had dared mention the political situation, until the *Vilna Maggid* at the graveside made references to "changes taking place" — and was forcefully removed from the platform and arrested. Literally thousands of *tzetlach* (pieces of paper) with all sorts of requests were thrown into the grave before it was closed — the soldiers made certain that they all reached their destination, not outside, for fear some might contain anti-Soviet propaganda.

◄§ Early Years

Reb Chaim Ozer Grodzensky was born in Ivye, a small town near Vilna where his father was *Rav* for forty years, preceded by his grandfather who had also served as *Rav* there for forty years.

Reb Chaim Ozer was gifted with an infallible memory — never experiencing "forgetting," as he himself remarked, until his old age. Hence, when asked to deliver the customary *drashah* at his Bar Mitzvah, he refused, instead inviting guests to "open any page in the *Ktzos Hachoshen* or in the *Nesivos Hamishpat* (classic commentaries on one section of the *Shulchan Aruch*), and I'll recite it from memory." They took up the challenge and he responded — page after page — without missing a word.

At fifteen, he went to the world-renowned yeshiva of Volozhin. In spite of his tender age, he was immediately accepted in Reb Chaim Brisker's select group. When twenty, he passed through Vilna, his fame preceding him. He accepted an invitation to address a learned group there, and overwhelmed them with his *shiur* (Torah lecture). Soon, every father of an eligible girl and

---

5. Apparently they appreciated how the Jews had valued their *Rabbin*. Or, perhaps, because their occupation was only three days old, they did not want to risk stirring up the population.

every *shadchen* (matchmaker) in Vilna was after him.[6] He followed the suggestion of his father, a *talmid* of Reb Yisrael Salanter, who advised him to marry the daughter of the Vilna *dayan*, Reb Lazer, son-in-law of Reb Yisrael Salanter.

He had expected to engage full-time in Torah study in his father-in-law's house, but after two years Reb Lazer died, and the *kehillah* of Vilna requested him to take his father-in-law's place. Since the time of the Vilna Gaon, Vilna never had an official rabbi. Instead, a group of *dayanim* formed the rabbinate — all of them elderly and great *lomdim* (scholars) and *poskim* (authorities in Torah Law). Now the twenty-two year old *dayan* joined their ranks and over the following fifty-five years emerged as the unoffical *Rav* of Vilna — for it was apparent from the start that his vast Torah knowledge was complemented by great wisdom. Eventually, no convention of *gedolim* took place without his participation — usually as presiding officer. Soon it no longer seemed odd to see men great in Torah, old in wisdom, gray in years, bending forward to catch every word uttered by the young man with the jet black beard.

◆§ The Flawless Memory Bank

His mind was a storage place for all sorts of information — names of places and people from all over the world were deposited there, never to be erased. Hence countless communities, from far-off Jerusalem to my home town, Lomza, when in need of a *Rav* or *Rosh Yeshiva* would consult him[7]; and his choice was always superbly suitable.[8]

While Reb Chaim Ozer did have a yeshiva, it was not a yeshiva in the usual sense, for he could not give the *talmidim* (students) much of his time. The group studied independently,

6. A *din Torah* actually arose regarding Reb Chaim Ozer, and was brought before Reb Yitzchak Elchanan, revered Kovno Rav. One claimant argued that since he gave him his *"derech in lernen,"* he holds a spiritual claim over him. Reb Lazer argued that he had a physical claim, for Reb Chaim Ozer would have been a soldier in the Czar's army — since he had arranged Reb Chaim Ozer's "green billet" (exemption slip). After Reb Yitzchak Elchanan had a Torah discussion with the young man, he said, "If I had a daughter I would want him for my own son-in-law." Neither of them knew that, under his father's guidance, Reb Chaim Ozer already made his own selection.

7. This follows the practice recorded in the *Gemara*: the city of Semunya asked Rebbi to recommend a *dayan* and *darshan* (preacher) for them — (*Yerushalmi Yevamos* 60:2).

8. For Dvinsk he recommended an unknown young man who was learning in his father-in-law's house in Bialystok, Reb Meir Simcha, later known by the name of his *sefer* — the *Or Same'ach*. For Lomza he recommended his *talmid*, the *Rav* of my hometown Ivye, Reb Moshe Shatzkes. When Rabbi Shatzkes arrived in Lomza, my father greeted him with a *"vort"* relating to the *Gemara* in *Baba Basra* 12a. "Ameimar said, 'A *chacham* (wise man) is superior to a *navi* (prophet), as it says '*Venavie l'vav chachma*' (may we bring to ourselves

and only on *Shabbos* would the boys gather in his home for discussions. Thus the name — "*Reb Chaim Ozer's Kibbutz.*" In spite of the limited hours he spent with his *talmidim*, he had vast influence over them and a number of great men emerged from this *Kibbutz* — among others, Rabbi Moshe Shatzkes, Rabbi Eliezer Silver (Cincinnati), Rabbi Avigdor Amiel (Tel Aviv), and Rabbi Yechezkiel Abramski (formerly of London, then in Jerusalem), זכרונם לברכה.

Indeed, his concern — and his memory — encompassed all, great and small: The *Minsker Gadol* had a very promising student of Bar Mitzvah age, whom he recommended in a letter to Reb Chaim Ozer for acceptance in his *Kibbutz*. Reb Chaim Ozer told the boy's father that he was impressed with the recommendation but since his *Kibbutz* had no *mashgiach*[9] (a faculty member who served as guide and advisor to the students), and he personally could not give the boy his full attention, he advised Slobodka which had a *mashgiach* and a *mussar* program (which concentrated on character development).

Six years later, the boy visited Reb Chaim Ozer at his *datcha* (summer house) near Vilna. Upon hearing his name, Reb Chaim Ozer, of course, recalled the letter, and was pleased that he had followed his advice and entered Slobodka. Then, as was his custom, he told the boy, "*Zogt epes* (Say a *dvar* Torah)." The young fellow explained that he was now deeply involved in the complicated subject in *Hilchos Shegagos*, and a famous *Rambam* on it. "If the *Rebbe* is not currently studying the subject it might prove difficult for him to discuss."[10] The young fellow immediately realized the *chutzpah* of his remark, but it was too late. The words had been spoken.

Reb Chaim Ozer good-naturedly said, "Test me!" Once they

a heart of wisdom)" *Tehillim* 90, 12. My father asked, "How does this prove wisdom's superiority? — Simply because we pray for it? We pray for many things!" My father answered, "*Tefilla l'Moshe ish Ha'Elokim* — If Moshe who reached the highest level of prophecy prays for the attainment of *l'vav chachma*,' then wisdom is certainly higher than prophecy."

On Rabbi Shatzkes's next trip to Vilna, he repeated the *vort* to Reb Chaim Ozer. Reb Chaim Ozer excitedly exclaimed: "This is *l'amita shel Torah* — the true intent of the passage! Is that typical of your *ba'alei batim* in Lomza?" He then listed dozens of cities and their *Rabbanim*, the quality of their *ba'alei batim*, and how such *ba'alei batim* make it obligatory for a *Rav* to ever advance in his Torah scholarship, to qualify as their *Rav*.

9. As Reb Chaim Ozer remarked to Reb Yeruchem Levovitz, *mashgiach* of Mir, "A yeshiva without a *mashgiach* and *mussar* is a *bor bir'shus harabbim* — an open hazard in a public place."

10. Reb Chiya said to Rav, When *Rebbi* (Rabbi Judah the Prince, who compiled the *Mishna*) is studying one *Mesechta* do not ask him about another *Mesechta*. Perhaps it's not [clear] in his mind at that moment (*Shabbos* 7b).

entered the subject, it proved as fresh in his mind as if he had studied it that very morning. When they concluded their discussion, the young man still seemed terribly ill at ease for his hasty remark. To ease the pain, Reb Chaim Ozer set out to walk him back toward Vilna. After a half mile, when they were ready to part, the boy wanted to accompany Reb Chaim Ozer back to his house. Reb Chaim Ozer refused, saying: "Then I'll have to *beglait* you again, and we could continue in this manner all day."

When on another visit the same young fellow asked him a *kushya* (question), Reb Chaim Ozer pulled out ten *sefarim* from his vast collection, and showed him the same *kushya* in all ten.

Years later, the young man became a Rosh Yeshiva in a distant land, maintaining a Torah corespondence with Rabbi Chaim Ozer all the while. In one letter, Reb Chaim Ozer wrote him that the Rosh Yeshiva of Brisk, Reb Moshe Sokolowski (author of *Divrei Moshe*) had passed away, and he recommended the young Rosh Yeshiva for this position. Parenthetically, he added that he personally advises against the move, for the situation in Europe would eventually force him to leave. The young Rosh Yeshiva took his advice, and instead of joining Brisk founded a yeshiva of his own, eventually becoming a leading figure in Torah circles.

❦ ❦ ❦

Rabbi Nissan Waxman, currently in Petach Tikva, recalls passing through Vilna with the Mirrer Yeshiva shortly after World War I. Reb Chaim Ozer helped him get to Slobodka where he studied for two years, followed by five years in Yeshivas Rabbi Yitzchak Elchanan in New York. On his return to Mir he stopped in to see Reb Chaim Ozer, and he was introduced as an *"Amerikaner ben Torah."* Reb Chaim Ozer interjected: "What are you talking about? I only recently sent him to Slobodka" — remembering a passing encounter of seven years before.

◄§ Druskenik — Yeshiva Town in the Forest

Doctors in Poland often advised their patients to recuperate in Druskenik, a town surrounded by forests and blessed with "dry air". As it was close to both Grodno and Vilna, Reb Shimon Shkop and Reb Chaim Ozer used to vacation there. And so did Reb Boruch Ber of Kamenitz and Reb Aharon Kotler also spent summers there. (Thus all the photographs in circulation of *Gedolim* in Druskenik.) The local Jewish citizenry waited all year for the summer months when every house became a "hotel" and every bit of space was rented out. Nonetheless, a *ben Torah* in need of a *datcha* was never at a loss, for the local *Rav* and his son headed a committee to arrange free room and board for *b'nei Torah*. As a result, a "yeshiva corner" developed in the forest, away from the more vulgar goings-on.

When I was a student in Baranovitz, I asked the *Mashgiach* for permission to vacation in Druskenik, adding that I had a relative there, so I would not be a burden on the committee. He granted me permission for a two week *datcha*. One morning while I was there, news spread that Reb Chaim Ozer was coming. The local *Rav* always had difficulty finding a suitable house for him, for although Reb Chaim Ozer claimed to need only a bed for himself and a bookcase for his *sefarim*, the *Rav* knew better. Reb Chaim Ozer not only headed Polish Jewry, he was the leader of world Jewry. The hundreds of daily letters with all sorts of questions and problems had to be answered — even in Druskenik. Nor did the lines of visitors, dignitaries and government officials stop because it was summer. The *Rav* finally selected a house of suitable stature, close to the "yeshiva corner."

A group of *b'nei Torah* kept a vigil on the house, waiting for the *tzaddik's* arrival. Finally the local *Rav* and his son brought him from the station, and we found his bearing striking — a rather short man with an unusually large head ... I was reminded of a description of the *Sha'agas Arye*, as possessing a large head, out of proportion to his body. His face seemed to glow with wisdom, his eyes full of goodness. Reb Chaim Ozer and the *Rav* entered the house while we remained outside. When they came out, we could hear him saying to the *Rav*, "I cannot accept the house. First I must check with her."

Someone whispered that the local Rav was out of step, and should have shown the house to the Rebbitzin. — *But isn't Reb Chaim Ozer a widower?*[11] whispered another bystander. — *Then, who is this "her"?*

It turned out that Reb Chaim Ozer had been referring to his cook. The kitchen was a distance from the dining room, and he feared it would prove too tiring for her for serving. In Eastern Europe, no decent man would eat in the kitchen ... Eventually, the cook arrived, loaded down with her pots and pans, and she gave her approval to the quarters.

---

11. He was a brother-in-law to Reb Elchanan Wasserman through his second marriage.

"Ish HaEshkolos" / 143

◄§ Source of Chessed

His house was wide open day and night. No appointment was required. His house was thus always full of people — the sick, widows, orphans, *Rabbanim*, *Roshei Yeshiva*, visitors from all over the world. One wondered when he had time for study, yet he published three volumes of his Responsa in his monumental *Achiezer*.

More amazing was his spiritual stamina. His only child, a girl of seventeen, became ill, was bedridden for three years, and died at twenty. Throughout this trying period, his *Klal* activities and his writing of his *Achiezer* did not diminish.

He personally handled funds for any number of charities. Thus to people the world over, the Joint Distribution Committee, Vaad Hatzala, the Haffkine Fund[12] all had but one address, for both givers and receivers: Reb Chaim Ozer's.

□ *A young orphan girl came to him for financial help just before her wedding. He asked her, "Tell me, my daughter, did you learn the halachos regarding family purity?"*

No, she did not.

He asked her to come into his office and be seated. He sat in his own chair and stared out the window while telling her in detail all the pertinent laws, never once averting his gaze.

He was, indeed, a father to all *Klal Yisrael* as well as to every individual member.

◄§ Agudath Israel

Reb Chaim Ozer was one of the founders of Agudath Israel and the pillar of the movement throughout his life, participating in every Knessia Gedolah as long as health permitted. When the Moetzes Gedolei HaTorah (Council of Torah Sages) was established, he was the first chairman and remained so throughout his life. When his *talmid* Rabbi Eliezer Silver became the founding president of Agudath Israel of America, he sent personal greetings. More, he instructed Rabbi Shlomo Heiman,

---

12. In the beginning of the century, millions of people in Europe and Asia, particularly India, died in a cholera epidemic. Dr. Haffkine invented a serum that arrested the epidemic. The Indian Government honored him by naming a university after him. When he returned to Paris, he became a *ba'al teshuvah* and left his entire fortune for yeshivos. The building of the Yeshiva in Kaminetz was in a great measure built from the Haffkine Fund. Hence Reb Chaim Ozer's remark: "Dr. Haffkine devised not only a serum against cholera, but also a serum for *Klal Yisrael* — that is, for the yeshivos."

revered Rosh Yeshiva of Mesifta Torah Vodaath, to participate in the first American Agudath Israel Convention in Far Rockaway in 1937, and to accept the vice-presidency of the budding organization. Reb Shlomo customarily shied away from public affairs, but Reb Chaim Ozer urged him to make an exception for "to associate with Agudath Israel in any way possible is a *Kiddush Hashem.*"

The Chofetz Chaim would not initiate any public action, or sign any public document, until he consulted with Reb Chaim Ozer. The Chofetz Chaim considered him as a living embodiment of Torah and showed him the utmost respect.

□ *Once when they were both to sign a public proclamation, the Chofetz Chaim refused to sign first, claiming that Reb Chaim Ozer personified* Kavod HaTorah *(the honor of Torah).*

Reb Chaim Ozer in turn deferred to the Chofetz Chaim, claiming that he encompassed both "Kavod HaTorah *and venerable old age."*

The Chofetz Chaim then counter-argued that Reb Chaim Ozer was more than Moreh De'asra *of Vilna; he was the* Moreh *of Klal Yisrael, as well. He should sign first.*

Finally Reb Chaim Ozer won the "argument," backing his claim with "Vekidashto — you shall sanctify the kohen" — even over his protest — and the Chofetz Chaim was a kohen. *The Chofetz Chaim yielded, providing that Reb Chaim Ozer sign alongside his signature, not on the following line.*

◄§ The Sha'alos Uteshuvos — His Responsa

Reb Chaim Ozer's brilliance as well as the scope of his leadership are reflected both in the *sha'alos* (halachic queries) that were sent to him from all parts of the world and in the *teshuvos* (responsa) he sent in return. He would write each responsum personally, not entrusting this to a secretary. His mind was so disciplined, that he would simultaneously write a responsum in halachah, give orders to two secretaries, and speak on the telephone.

His *psak* (decision) often reflected a concern far beyond the immediate question posed ... He was known to use an electric bulb in place of a *havdalah* candle; "people think that electricity is not a fire, and thus they permit themselves to put on electric lights on Shabbos," he explained. "So I make a point of saying the blessing 'Borei me'orei ha'eish — He created the lights of the fire' on an electric bulb to demonstrate that electricity is, indeed, a fire."

His last three p'sakim were typical:

☐ A number of talmidim of the Yeshivas Chachmei Lublin who had escaped to Vilna wanted to join Yeshivas Mir.

His psak: No! Every Yeshiva has a rightful place in Klal Yisrael, he explained. No one has the right to dissolve a Yeshiva; especially one like Chachmei Lublin.[13]

☐ A number of visas to leave Vilna had been granted and the question arose: who is more entitled to them, the old Rabbanim and Roshei Yeshiva, or the young ones? (He personally could have gone to the country of his choice, but he refused to abandon Vilna.) This was a she'eila in dinei nefashos — a matter of life and death — for it was expected that sooner or later everybody would fall victim to either the Russians or the Germans.

His psak: The older rabbis should get the visas, for the older men would work tirelessly to see to it that those left behind would also get visas.

☐ His final recorded teshuva (he submitted it to the Lutsker Rav, Rabbi Zalman Sorotzkin, for review before mailing it) was to the Swiss Rabbinate. Shechitah (ritual slaughter) had been forbidden in Switzerland for many years. This proved no hardship for Swiss Jews, for they relied upon imported meats. When the Nazis occupied all countries surrounding Switzerland, however, the rabbis asked Reb Chaim Ozer if it were permissible to stun the animal with an electric shock prior to shechitah, to conform with Swiss law.

His reply: No. After citing numerous sources, he ended his psak with the following words: "The Jews are an ancient people — old and gray from tzaros and enemies. Yet all its enemies of the past have vanished and the Jews are still in existence. In times such as these every one is called upon to demonstrate mesiras nefesh (to put his life on the line) even for a rabbinical ordinance — most assuredly in our case,

13. While Reb Chaim Ozer did appoint Reb Moshe Shatzkes Rosh Yeshiva for the Grodno yeshiva when its talmidim arrived in Vilna, he did not appoint anyone for Chachmei Lublin. Apparently he did not know a qualified chassidic gadol in Vilna and this was essential to preserve the character of the Yeshiva.

when a Torah prohibition is involved. My decision, thus, is that the proposal is prohibited."

He was called *"Ish Ha'Eshkolos* — The Man of Clusters." The Talmud explains the term: "Reb Yehudah said in the name of Shmuel: (it refers to) a man who has everything in him." *Rashi* enumerates: "True understanding of Torah, without falsehood, without forgetfulness, nor is he argumentative" (*Sotah* 47b). What a perfect description of that giant called Reb Chaim Ozer! With his passing, a *tekufah* came to an end, as the Dubner Maggid had explained.

What, then, can we call our present *tekufah*, which followed? Reb Elchanan Wasserman, among so many others, described it aptly: *"Ikvesa Dim'shicha"* — the chaotic era immediately preceding *Mashiach's* arrival.

Reb Archik

mussar emissary (teacher of ethics) to ba'alei battim, the lay community

Rabbi Aaron Yoseif Baksht זצ״ל
5629/1869 — 5701/1941

WHEN Rabbi Meyer Shapiro, the Rav and Rosh Yeshiva of Lublin, was asked why he changed his rabbinical positions with such frequency,he replied: "A rav can be compared to a nail. As long as he has a head, he can be pulled out from one place and set into another."

Rabbi Aaron Yoseif Baksht, who was lovingly referred to as "Reb Archik", served in no less than thirteen cities — from Stalingrad deep in Russia to Shavl in the heart of Lithuania. Yet he was known mainly as the "Lomzer Rav", the rav of my home town.

When a delegation came to the town of Suvalk to invite him to serve as rabbi in Lomza, Reb Archik refused. He explained that he had a *kollel* of young men whom he was teaching and training for the rabbinate. Since Lomza already supported a large yeshiva, he would not impose on the community the further responsibility of supporting a *kollel*.

When Rabbi Yechiel Mordechai Gordon, the Rosh Yeshiva of Lomza, heard this, he immediately made the trip to Reb Archik to personally plead with him to accept the *rabbanus*. Rather than compete with the Yeshiva, he insisted, the *kollel* would be an asset to the Yeshiva, as an inspiration and a direction for continuation. And knowing the people of Lomza, the Rosh Yeshiva assured the Rav that the community would certainly take care of both!

◅§ Arrival in Lomza

The city's entire population lined the road leading to Lomza, awaiting the arrival of the new Rav. With much pomp he was taken to the Central Synagogue where he delivered his maiden speech. With the voice of a roaring lion projecting his dynamic personality, expressing his *mussar* approach, he made a lasting impression on the entire community.

It was assumed that the Rav was fatigued from his trip and the welcoming parade, and he was taken immediately to the spacious apartment the *kehillah* had always reserved for the Rav. To everyone's surprise, the Rav insisted on visiting the Yeshiva first.

Entering the Yeshiva, he glanced into the *sefer* a student was immersed in. It was open at *Yore De'ah* 58, and he began his speech with this very paragraph. The subject was *risuk eivarim* (broken limbs), i.e. if an animal falls from a certain height, it is not kosher for ritual slaughter until it is examined for broken vital limbs. The animal is tested by allowing it to walk by itself. He widened the subject, quoting relevant sources from memory. The same rules apply to fowl; however, swimming is as valid a test as walking, provided the subject swims against the current, for a crippled or even a dead subject can be carried with the current.

"People who move with the current," continued the *Rav*, "following the trend, show no proof of life! '*Ve'atem hadveikim beHashem*' by clinging to G-d, by studying His Torah, opposing the trends, resisting the current — this proves that '*chaim kulchem hayom*' — that you are very much alive!"

◅§ "Know What to Answer"

By nature he was a man of bounding enthusiasm — a basic ingredient for imparting *mussar* (Torah ethics) ... Thus as a young lad in Volozhin, where he was recognized as a potential giant in Torah scholarship, he caught the eye of Rabbi Yitzchak Blazer (Reb Itzele Peterburger) — a disciple of Reb Yisrael Salanter, founder of the *mussar* movement — and Reb Itzele introduced him to *mussar*. He eventually moved to Kelm where he became attached to Reb Simcha Zissel Ziv, another disciple of Reb Yisrael Salanter. Reb Archik emerged as a giant in Torah and *mussar*, the two unseparable banners which he carried with enthusiasm all his life.

Reb Archik was a gifted orator. His *rebbes* therefore assigned him the task of spreading the *mussar* movement — not in the Yeshiva world, but in the streets, among *ba'alei battim* (laymen). He would debate *maskillim* and *apikorsim* with relish. His favorite argument that Torah is *min hashamayim* (of Divine source) was from *Vayikra* 11, where the two signs of *kashrus* are named — chewing a cud and possessing split hooves. The Torah lists the three animals that chew a cud but do not have split hooves — the camel, the rockbadger and the hare — and the one animal that does have split hooves but does not chew the cud — the swine. The Talmud in *Chullin* 59 comments: "The Ruler of the world knows that there are no animals but these that possess only one of the two signs of *kashrus*.

"Now," Reb Archik would exclaim, "in all these years no one has ever found an additional animal to disprove those sentences in the Torah! Isn't that proof that Torah is *min hashamayim!*"

To demonstrate the veracity of the Talmud he would quote his Rebbe, Reb Simcha Zissel: "In *Chulin* 127 the Talmud says: 'All animals found on earth have a counterpart in the sea, except the *chuldah* (weasel).' Now listen carefully," he would exclaim, "how the *Chazal* opened themselves to disproof. If they would say 'including the weasel' and we never found a weasel in the sea, that would never prove them wrong. Did anyone ever check all the oceans of the world for a sea-weasel? However when the *Chazal* dared state 'except the weasel' — if one would ever find a weasel in the sea, even a thousand years later, he would have proven the *Chazal* false!"

(This last statement became especially clear to me while visiting the aquarium in Eilat. There one can see a variety of ocean-animals which are found in the Red Sea. I was impressed by the sea-lion and others — but no weasel!)

✑§ "Ahavas Yisrael — Kavod Yisrael"

In his speeches he would make great demands on his community, raising the Jew to higher levels, criticizing constantly. However, should an outsider — a non-Jew or an irreligious Jew — criticize the *klal*, he would rise militantly to the defense. Once an American diplomat criticized his *kehillah* in his presence. Reb Archik, like a faithful shepherd, rose in defense of his flock.

While non-Jewish orphans would run the streets without supervision, often turning to a life of crime, the Jewish orphans in Lomza were cared for by the *"Chevrah Hashgachas Yesomim."* Two separate homes were maintained — one for boys and one for girls — where they would be kept until they reached 18, when they set out on their own, prepared with an education and a trade. Many of the boys would continue to study in the Yeshiva.

After the First World War, applications to the orphans' homes tripled. There was no room, nor was it within the capacity of the *Chevrah* to take care of so many children. A call went out to America, and as always, American Jewry responded quickly and generously. The Joint Distribution Committee sent sufficient funds and a new building with all facilities went up. The children from poor families with parents would quip, "We are not lucky enough to be orphans."

A delegation from the Joint, accompanied by a representative of the American Embassy in Warsaw, came to Lomza to dedicate the new building. In the presence of Polish Government delegates and the City Hall officials, the American diplomat delivered a speech criticizing the Jewish Community for constantly extending its open palms to America. Wrapped in diplomatic fine-talk he demanded that the community try harder to muster together its own resources without begging from America!

My uncle, Reb Yechiel Kamchi, who was one of the trustees of the *Chevrah* used to tell how shocked everyone was — but who could dare talk up against an American diplomat? And how could one reply to him without insulting the Joint delegation? They were charitable Jews who had furnished the necessary funds, and were certainly not responsible for the tactless speech of their embassy official. All eyes turned to the Rav. One could see from his face that a storm was brewing within him. The Rav began his speech calmly, telling of the various charity activities in the Jewish community of Lomza. "When it comes to charity, the Jews are second to none. And when the *Chevrah* finally did turn to America for help, it was because of the war, and the poverty it had brought to the people." He then quoted a Midrash, which tells of a woman who came before King Solomon to sue G-d Himself! She complained that she was a poor widow and that she had been collecting grain in the field — as she was entitled by law — when a fierce storm-wind blew away all the grain she had collected, and she and her little children were forced to hunger the entire night. The King summoned the wealthiest merchant in

Jerusalem, asking him how his business was faring.

"Excellent," replied the merchant. His ships were at sea, and a strong wind brought them to port three days ahead of schedule. So he hit the high market and made a killing. "Pay the poor widow," ordered the King, "for the same storm that made you rich made her hungry."

"Gentlemen," concluded the Rav, his eyes piercing the diplomat, "the very same war that orphaned these children made America rich! And it is no more than right that you pay the bill!"

✑§ Wisdom, Comparison, and Zeal

Two women once came to Reb Archik with a *din Torah*. They were neighbors who shared a clothesline and now each claimed an entire wash as her own. Reb Archik told them to leave the laundry with him and he would announce his *psak* (verdict) the following morning. After the women left, he took some of his own clothing and mixed it with the bundle they had left. The next day he called in one of the women and she immediately picked out her laundry, separating Reb Archik's from it, stating "These are not mine."

When the other woman's turn came, she looked over the laundry and stated with a conviction that betrayed her dishonesty: "The entire laundry is mine!"

The city of Lomza was astir over the practical wisdom of their Rav.

Among the many charity *"chevros"* in Lomza was a *Chevrah Gemilas Chasadim Al Mashkonos* — a free loan society on collateral. Thus many poor people would borrow before the market day and then repay the date after, when they had made their profit — living from hand to mouth. Some would repay in a month or six months or a year. The society's building had a *shul* in front with a storage area in the rear — always full of jewelry and other valuable items that had been deposited for collateral. One night thieves broke in and stole most of the valuables. People knew all the thieves in town, so the suspects were recognized. No charges could be made, however, for there were no clues. The Rav announced three warnings, promising no prosecution: he asked for a return of the items or he would proclaim a *cherem* (banishing the guilty parties from the Jewish community), because many poor people and widows had lost their last small treasures and the *Chevrah* was ruined, unable to pay for the damages and unable to continue in its charitable activities. With no results, the date of the *cherem* was set. The community gathered in the largest *shul*, black candles were lit, and the Rav opened the *aron hakodesh*, proclaiming in the name "of the Holy One, in the name of the Torah." Then a list of curses followed that made everyone shudder with fear ...

Before the year was over, two known thieves became ill. Not only did the physicians fail to prescribe a cure, they could not even diagnose the ailment, so strange were the symptoms; and the two died in a matter of days! That must have been the last *cherem* in all of Poland.

Reb Archik eventually left Lomza. At first it seemed that he would go to Lodz, the second largest city in Poland, and without a Rav for years. A former Rav of Lomza, Reb Ely Chaim Maizel, had once been Rav in Lodz and had brought order to the city. Again Lodz looked to Lomza, and invited Reb Archik. There were two stumbling blocks to overcome, however. First, how could a Chassidic city like Lodz accept a *mussar* exponent like Reb Archik? In addition, would they support his *kollel*?

Two members of the *kollel*, my uncle Rabbi Hirsh Y. Margolis and, *yibadel lechaim*, Rabbi J.H. Feldman (formerly of Baltimore, presently in Jerusalem) went to Lodz to surmount these difficulties. Both were Chassidim and had spent many years in the Yeshiva of Lomza and in Reb Archik's *kollel*. They negotiated with Ger (Gerer Chassidim were the most powerful faction in Lodz) and they almost succeeded in bringing their beloved Rebbe to Lodz. Then the Polish authorities vetoed the move. This was at the height of Polish-Lithuanian animosity and the Poles would not permit a Lithuanian Rabbi to become head of the second largest city in Poland. (Although there were many Lithuanian rabbis in Poland, they had won their positions before Poland became independent.) And so Reb Archik moved back to his native Lithuania and became Rav in Shavl.

ᴇ§ Surprises: Flight ... and Return

After World War II, I had thought that Reb Archik, his activity, and his entire world were totally wiped out. Then I had several surprises. While waiting for a train in the Paris Metro, a lady approached me, calling me by name. She was Reb Archik's daughter, who miraculously came out alive from the Shavl Ghetto. She recognized me, for my father would often take me along as a small boy on his frequent visits to the Rav. She told me about her brothers — rabbis in London, one of whom eventually settled in Jerusalem.

Then came the surprise of Ely Galupkin. In Winsheim-Nurenberg, the Vaad Hatzalah (the rescue arm of American Orthodoxy) opened a yeshiva for the survivors of all European yeshivos. There I met a Telshe *talmid*, Ely Galupkin. Discovering that he is a native of Shavl, I asked him about Reb Archik, and indeed he had a story to tell.

Reb Archik would study with him and his brothers, for he had a deep love for *b'nei Torah* and a craving for *harbotzas-HaTorah* — promoting Torah study. When the Soviets occupied Lithuania and began to arrest leading personalities, shipping them off to Siberia, the Rav was afraid of being arrested at any moment. He therefore handed over to Ely a valise full of manuscripts, his seals, all kinds of documents, plus thirteen *ksav Rabbanus* from the thirteen cities he had served as Rav. He asked him to hide the valise so the Soviets would not take these papers.

Then came the dreadful day of June 22, 1941 — the German attack on Russia. On the very first day, all cities along the border were bombed, including Shavl. Galupkin understood that the Russians had their hands full with the war and they would not bother the Rav anymore, so he returned the valise to the Rav. Reb Archik took out some of the papers, returned the rest to Ely and told him to take them and leave town immediately with his family, adding, "I am *batuach* (I have faith) that you will take good care of this and that you will return *leshalom*." When Ely pointed out that his father was out of town and there was no way of communicating with him, the Rav stamped his feet on the floor and ordered: "Get out! Get out of the city at once!" repeating his blessing: "I am *batuach* you will return *leshalom*."

With the valise under his arm, Ely went home to inform his mother of the Rav's order. On the way, a gnawing question dawned on him: What if the Germans push the Russians out of Lithuania and march into Russia? Does the Rav's order mean even to run into Russia? He turned around, under a hail of German bombs, in hope of clarifying the matter with the Rav. He found the Rav's house totally empty. He decided that this was exactly what the Rav had meant, and he rushed to his mother to tell her the Rav's command. She unhesitatingly gathered her sons and began the long march to safety.

On foot for many miles, then by truck and train, under a constant shower of bombs, with people falling to the left and to the right, they made it deep into Russia — all the while guarding the Rav's treasure, the manuscripts, with great *mesiras nefesh* and personal risk. In those dark days, with the absence of *sefarim* the boys would take out those pages and study them. There was *sh'eilos u'teshuvos* (responsa), commentaries and *mussar shmuessen* (ethical discourses).

When the war ended, the Galupkins returned to Shavl with the manuscripts, just as the Rav had promised. But the country was empty of Jews — the Germans, with the active, enthusiastic help of the Lithuanians, had wiped out Lithuanian Jewry. Ely realized that Soviet Lithuania was no place for a *ben Torah* and he decided to escape illegally from the U.S.S.R. While he was ready to risk his own life — for he would have to cross one border into Communist Poland, another border into Soviet occupied Germany, and then on into the American Zone — he did not dare risk the manuscripts. Thus he left them with his mother. Ely made it across all those borders to the Yeshiva in Windsheim, then on to the other Vaad Hatzalah Yeshiva in Bailly, France, and finally to the Telsher Yeshiva in Cleveland, Ohio, where he is now a Rosh Yeshiva.

Throughout these years he tirelessly tried to get the manuscripts out of Vilna, but to no avail. First his mother, an elderly woman, had received permission to emigrate to Israel years before the mass emigration started, and she took the manuscripts along. The Soviet inspectors spotted them and confiscated them. A shock wave passed through her old bones as she watched the Russian's hands rifle the holy papers. Risking everything, she managed to slip them out from under his hands and hand them over to her son who was waiting outside the plane. Later, the son tried to mail it page by page, first to Israel and then to the U.S., but they would always be returned with a note from the Soviet inspectors, stating that sending out these materials was unlawful. Finally the son got his exit visa to Israel. Again the inspector discovered the manuscripts, but this time there was no one to leave them with. For three days Galupkin refused to board the plane without the manuscripts. One can imagine his frustration, after having waited for five years for an exit permit; and now at the gates of freedom he refused to leave without these papers! Finally on the fourth day, he managed to hand over all his cash-savings to an inspector, and with the manuscripts in his possession, he finally arrived in Israel!

❀　❀　❀

How old was Reb Archik when he was tortured and finally murdered by the Lithuanians and Germans? Rabbi Galupkin has a most characteristic reply. Reb Archik used to tell him that he adopted a *minhag* (custom) from his late mother. Every day she would recite the Chapter of *Tehillim* (Psalms) that corresponded to her age. The year Reb Archik was murdered he would say with deep emotion every day Chapter 72: "On behalf of Solomon: O G-d grant Your powers of judgment to a King, Your righteousness to a King's son."

The Ponevezer Rav*

*a Torah giant
who directed the
reconstruction
of the European
Torah world in
the Holy Land*

Rabbi Yoseif Kahaneman צז״ל
5646/5729 — 1886/1969

I SPEAK not as a member of the Rabbinate of this country or as a member of the Bais Din. I speak as a *talmid* of the Ponevez Yeshiva when it was still in Ponevez, Lithuania. My relationship with the Ponevezer Rav goes back 43 years, when he first visited England in 1926, and he urged me and persuaded my parents to send me to Lithuania. I was, I believe, the first English born student to leave these shores to become a *yeshiva bachur* in Ponevez. For a short while I stayed in his home. I saw his wonderful family life, it was majesty; I saw him among his students, it was royalty; I saw him among his *ba'alei batim*, it was loyalty; and I saw him among his colleagues, it was dignity. I saw him in many parts of the world. He was a man without a name, he was known only as the Ponevezer Rav.

He was like an angel, someone with a mission. He was adored and idolized. I saw people run after him in the streets to kiss his hand. He was an unusual man, a rare type. I had a feeling

---

* The Ponevezer Rav was known to the Torah world as a Master Builder. This appreciation, from a *hesped* delivered in London by Dayan Moshe Swift, reveals that aspect of the Rav which was best known only by those who were close to him.

when I was in his presence that there was something angelic about him. He had indomitable energy, for over twenty years he lived with only one kidney and was under a strict diet. He hardly enjoyed a full meal, he hardly slept four consecutive hours. His mind was alert, his love for people, *Ahavas Yisrael*, was indescribable. He had an unsatiable appetite for Torah and his love for *Eretz Yisrael* was like the prophets in Temple times. Like Rabbi Shimon ben Gamliel who kissed the floor of the Temple, every grain of sand was holy to him. He was the real "Zionist." He lived for it and he died for it. To him, the link with Israel was not the language, it was the Jew himself.

To see him was to see a living embodiment of G-d, Israel and Torah combined in one ... The Rabbis say that Moshe *Rabbeinu* was promised that he would never be forgotten, because down the ages the prophet's voice could be heard, "Remember the Torah of Moshe my servant." Yet when Moshe died it was only a section of the people who wept for his passing. "The Children of Israel wept for Moshe." The Ponevezer Rav was compared to Aharon the *Kohen Gadol*. He wore not only the crown of Torah, he also wore the crown of *Kehunah*. When Aharon died the Torah says, "The whole House of Israel wept."

Until I met him I never understood what the wisest of all men meant in his Song of Songs when he broke out in ecstasy and spoke of the *cholas ahava*, the sickness of love. He was literally sick all his life with the love of his fellow Jew.

☐ *In one of my heated arguments with him in the United States when, as was his loving nature to embrace every Jew, I said to him, "You come and go, but we have to struggle here and disentangle ourselves from the entanglements in which these men involve us." He looked at me with his angelic eyes and said, "A Yiddishe Neshamah. These people are sick." I retorted and I said, "You love too much. You love like Yitzchok Avinu whose eyes were so dim that he could see not wrong, not even in Eisav."*

He was the greatest *Oheiv* that I have ever known. The Rabbis say that when Isaac was bound to the altar the angels cried and the tears dropped from their cheeks directly into Isaac's eyes from so far away. The Ponevezer Rav felt the pain of another Jew from miles away. He was indeed a patriarch.

I can think of no rabbinic figure since the Chofetz Chaim — whose pupil he was and who inspired him in his life's work —

whose name was so worldwide and who was so internationally known as the Ponevezer Rav. They used to say during the war that Winston Churchill was worth ten divisions in the army. A thousand men ... could not achieve what one Ponevezer Rav was able to do: the Torah he built, the orphans he comforted, the widows he helped, the mouths he fed — the students he taught, tens of thousands, may well be countless all over the Jewish world, [and] he exercised a benign influence.

When the Rabbis portray the death of *Moshe Rabbeinu*, they speak of the Almighty eulogizing his passing with the words מי יקום לי עם מרעים, *"Who will rise up for Me against these evil-doers?"* There are two ways of translating these words. The world needs two types of rabbis: One, who will rise up against evil-doers, tell them of their wrongs, condemn them when necessary, reproach them. There is another way, too, to be an advocate for them: to say, *forgive them for they are ignorant.* The Ponevezer Rav was of the second type. The angels cried and they said, החכמה מאין תמצא. I translate that as meaning that wisdom may come *mei'ayin*, from nowhere, if yeshivos are built and Torah is studied and every effort is exerted and every muscle is strained ... This was the Ponevezer Rav.

The heavens wept, and said, אבד חסיד, *a pious man is gone.* The stars and the planets, and the sun and the moon wept, and said, לא קם כמשה, *no one has arisen like Moshe.* This to me is the personification of the Ponevezer Rav. Everybody seems to cry at his passing. In our generation there was none like him. He fed two thousand mouths a day. He was in the process of building seventeen yeshivos.

וימת יוסף וכל אחיו וכל הדור, *And Yoseif died, and all his brothers, and all that generation* — with the death of this great Yoseif there moves out into history an entire epoch of that generation and of his brethren. He was the last of all the Lithuanian Rabbis. Of seven hundred *rabbanim*, he was the only one who was saved for us from the annihilation of Lithuania. The Rabbis say that when Moshe died, not only did the people weep, not only did Yehoshua weep, the Almighty wept too. A great light has been extinguished.

On Rosh Hashanah we quote in the *Zichronos* the reference to the Shofar which was sounded at Sinai. וקול השופר הולך וחזק, *The sound of the shofar waxed stronger and stronger.* Our Rabbis say, שופר מהיכן בא, what produces a voice that never weakens while all other voices become weaker and weaker? All the world's philosophies and ideologies and civilizations face bankruptcy. The indecency, the immorality, the violence — how does the world look today? They face bankruptcy while the voice of the shofar הולך וחזק ... where does that sound come from? — שופר של איל, *the ram that was offered up by Abraham in place of his son.* And again they wonder, but surely that ram was an *olah*, completely consumed by fire! But they reply, גבל הקב"ה עפרו והחזירו במה שהיה, *The Holy One collected the ashes, moulded them, shaped them, and transferred them to their original state.* The voice of Jewish sacrifice that began with the *Akeidah* is a sound that can never be silenced. While every other voice is crushed and every holocaust is silenced and even forgotten, the voice of Jewish sacrifice rises above it all.

The Ponevezer Rav saw the *olah*, Lithuanian Jewry, completely annihilated; among them over seven hundred *gedolei Torah*, scholars and students. Great *yeshivos* like Slobodka and Ponevez fell; great Jewish communities like Shavl and others, the cream of world Jewry, were completely wiped out. He was the only surviving *Rav*. He was the shofar, saved from the ashes, moulded and shaped from all these *Rabbanim*, from the whole of Lithuanian Jewry, saved from the *Akeidah*, calling to the Jewish world.

He told me again and again, he felt that this was his purpose in life. He felt that he bore upon his shoulders the burden of seven hundred *Rabbanim*. It means that we Jewish people today bear upon our shoulders the burden of six million Jews. So in paying our humble tribute to this great master and teacher, this angel among men, this giant among humans, it is a challenge to us to maintain and to double our efforts in maintaining the institutions that he built and was in the process of building, and never to forget our own responsibilities to [all] Torah institutions.

Rabbi Michael Ber Weissmandl

*he struggled
with all he
possessed to
save Europe's
condemned
Jews*

5674/1903 — 5718/1957

BIOGRAPHIES are moving increasingly into the forefront of literature today. The reason for this seems to be the lateness in age of our culture and the complexity of our civilization. The immensity of the problems of today's world has lessened the opportunity of the average man to play a part in it. Overwhelmed by anxieties, he has apathetically handed over his problems to the professional in order to be relieved from a responsibility he can no longer endure. Hence, man has become unable to confront the steadily widening periphery of his dilemma and to react to it as an individual. Our media of communication, unprecedented in scope and intensity, spread manufactured, ready-made opinion, conditioning man to an "outer-directed" mass-product.

Man has lost significance in his own eyes and that is why biographical literature has become so interesting and important to us. Our time is hungry for the individual it can no longer produce and has to search for him and dig him out of the past. The biographical hero in literature has to be isolated from his time and disjoined from the world around him. His experiences and conflicts with life are set into a sharp contour of individualization, and the more this is the case, the more fascinating and interesting is the esthetic enjoyment.

It is however not in a biographical sense in which a study of the personality of Michael Ber Weissmandl is attempted here. In the world of authentic Jewish ideas, biography as a literary exercise has no place. Here, the aim is not the isolation of the hero from his time and people; on the contrary, the interest in a hero is proportionate to the degree of intensity in which his life demonstrates and reflects the very essence of his people. His experience with life is our concern only insofar as it widens the scope of our own confrontation with the world, Our biographical dealing with a man of extraordinary caliber is, therefore, not an esthetic but rather an eminently religious experience.

With the growing distance of time, Michael Ber Weissmandl is emerging with increasing clarity as a unique historical figure. In the post-war literature dealing with the fate of Central Europeans, especially the Slovakian and Hungarian Jews, as well as in the major war-crime trials, the name of Michael Ber Weissmandl appears again and again; especially at the Kasztner and Eichmann trials in Jerusalem in 1955 and 1961, during which letters, telegrams, and memoranda written by Rabbi Weissmandl and sent to the free world between 1942 and 1945, have been read in court. The sensational testimonies have revealed as a fact that Rabbi Weissmandl opened possibilities to rescue hundreds of thousands of Jews. Michael Ber Weissmandl was the one who got into contact with two Slovakian Jews who escaped from Auschwitz and gave the first eyewitness description of the systematic extermination which was until then only a vague rumor and not really believed by anyone. Michael Ber Weissmandl was the one who sent a detailed map of the camp together with the sworn testimony of the two men to the outside world. Michael Ber Weissmandl was the one who probed the Nazi mind with a point blank offer of money. Nobody would have believed it — for $50,000, Wisliceny, Eichmann's deputy, stopped the deportations for a long period of time. This was what encouraged Rabbi Weissmandl to suggest a bold proposition — the so-called "Europa Plan," which provided to bring to a halt all deportations from all of Europe for the payment of a huge sum of money. Wisliceny himself went to Berlin and personally submitted the plan.

Responsibility for the failure of those negotiations, Michael Ber Weissmandl was convinced, rests upon the assimilated Jews in the West who contented themselves with public speeches and demonstrations. He recalled that after such a demonstration in

New York, Wisliceny told him that Hitler was incensed and determined to intensify the persecution. Above all, Michael Ber Weissmandl accused the Zionist Jewish Agency in Palestine and Turkey of having frustrated his efforts. There are letters Weissmandl had the opportunity to see after the war, which give evidence — undisputable historical evidence — not only of a fatal blunder, but of deliberate and cynical frustration of his frantic appeals for money.

□ *Brothers, children of Israel, have you all become insane? Don't you know in what hell we are living? For whom do you keep your money? Do you really want to wait until we send a special messenger to plead with you, to give us what is coming to us? To you, all our pleas don't even seem to have the effect as that of a beggar at the door; after so much urging you have thrown pennies at our feet. You are murderers! You madmen! Who is the one who gives? You who are throwing pennies, looking at us from the heights of your eminence, or we, who give blood and tears from the depths of our hearts?*

□ *And you, our Jewish brothers in all the free countries; and you, leaders of nations: How could you be silent in the face of this great murder? In it, about 600,000 Jews have already been put to death, and every day now, tens of thousands are being murdered. With their devastated hearts those murdered Jews cry to you: 'You are cruel murderers yourselves, because of your cruel silence. You have the means in your hands to avert and to stop these happenings at this very moment. For the sake of the blood of millions and the tears of hundreds of thousands, we ask you, we beg you, we demand, that you should act right now!*

Selections from letters written by Rabbi M. B. Weissmandl during the war years and cited at the trial proceedings of Grunwald-Kasztner in Jerusalem (from Shalom Rosenfeld's *Criminal File No. 124* / Tel-Aviv, 1955).

One such letter decried his constant asking for money, with the argument that one cannot ask the Western Powers to accede to the transfer of money to the Nazis, when Allied blood was being shed in the struggle against them. "We also have to shed blood," the letter argues, "because it is necessary for the establishment of the Jewish Homeland — *Only with blood will the Land be redeemed.*"

"One cow in Palestine is worth more than all the Jews in

Europe" — was the immortal statement of Yitzchak Grunbaum, one of the leading figures in the Jewish Agency at that time.

One must understand the motive and the nature of Rabbi Weissmandl's statements and vehement accusations. Though he addressed himself to a political group, dealing with practical issues of enormous dimensions, his motivation was not "political" — it was basically religious, because Rabbi Weissmandl was a religious man par excellence. He conceived Jewish Nationalism as the great sin of assimilation in a national disguise, as a substitution for a universal religion which, like all religions has the purpose to give sense to one's life and solve the personal and collective dilemma of man in this world. One has to understand what went on in the mind of this man who stood in the midst of the fire, waiting day after day, month after month with terrible anxiety for that answer to his hundreds of frantic letters, telegrams and messages. He could not comprehend what had happened only until it was all over. It was only after the war when the crushing realization dawned upon him that a group of people, having lost their roots, in possession of power and influence, commanding publicity, journalists, politicians and professional pulpiteers, with almost irrational delusion had substituted an ideal after their own image, for the most basic, the most elementary and vital Jewish command of that hour — to save Jewish lives.

Rabbi Weissmandl's book *Min Hameitzar* contains a wealth of letters and documents which by themselves tell the story of Jewry in Slovakia and of their frantic attempts to wrestle themselves out of the iron clamp of destruction. There is nothing written by a Jew during that time comparable to these letters.

One has to picture in one's mind the ghastly situation in which those letters were written; the intricate and round-about ways — and the danger involved — in hiring diplomatic couriers to deliver them and the large sums of money paid to the messengers. These attempts to arouse the free world were repeated again and again with increased anxiety and despair. One also has to imagine the consternation and the abyss which opened itself before the eyes when the messengers came back first empty handed, later with short notes from which it became clear that the reports simply were not believed and besides, no money was available anyway.

How far this unbelievable conspiracy has captured the Jewish masses, and how impossible it is for any different thought to penetrate their minds, even to the point of mere evaluation, can be seen in the starry-eyed vehemence of the reaction to any reproach. With blinded eyes and closed ears, any voice raised in protest and accusation is immediately suppressed and deafened by the thousandfold cry: "Traitor," "Enemy of the Jewish People."

These facts are read with consternation and unbearable shame. How can it be explained that at a time during the last phase of the war, when the Nazis were willing to barter Jews for money, partly because of personal greed, partly because of their desire to establish contact with the Western powers which, they believed, were under Jewish influence, how was it possible, one asks, that the Jewish leaders did not move heaven and earth to save the last remnant of their brothers?

Weissmandl gives us the answer. And the answer does not deal with missed opportunities, errors of judgment, etc., as the main keys to the question. The entire wrong approach, the delusions, the horrible failure, are only results; results of the un-Jewish mentality of those Jews who had the money, the power and the apparatus in their hands. They have shunned the "old-fashioned" methods of clandestine operations and bribes as not glamorous and heroic. Demonstrations and rallies in Madison Square Garden yield uncomparably more publicity — and of course there was the aim of the "Jewish Homeland," which must not be compromised by undue demands from the Allies.

All problems, including that of saving Jewish lives, had to be subordinated to that one and only goal. It was Michael Ber Weissmandl's unshakable belief, for which he claimed to have ten-fold proof, that the few avenues of rescue which opened themselves during the holocaust were deliberately ignored by the Zionist leadership because those avenues of rescue were leading to places other than Palestine, and any undertaking along that line might thwart the expectations towards the establishment of the Jewish State. This attitude of a multitude of arrogant busybodies, the self-appointed leaders and spokesmen for world Jewry during the most tragic time in our history, has put into focus the great dilemma in which the Jewish people find itself *even today*. An intelligentsia which has become estranged from historical and authentic Judaism, has formed itself into a latterday secularistic national-political movement, which is interpreting Judaism and has usurped its representation with skill and effectiveness, utilizing Jewish suffering and persecution to intensify the notion, that only a Jewish State will "normalize" the Jewish people and solve the "Jewish question," once and for all.

Michael B. Weissmandl came to America after the war, completely broken in body and in spirit — and the establishment of the State of Israel was on the agenda of the United Nations. With incessant compulsion, he hunted for documents and rummaged through the libraries and archives among the mounds of material which had been collected after the war. He was tracing his own letters and communications, some of which found their way to the highest authorities, like his proposal to bomb the rails leading to Auschwitz. *Allied bombers did successfully strafe the oilfields of Ploesti, Rumania, but they let the trains to Auschwitz roll undisturbed until the last minute, a fact which the Nazis amusedly interpreted in their own way.*

The more the condemning evidence mounted — that the free world stood idly by while the Jews were systematically slaughtered — the more the mystery took shape with impressive contours. When it became clear that the few diplomatic and military gestures which were made before the very end of the war by the Pope and President Roosevelt to the Regent of Hungary, and also to Tiso of Slovakia, could have saved untold lives if they were made earlier, in addition to the fatal stupidities of the Jewish leaders, the phenomenon widened to a dimension which reaches beyond ordinary comprehension. Blames and recriminations become pedestrian and somehow meaningless.

To Rabbi Weissmandl, the entire catastrophe represented a phenomenon of the highest religious validity. It is precisely this reaction of Rabbi Weissmandl as he emerged after the war and which marked his personality, which is of importance to us in a biographical study because it is a *religious* experience of singular significance.

We have to put Rabbi Weissmandl against the background of the catastrophic years 1941-1945, as this was the turning point in his life, and regard his remaining years in the U.S.A. as the framework of his reaction to the war experience. The personality of Rabbi Weissmandl as he emerged after the war, appears under a twofold aspect. One is the aspect of his personal tragedy which he shared with many who suffered as he had. The second aspect is the collective tragedy which was so emphatically pronounced by his total personality, an aspect which he shared with nobody. *He could not forget.* Particularly this is what interests us here. *Is this reaction to a tragedy an incidental matter of an individual temperament, or does it have significance of a higher order of eminently Jewish religious validity?*

The question implies more than the investigation of a theoretical concept; it reaches deep into the "either-or" realms of our lives.

Here lies perhaps one of the most baffling phenomena in the history of Jews. It is the fact that they have entirely forgotten to ask the question "WHY?" Speaking about Jews in this context does not mean individuals or groups who have come to conclusions and solutions which lie outside the authentic mainstream of the Jewish people, like assimilation in its liberalistic-humanitarian or nationalistic manifestations. What we mean here is the Jew as the *homo religiosus* par excellence. How was it possible for him to forget so completely what had happened? The trials, which are occasionally held, still force the evading memory into some form of historical consciousness, just as the plays performed and the books written have added to art and literature. But what has all this to do with the question, "WHY?" which was not asked? How could we so surefootedly step back into a reality which not long ago vanished into a phantasmic nightmare? Where is the restlessness of our soul and mind?

The question "WHY?" presupposes an eminently religious outlook. It presupposes a given order in the world and sense in life; it implies want of moral justification, and it creates an intimate mutuality and reciprocity between man and event, man and nature, and ultimately man and G-d. Seen with the eyes of the religious, man is not a product of nature, but nature is a product of man. The question "WHY?" is basically different from the question "HOW?" The question "HOW?" is the question of the scientist whose interest lies not in the event but rather in the law which is either confirmed or upset by it. The answer to the question "HOW?" is always mechanistic and causal, it does not take human consciousness into account and is therefore basically amoral. The scientific approach, since it has shrunk from universalism to specialization, is today less capable than ever to grasp a phenomenon in its totality.

The question "WHY?" is a profoundly religious question and *the* Jewish Question par excellence. It establishes relationship between the event and man's consciousness — and that is what counts — not the answer.

What makes the life of Michael Ber Weissmandl significant and important for us? In what way does it reach beyond the personal and enter the wide scope of norm-giving Jewish authenticity? To put it in the most simple and unmistakable terms — *was*

Michael Ber Weissmandl as he came out after the tragedy, acting "normally? Or is it we, who have reconciled ourselves with the order of things, who represent "normalcy"? This radical question, as simple as it is, is the eminently decisive question for our lives.

⮐ Chassidic Leaders

*The warmth, vibrancy, and
singular vision of Chassidic Rebbeim*

Come With Me to the Tisch

Friday night with the Vizhnitzer Rebbe

Rabbi Chaim Meir Hager זצ"ל
5641/1881—5732/1972

Rabbi Chaim Meir Hager, who had been revered as Vizhnitzer Rebbe for 35 years, passed away in Eretz Yisrael on the Thursday night before Pesach, 5732. On the following day, an estimated 50,000 mourners accompanied his aron to its final resting place.

He had a huge following, including the thousands of settlers of Shikun Vizhnitz, and the hundreds of students of the Vizhnitzer Yeshiva, both in Bnei Brak; he was a member of the Moetzes Gedolei Hatorah (Council of Torah Sages) of the Agudath Israel of Eretz Yisrael; he was the scion of a noble Chassidic dynasty; but, perhaps equal to all of these elements, his personal warmth, the majesty of his tisch, and the triumph of joy over adversity that he personified, won him vast admiration beyond the confines of any one group.

THE *shtiebel* on Ross Street in Williamsburg was packed. People were literally hanging on to the walls. I was perched on the oversized cast-iron radiator in the corner, one hand mopping my brow with my handkerchief, the other hand holding on for dear life to the *gartel* of my partner on the radiator. We didn't know if the radiator was warming us or if the heat was generated from the assembled multitude. This was a multifaceted group of Chassidim from Galicia, Bukovina, Rumania, Hungary, Marmorosh, Transylvania — indeed from all over the globe, bent on one purpose: spending the *Shabbos* with the Vizhnitzer Rebbe, who had just arrived from *Eretz Yisrael* to seek support for his beloved project, the building of Shikun Vizhnitz in Bnai Brak. His avowed purpose was the rejuvenation of *Chassidus* after the Holocaust, which left many in despair; reciting *Kaddish* over *Yiddishkeit, frumkeit* and especially *Chassidus*. In our minds, we were mulling over the Rebbe's words regarding the Baal Shem Tov's promise to his great disciple and *shliach tzibbur*, Reb Yaakov Koppel Chassid, from whom the Rebbe was a seventh generation descendant — *Your issue will lead Klal Yisrael to welcome Mashiach.*

Suddenly all was quiet. The Rebbe silently made his way through a hastily formed lane, the throng held back by broad-shouldered Chassidim. He took his place at the head of the table and, with outstretched arms welcoming the *Shabbos*, he began, *"Gut Shabbos, Gut Shabbos, Gut Shabbos, heiliger Shabbos, taiyere Shabbos, shreit shet, Yiddalech, Gut Shabbos."*

Thus, at about eight o'clock, began the *tisch* which was to last into the early hours of the morning. *Shabbos knows no night,* the Rebbe would say, quoting *Rashi* in *Masechta Shabbos — Friday is considered the night of Shabbos. Shabbos is completely day, made up entirely of light, life and purity.* He recited the *Shalom Aleichem* in the *nusach* made famous by three great Vizhnitzer Rebbes before him, intoning each phrase distinctly and in his own unique manner. *Shabbos shulem u'mevoroch — Shulem aleichem, malachay hashoreis, malachay hashulem, malachay elyon!*

He sang with a clear and resonant voice, broken from time to time by a sob — a tear shed out of the joy with which he greeted the *Shabbos* — and by a deep *krechtz* emanating from the soul which longed with such great anticipation for *Shabbos HaMalkah* — the Sabbath Queen.

He went through the recitation of *"Shalom Aleichem"* and the entire *"Ribbon Ha'olamim"* without singing, merely chanting the words. Upon its completion he picked up the *hadassim* filled with spices and recited the *"Boray minay besamim."* Thus, with an addition to his great soul and the scent of *m'danay asa*, he began to say *"Aishes Chayil"* in a half singing, half chanting tone

— a tradition brought down from the holy *Zeides* of Kosov, who labored and toiled in the cradle of *Chassidus*, in the mountain valleys where Russia, Poland, Rumania, and Hungary touched each other. The *u-bu-bu-boy* and the lingering sounds of the Vizhnitzer *nusach*, elongating many words and dragging the syllables of others, were the trademark of the dynasty founded by Reb Yaakov Koppel Chassid, established in the Galician village by his son Reb Mendel and fortified by his grandson Reb Chaim. The next generation had its own Reb Mendel, known as the *Tsemach*, from whom sprouted the present dynasty. As the son-in-law of the great Rizhiner, he set up his court in Vizhnitz, a hamlet in Bukovina, not far from the palace of the Rizhiner in Sadegura.

The Rebbe continued to recite the *"Askinu Seudasa,"* with the unmistakable *nusach*, revealing in each phrase his thoughts and emotions. One could feel the expression of *"simchah b'lev nishbar"* — rejoicing with a broken heart — a melody peering out of the cracks of a heart, overflowing with the joy of the advent of *Shabbos*. His progenitors dwelled upon the mysteries of the *Shabbos*, the holiness of the *Shabbos* in all of their writings. He, the Rebbe, was attempting to convey the joy of the *Shabbos*. To all who entered his sphere of influence he opened a door to the enjoyment of the *Shabbos*; to sense its happiness and to open one's heart and soul to its flood of purity and sanctity, contentment and ecstasy.

The *shtiebel* was filled with all kinds of Jews, all types of Chassidim, attracted to the Rebbe's voice and look as to a magnet. He led, he directed, he guided with a wink, a gesture, a movement. The entire group swayed, as he swayed; sang, as he sang; cried, as he cried; smiled, as he smiled; everyone, as if transposed from this world to another, elated, uplifted, and overjoyed. This was his magical power of *"taking the olam,"* the entire group, molding them into one unit, ready to do the Will of the One Above.

He proceeded to make *Kiddush*. As he uttered the words *"Yom hashishi,"* we all strained to get a glimpse of his face. With the entrance of the *Shabbos* his entire appearance changed. It was as if he had grown a foot taller. His bearing, so regal all week long, was even more pronounced on *Shabbos*. He was immaculate in dress. Every hair of his beard was in a pre-ordained place. His *payos* were neatly curled and smoothly blended into his beard. His face was radiant with joy. Yet he was *"poshet tsura v'lovesh tsura"* — his facial expressions changed with the mood of the words he chanted. He intoned the words of the *Kiddush*, some hurriedly and others he lingered upon; stressing, explaining, emoting — all part of the same process of involving all around him in the happiness he felt in the *Shabbos*. Here before our eyes was the Rebbe who personified the humility of Kosov, the majesty of Rizhin, the wisdom of Ropshitz, the piety of Chernobyl and the kindness of Apt. In his veins flowed their blood and in his conduct he eternalized their message. His path was a synthesis of all of these great dynasties and he sought to recreate their former greatness in his renaissance of *Chassidus* after the great holocaust.

No sooner had he finished the *Kiddush*, partaken of the wine, when he immediately lifted his hands to conduct the entire *olam* in a new song — a melody he had composed on his way to America. He enjoyed a new *niggun* and lent his ear to every type of song. He once told us that his entire body is one *niggun*; from the tips of his toes to the top of his head he echoed with song.

The entire *shtiebel* trembled as the sound reverberated, as all were pervaded with his joyful presence. He was in full command at all times. He glanced around the room and scrutinized us all — nothing escaped him. He recognized faces he hadn't seen in forty years and he embraced relatives he hadn't seen since before the war. He drew everyone close with his sharp and friendly look.

Thus, the *tisch* continued and the first course was served. He nibbled at the fish and distributed the *shirayim* — being meticulously careful to hand out the fish on a special fork to those he knew as uninitiated in the habits of the Chassidim. He would avoid violating anyone's feelings and strove to make everyone feel at home.

After the distribution of *shirayim* to the dignitaries, the platter was pounced upon by the Chassidim who were even satisfied to have only touched the platter. Others, who were more lucky, diligently divided up their spoils with their neighbors and to all newcomers — especially to those who were not Chassidim. Remember, this was Vizhnitz where *all* were drawn close to the Rebbe by the Chassidim who were taught to attract *all* — even the most distant. Their motto was summed up in the words of the Rosh Hashana prayer of *V'yishme'u rechokim v'yavo'u*, "Those distant will hear of you and come close to you."

All is silent. The Rebbe begins to chant the "*Kol Mekadeish*" with the tune of his forefathers, repeating some words and stretching out others. He repeats the word "*maychalelo*" three times. The last time he pronounces it as "mochal-lo," hinting at a Chazal that states — "If a man keeps the Shabbos, even if he was guilty of idolatry, his sins are forgiven."

The Chassidim press forward, eager to see the Rebbe, and to swallow each word he recites. At times, the Rebbe pauses to wipe a tear from his eyes, but he is not crying. He is enjoying the Shabbos and expressing his happiness. His voice rings loud and clear, and it tears into every heart. It is difficult to forget his imposing presence, his resonant voice and his loving smile.

The " Kol Mekadeish" is followed by a lively niggun, a dance melody, and the Rebbe is careful to make sure that all are responsive to his urging to participate. Soon the entire room is reverberating — everyone is awake, swaying back and forth to the rhythm.

Following the soup the Rebbe pauses and then begins the "Menuchah Vesimchah." This is no ordinary tune. It is a symphony. Its composer was the great Reb Nisson who had sung in the court of the Rebbe's father (known as the "Ahavas Yisroel" after his sefer), Reb Yisroel, of blessed memory. The Rebbe sang the first movement. It was repeated by the entire group. He then carefully taught the group the refrain and was gratified by the quick response and some able voices. His pleasure was obvious, for his face shone. But pity the one who went off key! No matter how many people were assembled, his sensitive ear would rebel at a false note and he would pound on the table with his fingers, interrupt the singing, and have the olam repeat the melody perfectly.

"Menuchah Vesimchah" sometimes took close to twenty minutes by the clock! But who was looking at the clock? We had lost all sense of time, as if transposed into a Gan Eden — some Olam Haba beyond space and beyond time. Our joy knew no bounds as we sang and opened our ears to the voice of his singing, for he pierced many ears that were tone-deaf and many hearts that were laden with grief and adversity. He taught us how to daven, how to chant, how to sing, and we felt closer to him with every note. He blended everyone into one symphony of prayer and song. From hundreds of individuals, drawn from dissimilar backgrounds and temperaments, he welded together one solid group of Chassidim bent on one purpose — tasting the joys of the Shabbos.

While eating the main course the Rebbe was humming to himself and mulling over in his own mind the thoughts he was going to say in his *d'var Torah*. Even though he was so engrossed in his own thoughts, he was alert to the entrance of any visiting dignitary — Rebbe or Rav or Rosh Yeshiva. He had each seated according to his station and was reverent and respectful to all, sidestepping his own dignity to honor all. His frequent question asked of his guests was, "Where does one find *simchah*? Can joy be purchased in a special store?" I once gathered enough courage to answer him that happiness was to be found by the Rebbe. His face lit up, and smiling from ear to ear, he bestowed his usual blessing: "*A zees leben oif dir, mein kind.*"

His *d'var Torah* was always preceded by a serious *niggun* sung in undertones, and erratically interrupted by the Torah itself. His Torah words were filled with mystical combinations and numerical equivalents, laboriously put together. He always stressed the theme of *Shabbos:* enjoying the *Shabbos*, hallowing the *Shabbos*. He would always inject some *mussar*, criticizing those who slept away most of the *Shabbos*. He implored all to taste the *Shabbos* and to sense its beauty, holiness, and joy. No heart was left untouched and no mind was left unchallenged. He had something to say to everybody — to the great scholar and the simple Chassid alike. He appealed to all, embraced all, and inspired all.

The *bentchen* was followed by a joyous dance, with the Rebbe stationed in the center, observing all who danced. Here he recognized a face he hadn't seen in ages and there he patted a Chassid on the back, thanking him for some long forgotten favor. People who had in some way been of service were astounded to hear him offer his thanks and blessings to them after decades of separation. He never forgot a face, a name, a good deed. As the dancing proceeded, he immersed himself into it, constantly urging the *olam* from his station to increase the intensity of the singing and dancing. The *olam* responded with more ecstasy and greater enthusiasm.

After a while the table was reset with fruit and kugel, and the Rebbe sat down for what was known as the Second *Tisch*. The older Chassidim went home, and the younger people, with greater resources of energy, remained. It was well past midnight. After distributing the fruit and kugel, the Rebbe would retell oft-told stories of his great ancestors and of other great Chassidic leaders. Special songs were sung upon various occasions. Most often he had one of the Hungarian Chassidim sing the song of the Kalever that dealt with the coming of *Mashiach* ("*Shirnok Rinok*"). After each stanza he would sing the Hebrew words as tears rolled down his cheeks. He always followed this *niggun* with a very joyful dance-song, which sounded like a triumphant welcome to the expected *Mashiach*.

At this second *tisch* the Rebbe began to call over the *bachurim*, requesting that each say a *d'var Torah*. After each *bachur* divested himself of his *d'var Torah* the Rebbe would add to it, correct it, and make sure that the source be given due credit. He would literally trade *d'var Torah* for *d'var Torah*, and embellished each one with stories from the lives of the authors. At this *tisch* he would usually sing "Kah Ribbon Olam." The *niggun*, the gestures, and the trembling voice alerted all to the holiness of *Ma'amad Har Sinai* and all rose to their feet to honor this momentous occasion.

Following the Second *Tisch*, the Chassidim danced to either a wordless *niggun*, or to the famous "Hashir V'hashevach," or to the Vizhnitzer "Shevach Ykar U'gdula." Once experienced, it was difficult to forget the sight of the Rebbe in the early hours of the morning as alert and enthusiastic as a youngster, urging all of us on to greater heights of joy and ecstasy.

The Rebbe sat down to a third *Tisch* where the *bachurim* were the center of attraction. There each had to say his *d'var Torah* and listen to the Rebbe's comments. At this *tisch* he distributed *korsh* (a cake made of yellow corn meal), served with herring and *shnapps*. By this time all sleep had been forgotten and the remaining *olam* was as alert and as eager to enjoy the *Shabbos* as the Rebbe. But it was getting late and at about 2 a.m. the Rebbe would begin to ascend the steps to his apartment above. He turned around to us, and seeing that we longed for more he began to sing the "Odeh Lakeil." The building echoed with our singing of the refrain, and as he mounted the steps, the Rebbe turned around and sang another stanza. The song spoke of rejuvenation and of constant devotion — themes the Rebbe had made popular. He stressed them and literally seared these thoughts into our minds. The song completed, we took our leave of him with the same *Gut Shabbos* with which he had begun the *tisch*.

He was now alone, in his own room, and most everyone had left. Only a few of us lingered, and we listened. Alone, the Rebbe was dancing a *Shabbos* song by himself; he was dancing around his own *tisch* laden with *sefarim*, singing aloud to himself. No weariness and no exhaustion marred his *Shabbos*. He sang and danced until the rays of the sun entered his room.

All is quiet but all is not over. His spirit continues to sing and dance in our lives and homes.

The Gerer Rebbe

*a tribute to a
chassidic leader
who rebuilt his
decimated flock
in the Holy
Land*

Rabbi Yisroel Alter זצ״ל
5655/1895—5737/1977

*Where did all these people come from? What drove
them to crowd the streets?*

*It is barely 4 p.m. The radio had broadcast the bleak
tidings at noon. To all except the closest, the news was totally unexpected. The morning papers surely had no mention
of the Gerer Rebbe's passing. Even the more popular afternoon dailies did not report it. Who, then, amassed this crowd
of 100,000 mourners — or 200,000, as police estimated them?*

*What contact did these tens of thousands of Jews have
with Gerer Chassidus, or with the late Rebbe? They never
caught a glimpse of his features on the TV screen — he kept
himself as removed from the instrument as he would from
fire. Radio? His few chosen words were never squandered on
radio frequencies. The papers seldom reported his activities
— his entire demeanor was in total opposition to the games of
publicity-seeking. So what triggered this flow of humanity
to flood Jerusalem's streets in tribute to this man in just three
to four hours?*

*The range of the representation is staggering. And so is
the contrast they present ... the faces: The obviously Chas-*

sidic bachurim *and* yungeleit, *whose every expression and gesture bespeak devotion to Torah and Chassidus ... middle-aged men, elegantly dressed in modern attire, tears flowing down their cheeks, unwiped ... Jerusalem natives, in full Me'ah Shearim garb, white crocheted skull-huggers peeking out from beneath their black velour hats, the gravity of generations weighing down their features ... The young Sabra generation, representing the Yeshivot Tichoniot, much in evidence — heads usually cocked audaciously, crowned by* kipot s'rugot, *now hung low ... And so many Jews, who bear no particular stamp of affiliation.*

A glance upward, and the eye sweeps over balconies and rooftops, crowded with yet more Jews ... The rich bouquet of Sephardic Jews of all hues and shades, the mix that only Jerusalem can boast ... mothers with their young, some cuddling infants in their arms.

One look around, and it is obvious that they are not spectators at all, but fellow mourners grieved over the terrible irreparable loss.

It was the response of those who had known him as Rebbe ... of others who had found in him the deep concern of a father — their father ... of still others who saw in him a rebuilder of shattered people and communities ... of yet others who had appreciated the leadership role he had assumed in the affairs of religious Jewry in the Holy Land — in Agudath Israel, Chinuch Atzmai ... But primarily it was the instinctive response of every Jew to the trauma of losing a great man. All knew the loss and felt its pangs with an immediacy that drove them into the streets to mourn — both the simple Jew who could not point to more than the simple fact, the "Ma zos," and those who knew: Those who savored the fine points of Kotzk, how they were perpetuated for four generations of Ger, only to be destroyed, and then rebuilt again in the Holy Land. How the specifics of Ger — the fierce devotion to Torah, the uncompromising pursuit of truth, the jealous watching of minutes, the careful training of the youth, the sparing of the words — how they were all recreated by this prince of Ger. They live on, but he is gone.

✑§ Ger — A Dynasty of Torah and Chassidus

The late Gerer Rebbe, Rabbi Yisroel Alter, was scion of a family of nobility, and heir to a demanding Chassidic tradition that had its spiritual source in the fountains of unadulterated truth that flowed from Parshys'che and Kotzk.

□ *An impoverished Jew came to the Kotzker Rebbe and begged him, "Help me! I haven't a bit of food to feed my family!"*

"That's not a problem. Just daven to Hashem with emes.*"*

"But I don't know how to daven with emes.*"*

"Then you do have a serious problem!"

Kotzk was not known for miracles. In its pursuit of truth — in Torah study, in life, in *avodas Hashem* — there was no time for miracles. But the truth that emerged from Kotzk was indeed miraculous.

Rabbi Yitzchok Meir, disciple of Kotzk, was the first Rebbe of Ger. His penetrating *Chidushei HaRim* on Talmud is widely studied. His thirteen children had died during his lifetime. His grandson, Reb Arye Leib, succeeded him. He was known by the title of his commentaries on Torah and Talmud, *Sfas Emes* (Truthful Speech), which are basic volumes in every Talmudic scholar's library.* Indeed, Ger is renowned for its emphasis on Torah learning, for all of the Gerer Rebbes were also leading Torah scholars in their generation.

His son and successor, Rabbi Avrohom Mordechai Alter, continued in this tradition. He had amassed a huge library of *sefarim*. There were those that claimed that most of the books were superfluous, for he had committed their contents to memory in his first perusal.

□ *During a visit to Berlin, he inspected the private library of a bibliophile. His host took out an old* sefer, *whose author was unknown to him — both the title page and first page of the work were missing. Reb Avrohom Mordechai asked permission to take the* sefer *to his room and his host readily*

---

* The great Rabbi of Sochatchov, son-in-law of the sainted Kotzker, author of the *Avnei Nezer*, is said to have maintained two bookcases, one for *Rishonim* (earlier commentators) and another for the *Acharonim* (later ones). The volumes of the *Sfas Emes, written at the turn of the century, were found to be amongst the Rishonim ...* To study some portions of the Talmud without the *Sfas Emes* is unthinkable to the modern day scholar.

agreed. The following day the sefer *was returned with the title page and first page — written in by hand.*

He is said to have left dozens of volumes of his own written commentary, which were never recovered from the destruction of World War II.

☐ *Reb Avrohom Mordechai was extremely reluctant to assume the leadership of Gerer Chassidus, deeming himself inadequate to the assignment. " 'He who commanded oil to burn can command vinegar to burn' — My sainted father was the 'oil' and his flame illuminated. I am the vinegar..."*

The growth Ger had experienced under the *Sfas Emes* was duplicated many times over under his son's leadership. While the town of Ger was over an hour's train-ride from Warsaw, and involved a long, difficult and expensive journey through the hills and valleys of Central Poland from other regions, 10,000 Jews would routinely undertake the trip to spend a Shavuos, a *Yomim Noraim* or a Succos in the company of their sainted leader. It was always considered a homecoming of sorts for Gerer *Chassidim* who, until the precious moments of greeting the Rebbe with "*Shalom*," considered themselves spiritually unfulfilled.

To be part of Ger for even a short while was to leave worldly concerns back home, to know the true meaning of serving Hashem with *emes*, to don the royal *levush* of Chassidic garb, and to muscle your way amongst the throngs for a glimpse — A word? That was a priceless commodity in Ger. For those few hours, the Chassid underwent a lapse of identity and it mattered little whether he was from the aristocracy or one of the numerous poor of Polish Jewry. Now he was a chassid ... It is said that the world-renowned giant of Talmudic scholarship, Rabbi Menachem Ziemba, would sit anonymously at the foot of the Rebbe's *tisch*, imbibing the atmosphere, drinking in each cryptic word.

The ranks of Ger swelled to include some 250,000 followers. Indeed, Gerer Chassidim were the dominant force in many phases of life in countless Polish cities, towns, and villages.

⋨ Rebuilding the Ruins

That was yesteryear, in pre-war Poland of the 1920's and 1930's, under the leadership of the Gerer Rebbe, Rabbi Avrohom Mordechai Alter. Then, Hitler intervened with his plan to wipe out Jewry, and this majestic empire ended up in total ruins. The Rebbe and three of his sons escaped destruction, finding refuge in *Eretz Yisrael.*

One question hovered above the smoke: Could illustrious Polish Jewry, now in ruins, ever be revived? Would this spiritual edifice ever again reach the epitome of G-dliness, Torah, and *Chassidus?* The Rebbe died in 1948, leaving the mantle of leadership on the shoulders of his oldest son, Rabbi Yisroel Alter. He had also suffered personal losses, for amongst the millions of *kedoshim* were his wife, their son and daughter, and their families.

At the time of his father's passing, Jerusalem was under siege. Despite the threatening Arab armies and the terrible food shortages, *chutz l'Aretz* was only a memory, never to be considered as an option for escape — not for himself, nor for others ... To a *Rav*, a refugee from the concentration camp, inquiring whether to settle in America or to stay in *Eretz Yisrael*, he remarked — "This may be *Medinat Yisrael*, but *chutz l'Aretz* doesn't compare to it." Indeed, he rarely left Yerushalayim and never left the Holy Land once he arrived there.

It was time to rebuild, to strengthen his own soul and to work for Jewish continuity. For Polish Jewry, and particularly for the remnants of Gerer Chassidim, he was a link to a world that was no more.

The Emerging Rebbe

Rabbi Yisroel Alter was always recognized as a brilliant scholar. When only five, his grandfather, the *Sfas Emes*, prophesied greatness for him. Not given to little jokes, he referred to his favorite grandson as "Reb Yisroel." When Reb Yisroel was 16, that genius of scholars, the Rogatchover, is said to have remarked, "This young man knows *Shas!*" When still 15, he was engaged to be married to the daughter of a renowned Polish Torah Gaon, Reb Yaakov Meir Biderman, son-in-law of the *Sfas Emes*. In Torah correspondence that he exchanged with his father, the latter would address him in terms reserved for those destined for greatness — unusual in Ger, but not in his case. Before long, Polish Jewry recognized him as an outstanding Torah scholar.

The Gerer Priority: The Youth

The Chassidic courts of Kotzk, the "*Rim,*" and the other Rebbes of Ger had a preponderance of young men. Rabbi Avrohom Mordechai especially had gone out of his way to encourage younger Chassidim, much to the consternation of some of their seniors. But in time, the barriers between old and young all but vanished.

"*Sharfe yungeleit* — sharp young men" they were called — sharp-witted, sharp in intellectual acumen, and sharply outspoken in their fierce intolerance of indolence, hypocrisy, and complacency. The Rebbe assigned the supervision of the *yungeleit* to his son, Reb Yisroel, and he took to the task with a zeal that never waned.

Batei midrashim cropped up all over Poland — in Warsaw, Lodz, Cracow, and other communities — where Gerer youth crowded their days with Torah and *Chassidus*. Some were full-time scholars, others were out in the world of commerce, but all had made the *bais hamidrash* the focal point of their days ... They were prominent among those who streamed to Ger to more fully experience the *kedushah* of a festival, the awe of the Ten Days of Repentance. And they were outstanding among those who had heroically demonstrated the tenacity of their convictions by learning and living Torah around the clock in Ghettos under the worst of the Nazi terror. (Some of their exploits are recorded in Moshe Prager's אלו שלא נכנעו.)

No sooner had the previous Rebbe, Rabbi Avrohom Mordechai, arrived in the Holy Land, but that he again focused on the needs of the young, and began to build Torah. First he devoted attention to the Yeshiva Sfas Emes in Jerusalem, which he had founded on one of his five previous trips to the Holy Land. Sfas Emes was greatly expanded by his heirs, Reb Yisroel, and, *yibadel lechaim*, the present Rebbe, Reb Bunim Alter. Reb Yisroel continued to honor this priority of devoting special attention to the *bachurim* and *yungeleit*, for they were his pride of the present and hope for the future. This was of extreme importance, for at the time he took over the leadership of Ger, the outlook for the future was bleak, indeed — a *Chassidus* without *Chassidim*.

In the words of David Zaritzky, well-known Israeli writer:

His task was more difficult than that of his great father, for he was standing on ruins; from under his feet curled the smoke of crematoria, of charred Batei Midrash, and their members. Around him gathered half-dead, fully-despondent Chassidim, whose attachment to Ger was their sole spark of life, surviving lost parents, wives, children.

Not only did he rebuild the Ger empire, he rebuilt tens of thousands of people, endowing them with new neshamos, forming new features on their faces — it was a brand-new start, from Bereishis ... It was not simply a matter of teaching them to think like Chassidim, but to think like human beings, then like Jews ... like Chassidim, and then ultimately in the singularly Gerer approach.

He created it all. Quietly, with a soft word, a sharp gesture, an understanding nod. He quickly perceived not only the kvittel *(the paper with the name and request written on it), but the person as well. The person? — he himself did not know what he wanted, so first the Rebbe taught him to want, then what to want. Finally, he taught him to ask for what he wanted — then he allowed himself to smile.*

In three decades, the Gerer Rebbe built a network of Torah institutions which were to educate thousands of children. Gerer Chassidim from Europe and the Americas sent their children to learn in the Torah institutions of Ger and from the Rebbe's greatness. They joined Israeli youngsters in the Yeshivos *Sfas Emes, Chidushei HaRim,* and numerous *kollelim* spread across the land. The *kollel* in Bnei Brak *(Bais HaTalmud LeHora'ah),* for example, is well-known for having produced some of the outstanding Torah scholars in the land.

His involvement in building Torah went beyond his own *Chassidus;* the Gerer Rebbe was one of the founders of Chinuch Atzmai (the Torah School network in Israel), actively serving on its Board of Governors. Besides guiding the growth of many other Torah institutions, he was also at the side of his cousin, Rabbi Pinchas Levin, who was leader of the Beth Jacob movement in Israel, and headed the Jerusalem B.J. Seminary.

His interest in Torah youth was also not limited to his own. Thousands of yeshiva students visited him regularly and this writer personally witnessed his closeness with the *talmidim* of Chevron, Kol Torah, Etz Chaim and other Jerusalem yeshivos. While *levush* — the traditional Chassidic attire — is of great importance in Ger, it mattered little to the Rebbe how a visitor was dressed; that was merely *chitzonius,* exterior. What was more significant on such occasions was *p'nimius* — the inner content of Torah and *midos.*

The Rebbe's building plans also reflected a concern beyond parochialism. He ordered the building for the Yeshivas Chidushei HaRim to be constructed in an extremely modern section of Tel Aviv, predominantly inhabited by secular Jews. The Rebbe felt that the Yeshiva could have an inspiring effect on the whole community. ... During his last years Ger began constructing Chatzor, a new settlement town in Galilee. Ger always had a special attachment to the Holy Land, and encouraging building in *Eretz Yisroel* was one of the Rebbe's important goals. His own father, Reb Avrohom Mordechai, would stress that the *mitzvah* of settling and building *Eretz Yisrael* is applicable in our times, and was above political considerations.

◄§ Leader of Klal

The Rebbe enhanced his many innate qualities by a relentless pursuit of personal perfection, making him into a Torah giant. This, however, did not lead him to withdraw from public life, and he forcefully used his unusual perceptive abilities in public leadership.

Like his father before him, who had joined the Chofetz Chaim and other leading figures of his time in founding Agudath Israel, he too chose to be one of the prime movers of the Agudath Israel movement. It was there that he saw his hopes for unifying Torah Jews — *Chassid* and *Misnagid* — into one strong movement. The Gerer Rebbe was one of the pillars of the *Moetzes Gedolei HaTorah* (Council of Torah Sages), and there was hardly a problem affecting Jewry in which he was not involved. Indeed, he felt it a sacred trust, and was often heard to refer to "my father's Agudath Israel."

He shunned personal publicity and offered his signature only where he saw a long range benefit to *Klal Yisrael*. Agudath Israel was his vehicle for public expression and on almost every occasion he sought to strengthen the movement in the *Yishuv* as well as anywhere around the world. He felt a special kinship with the Agudath Israel of America, and often wrote his followers in the United States to assume active roles in its affairs. Outside of Agudath Israel proclamations, he was not given to issuing public statements.

He was extremely close with other *gedolei Yisrael* — it mattered little what the background of the *gadol* was. Although he had occasional ideological differences with other Chassidic leaders, these never interfered with his relationship with them. The Rebbe never waited for a famed Torah scholar to visit him, but was quick to travel to see them — such as the Chazon Ish, Rabbi Issur Zalman Meltzer, Rabbi Eliezer Silver, and Rabbi Aharon Kotler. Torah, more than anything else, was his criterion for determining greatness, and he responded accordingly. People knew the extent of his involvement in *Klal;* they also sensed the depth of his devotion to being a loyal servant; their only questions were — When? — How?

Unity and peace amongst Torah Jews are known to have preoccupied his last days. One of his last actions was to take the initiative to heal a breach in political activity that had grown between him and the followers of the Ponovezher Rosh Yeshiva, Rabbi Eliezer Schach — a split that had resulted from the Rebbe's policy of extending Agudath Israel's areas of cooperation to include some debatable factions. As if to underscore this fierce determination, he was stricken as his lips uttered "Shalom," the final blessing of *Bircas Kohanim*.

✺ The Value of Time

The Gerer Rebbe seemed to have an obsession with time. No material commodity was more precious as a tool in *avodas Hashem*. His clocks and watches were meticulously synchronized and never had he arrived even one minute late for *tefillah*. *Z'man tefillah* (the halachically prescribed time for prayer) was scrupulously observed in Ger.

One could see his face nervously perspire at the slightest hint of wasted time. His every minute was accounted for and he often appeared edgy at public gatherings, in grief over time slipping by. Nor could time be measured without precision, and even his driver learned never to be late ... "Farbreng nisht der tzeit — don't while away the time" he was often heard to say.

> □ *Following the Yom Kippur War, the Rebbe was besieged by visiting delegations from all over the world. He detested discussions on the political and military situation. To all queries he had one answer, "We must pray."*
>
> *Once a distinguished American Rabbi asked him, "What do you say to the current situation?"*
>
> *Replied the Rebbe: "I say* Tehillim.*"*

Time also meant organization, and as if to preach by example, his day was a model of structured planning. There was time set aside to pray, to learn, to receive *Chassidim*, to take interest in his institutions, to lead in the affairs of Agudath Israel and *Klal Yisrael* ... To be *koveya ittim*, setting aside time for Torah study, was the substance of many of his messages to his followers.

When he was not busy receiving Chassidim or occupied with his involvement with *Klal*, he was totally immersed in Torah. His *Rebbetzin* was known to complain that he never slept, even after a serious operation in 1972. A familiar sight in Jerusalem's Ge'ulah section was the Rebbe strolling through the deserted streets well before daybreak. His *bachurim* were expected to have begun their day in Torah learning and he would not hesitate to awaken those who were not so quick.

Dawn: It was a time to take a deep breath of the brisk Jerusalem air — and to sigh for the woes of the individuals and the *Klal*. Equally as important was the opportunity it offered to signal the start of another day of *avodas Hashem* to his followers ... *Chassidim* remember the Rebbe performing essentially the same role in Poland, where he had also watched over the youth.

The before-dawn stroll was also a time when soldiers from the Schnellers Army Base (just opposite the courtyard of the Rebbe) would jog — and often would respond to a nod with "*Boker tov, Rebbe.*"

⊷§ The Private Encounter

The Rebbe had the unusual ability to sweep over a crowd of hundreds with one glance ... Somehow, each of the people in the crowd felt he had locked eyes with the Rebbe for one brief but powerful moment. In private consultations, he literally spent only minutes with each Jew who came to see him, yet he was able to swiftly profile the problems of the man before him. Scores of people would queue up outside his office and within a half-hour he would have seen everyone; each problem thoroughly aired and every response measured — but all in lightning time. He was privy to tens of thousands of problems — spiritual, economic, medical — and pronounced his advice within minutes. Surprisingly he would recall these brief encounters 10 and 20 years later, referring to names, dates, situations — asking after the welfare of those troubled. Sadness and joy passed quickly before him — through him — yet he was able to adjust his mood to a fresh start with each person.

Each man walked out with a substantial response. To a young yeshiva student who had been summoned home with dozens of telegrams on the eve of the Six-Day War, he said: "If you are afraid, stay here. If it is a matter of *kibud av v'eim*, go home." In little less than 30 seconds, a response, a *halachah*, and Torah philosophy.

An elderly Jew from Romania with a wholesale toy business in Tel Aviv, told his tale simply:

> My wife became seriously ill with yener machalah (a veiled reference to cancer). The doctors could not decide: "Operate." "Don't operate." People in the street said to me,

"Take a trip to the Gerer Rebbe. Everybody goes to him for advice and a brachah." So I traveled to Yerushalayim.

When I was younger I used to seek brachos at the courts of the Romanian Rebbes. And the procedure was simple. I'd put a sizeable pidyon (contribution) down on the Rebbe's table and he would devote a considerable amount of time to hear me out, question me on all the details, and rain down a host of brachos on me ...

At the Gerer Rebbe's, everything was different. That he doesn't accept pidyonim, I knew; but I had no idea everything went so fast. Before the people ahead of me even get inside they're out. What am I to do? I didn't even prepare a kvittel because I'd have to fill up a whole notebook with details.

I was very upset, and suddenly I was inside. To this day I don't understand what happened. I said only, "My wife's life is in danger," and the Rebbe understood everything. He asked me all kinds of questions and I felt sure it was taking a lot of time. He said "Don't operate!" and gave me a strong brachah. I felt wonderful. I looked at the clock when I came out — the whole thing had taken maybe two minutes. I still don't understand it. I know that "A tzaddik decrees and God fulfills." But I had not come for a brachah alone, but for advice as well. How did this tzaddik read my mind?

(from "An Appreciation," by Moshe Prager)

When he spoke, his answers were a remarkable blend of caution and razor-sharp wit. He yearned for the sharpness of Kotzk and he was overheard to have said, "Oh, how I wish I could lead like Kotzk!" But he considered the generation too weak for such leadership.

To Chassidim, Misnagdim, b'nai yeshiva and unaffiliated Jews, he was the Gerer Rebbe. Regardless of who you were, you were untruthful if you denied that your knees knocked in fright when you stood before him. — I heard this from people with no connection to Chassidus! His penetrating eyes were enough to make anyone quiver. But soon you were reassured, and once you walked out you realized that the Gerer Rebbe had left you with a lifelong impression.

The late Rav of Ponovezh once remarked: "Before the war, when my heart ached, I traveled to Radin to see the Chofetz Chaim and I felt better. After the war, I travel to Jerusalem to see the Gerer Rebbe and I feel better."

Such was the power of the late Gerer Rebbe — to penetrate minds, to soothe and to inspire. To people, big and small, he was the "big brother," the surrogate father, on whom to pour out all the world's woes ... Grandfathers saw in him the vanished patriarch in whom one could trust.

Whence the diversity of the Rebbe's followers? He had opened his door to everyone, and there is something about the Jewish soul, the *pintele Yid*, which homes in on its source.

The Loss and the Legacy

What did the Rebbe leave behind for us? A rebuilt, revitalized *Chassidus*, consisting of thriving institutions and devoted followers ... an enriched *Klal Yisrael. Seforim?* It is widely believed that, like his father and grandfather, he had recorded his Torah thoughts. No one is certain, but he did say, "Although there are differences of opinion amongst Torah leaders whether or not to write Torah, I say that in our impoverished generation everyone should write."

And he left us with indelible memories of a penetrating glance, a sharp word, a *tisch* ... and a funeral — the silent procession of multitudes, where the only sound was the shuffling of feet and the wiping of tears ... A silence.

□ *In Judaism there is a kind of inverse relationship between authority and words, and never was this more acutely demonstrated than in the "court" of Rabbi Yisroel Alter. A man of immense presence, a person who said a thousand words with a mere glance, the Rebbe needed to say almost nothing to work an internal revolution in his followers. A single sentence from him appeared to carry the authority of generations ...*

The Gerer Rebbe became a "Rebbe's rebbe," as Chassidic leaders from all over the world sought his counsel and submitted to his leadership. Following the death of the Amshinover Rebbe of Jerusalem, the Gerer Rebbe reputedly motored from his residence in the Ge'ula section of Jerusalem to the Bayit Vegan section. There he met with the grandson of the late Amshinover Rebbe and spoke with him for about half an hour, convincing him to carry on the Amshinover line and assume the position of Amshinover Rebbe.

A half hour. How frequently do we throw away a half-hour's words? If the Rebbe spoke half an hour, it had to be an unprecedented occasion. *In measuring words, a person deepens his wisdom and impact. Thus it really wasn't ironic that when the Gerer Rebbe died, thousands were left speechless, and, in accord with Polish Chassidic custom, no eulogy was delivered. Nothing needed to be said. The loss spoke for itself.*

(from an article in the Denver Intermountain Jewish News, by Hillel Goldberg)

Silence. How fitting a tribute to man who led with such an economy of words!

The Novominsker Rebbe

*a talmid
remembers his
private Talmud
sessions with
the Rebbe*

Rabbi Nochum Mordechai Perlow זצ"ל
5656/1896—5736/1976

I AM CERTAIN that there were others who knew the
Novominsker Rebbe better than I did. But, then again, we
learned together on a regular basis for the past few years. The
three of us — the Rebbe, Yitzchok, and I — spent thousands of
hours together, and I had the privilege of knowing him, his unwavering *hasmadah* (diligence), and his love for Torah, as few
others did.

To be sure, we also caught glimpses of his unusual *midos* —
his face would light up with joy whenever he learned of the success of someone else's undertaking: a *Rebbe* attracted a host of
new followers — marvelous! A *Rosh Yeshiva* expanded his institution — wonderful! Another's triumph was the most precious
of occurrences. As for himself, he would shrug: "Me a *Rebbe*?
Never! I'm at best a *Chassidishe Yid*. But I'm nowhere near the
achievements of my father."

We, however, did know him as a *Chassidishe Rebbe* ... The
last time I saw him alive — just a day before his passing — I had
traveled to Brooklyn from the Catskills to consult him on a
chinuch (educational) matter regarding one of my children.

Actually, his circle of followers was far wider than one might
have supposed:

☐ As far as we members of the bais hamidrash were concerned, "Sidney" was a mechalel Shabbos befarhesya — a public violator of the Sabbath, who deserved no place in our bais hamidrash. He had Yahrzeit one Shabbos, and the Rebbe went out of his way to wish him ""Lechayim" after davening.

We had misgivings: Sidney's hair had been well groomed and combed, and his smooth cheek reeked of aftershave lotion — pungent reminders of fresh chillul Shabbos. After havdalah, we respectfully approached the Rebbe: "Was it really necessary to give Sidney such kavod? He so obviously had violated the Shabbos!"

Said the Rebbe, "Shouldn't somebody tell him?"

Yet the Rebbe's definition of Yiddishkeit had its very strict demands:

☐ A distant cousin who taught in Jewish Theological Seminary boasted to him that he influenced his students toward Chassidus. Why, he even had them over for a Friday night tisch!

Commented the Rebbe, " ... Like trees that blossom profusely, but never bear fruit."

Others also knew his total suspension of self, his involvement in the situation of others. Our advantage was that we "learned with him."

◄§ The Kvius

When we would arrive at the *bais hamidrash* early for our *kvius*, we could hear the *Rebbe* struggling with breakfast in the kitchen, one floor above. And it *was* a struggle. Since radical stomach surgery nine years earlier, it was very painful for him to swallow any food; yet he had to eat to survive.

A few minutes later he would enter the *bais hamidrash*, fall into his chair, with barely enough strength to open the *Gemara* and turn the pages. But once we began our studies, he would argue heatedly, shouting, jumping to his feet, running to fetch a reference *sefer* to prove his point.

"Shas on his fingertips" meant just that. He would unfailingly refer to the exact page of a *Gemara*, flip open the pages, with finger ready at the position, pointing to a *Tosafos* ... all the while citing in advance *Tosafos's* three, four or five *tirutzim* (answers) to a particular question.

More than once, the *Rebbetzin* entered, interrupting a spirited argument, "What are you doing to him? Stop!" she would plead. Whereupon, the *Rebbe* would protest, "Do you want to rob me of my life?"

Torah, indeed, was his food, his life-stuff, his very breath. At times he would enter the *bais hamidrash* gasping for air, coughing, "I don't think we can learn today but we'll make an attempt."

In a matter of minutes, he was totally involved — voice raised, emphasizing a point with his fist on the *shtender*.

The margins of his *Gemara* were crowded with annotations in his script. Yet, in our experience, whatever we studied together, he approached with a freshness, unencumbered with previous judgments, taking one word, one line at a time.

His Concept of Klal Yisrael

Although the Novominsker Rebbe represented a very particular type of Polish *Chassidus*, his concept of *Klal Yisrael* was far from parochial. His deeper differences with the Satmar approach toward Israel are well-known, yet a copy of the Satmar Rav's definitive "*Va'Yoel Moshe*" was seen at his bedside ... If a *sefer* expressed the opinion of a legitimate group within *Klal Yisrael* or of a Torah leader, he wanted to know it.

The underpinnings of his understanding of *Klal Yisrael*, however, were Torah. For this reason, it seems he took special delight in *Daf Yomi* as a binding element of Jews the world over. In fact, quite apart from our regular sessions together, which were usually devoted to *Tur-Shulchan Aruch*, he made *Daf Yomi* his *kvius*, the focal point of his Torah study, which he would pursue standing, giving it his greatest concentration. He glowed with appreciation when I told him, how, on one particular day, I saw different Jews — in Bnei Brak, on a TWA plane, and then in the airport in London — all studying the same page of *Gemara*, following the *Daf Yomi* schedule. He always had the *Gemara* — the volume containing the current *Daf Yomi* tractate — at his side. Friday afternoons before *Minchah* on *Shabbos*, and *Motzoei Shabbos* after *havdalah* ... Yom Kippur eve, as well as right after the fast ... on Purim ... On his bedside table, on the *Shabbos* that he passed away, lay the *Daf Yomi* volume of *Pesachim*.

□ *We were in the middle of our regular seder, when the Rebbe made reference to a particular commentary, jumped out of his seat and quickly scaled the ladder to reach the sefer* to underscore his point. (He never asked anyone else to do his legwork for him.) On the way down, he tripped, and fell on a wooden box lying at the foot of the ladder. He suffered a terrible flesh wound and he gasped in pain. We attempted to pick him up, but he lifted his hand. "Please ... we need a doctor ... Leave me where I am."

No sooner had Yitzchok run for the doctor than the Rebbe turned to me and whispered, "Benish, gib mir a Gemara Zevachim" ... the current Daf Yomi Mesechta. When the doctor entered a few minutes later, the Rebbe was on the floor, his position unaltered, except for his two hands stretched over his head, holding the Gemara Zevachim open like a canopy.

☐ Before a trip to Miami in 1975 — incidentally, the first time he ever went South for his health — he was packing his belongings: I found him squatting in his library with a flashlight, searching for meforshim (commentaries) on the next Daf Yomi tractate, Eruvin. He collected eleven different volumes, satisfied that he was prepared for the trip.

◆§ Meeting The Needs of Klal

The Novominsker Rebbe may not have been a very well-known public figure, but his deep concern and insights made him highly appreciated behind the scenes. It may seem contradictory, but he was active both as a member of Agudath Israel's Presidium, which concerns itself with day-to-day organizational matters, and as a member of its Moetzes Gedolei HaTorah, which is a policy-making body.

During the Yom Kippur War, we had the opportunity to observe him from close: the anguish and loss of sleep that further creased his face, the numerous calls from outstanding Torah leaders and Knesset members in Israel, the conference calls. And his calm demeanor and total immersion in Torah and tefillah when their time had arrived.

☐ On Shemini Atzeres, as was the custom of the Rebbes of Novominsk, he would hold a small Sefer Torah and spend as much as an hour expounding on Midrashic interpretations of Chapter 30 of Mishlei:Eishes Chayil (Woman of Valor), which is an allegoric tribute to Torah. On this particular Shemini Atzeres, just ten days after the outbreak of the Yom Kippur War, he said, "One is commanded: אוהב את אשתו

כגופו ומכבדה יותר מגופו—*to love his* Eishes Chayil *as much as his own person, and to honor her even more.* Klal Yisrael *is threatened. Who can think of his body? What standard does it offer us for loving the* Eishes Chayil *,Torah? But the honor we must give is on a greater scale. Let us give kavod to the Torah.*

He was like a sturdy tree: with roots sunk deeply into the old world, its branches stretched out into contemporary society.

He often said: *Problems repeat themselves. So, we must assume, do their solutions. What would Reb Chaim Ozer say to this? ... What did the Gerer Rebbe do? — or the Chiddushei HaRim?*

Another of his frequent comments: *Yaakov Avinu was the "Rebbe" of our conduct in Golus. When he came to Shechem, he performed two services for the community: He minted coins and constructed bath-houses. The message is obvious. We must establish the means to carry on exchanges with other groups, but we must have the ability to wash off from ourselves the effects of each Golus exchange.*

One might say that this was the life pattern — involvement and, yet, isolation.

He would frequently say, "What can I do for this situation? What can I do ... ?"

Discussing the plight of South American Jewry, and the founding of the *Kollel* in Argentina, he said, yearningly, "If I thought I could be of help there, I would go there, sick as I am — perhaps I would see some *Poilishe Yidden* and influence them to say *Shema Yisrael* again or to send their children to a Talmud Torah."

□ *In 1974, he told us that he would be interrupting his regular sessions during* Aseres Yemei Teshuvah *(between Rosh HaShanah and Yom Kippur) because he was traveling to Toronto on behalf of the Russian Immigrant Rescue Fund. I felt close enough to the Rebbe to protest: "If you will allow me, this is the kvittel season, when people come to you. They need you and ...*

"I intimated that he was somewhat dependent on them.

Replied the Rebbe: "If they need me now in Toronto, I must go now. The Yid with the kvittel, if he really needs me, will wait until I come back."

⊸§ If He Had Known ...

When the Rebbe was born, his paternal grandfather Reb Yaakov Novominsker was so ecstatic over the birth of his first grandson — a direct descendant of the *Besht* (Ba'al Shem Tov) — that he recited the *brachah* "*Shehechiyanu*" in full. It seems as if his saintly grandfather had visualized that this descendant of the *Besht* would spend half a century in the United States, giving so much to *Klal Yisrael*, yet suffering not at all from exposure to the corrosive elements of American society.

Reliable Chassidic sources relate that the Chozeh of Lublin, during the sixteen years of his life that he was privileged to live contemporaneously with the Rebbe of Berditchev, would devote an hour a day to give thanks to *Hashem Yisborach* for this *zechus*, and to praise Him for having planted such lofty *neshamos* in our midst (see *Tiferes Shlomo*). Perhaps we, too, should sing praise for having had the *zechus* to share our life on earth with such a lofty *tzaddik*, whose very existence was so inspiring to those that knew him.

"My Neighbor, My Father, The Rebbe"

*an appreciation
of the late
Satmar Rav as
seen by a
talmid*

Rabbi Yoel Teitelbaum זצ"ל
5647/1887—5739/1979

Klal Yisrael suffered an irreplaceable loss with the passing of the Satmar Rav on 26 Menachem Av 5739 at the age of 92.

The Satmar Rav, a direct descendant of both the famed Yismach Moshe and the Chavas Daas, was recognized as a young man for his unusual lomdus, hasmadah *and* tzidkus *— Torah scholarship, diligence and piety — assuming his first rabbinical position as Rav of Muzheyer at the age of seventeen. By the outbreak of World War II, he was Rav of the thriving community of Satmar and had emerged as one of the leading figures in Hungarian Jewry. He distinguished himself with his heroic adherence to Torah under the most brutal conditions of the Nazi concentration camps. After a brief stay in Eretz Yisrael, the Rebbe came to America in 1946 and settled in the Williamsburg section of Brooklyn.*

It was in Williamsburg that the Rebbe painstakingly helped thousands of fellow survivors reconstruct their lives, at the same time reconstructing a thriving Chassidic community — taking advantage of all technological advances of contemporary America, while shunning its values and the more apparent aspects of its life-style. As a result, at the time of his passing, the Rebbe presided over a tight-knit, highly disciplined community numbering in the thousands, with major settlements in Williamsburg and elsewhere, including their flourishing Kiryas Yoel in New York's Monroe Township, Monsey, Montreal, and of course, Jerusalem, where he was Rav of the Eida Hachreidis.

Indeed, the Satmar communities are all distinguished by a kehillah system that include complete control of shul, kashrus, education, and in many cases, social welfare. Thus, the Brooklyn kehillah embraces an educational system of 5,000 students embodying a complete girl's school and yeshivos spanning nursery through Kolel, as well as an extremely effective tzeddakah-medical-welfare system and wide-reaching Bikur Cholim network, directed by the Satmar Rebbetzin. This, in a smaller format, is duplicated in the rolling expanses of Kiryas Yoel — the Satmar sponsored suburban settlement.

The Rebbe was renowned for his extremely strong stand against Zionism, even refusing to accept the existence of the State of Israel — differing markedly with Torah authorities of Agudath Israel in this. For that matter, he opposed the very concept of an organized coalition-structured Orthodoxy as personified by Agudath Israel. Nonetheless, he was respected — even revered — in other circles for his vast scholarship, tzidkus, personal humility, astute wisdom, and unwavering tenacity.

The 100,000 people that crowded the streets of Monroe to bid farewell to the Satmar Rav included followers and admirers, Chassidim and Misnagdim, Europeans and Americans, paying homage to one of the greatest of contemporary Jewish leaders, who had taught and led his people as a Rav for seventy-five years ... He will be missed — not only by those who followed his particular ideology, but by Orthodox Jews of contrasting viewpoint as well who saw in him a tower of principled leadership.

O F THE hushed tens of thousands that came to pay their last respects to the Satmar Rav at his funeral, a large number were members of other communities — various Chassidic groups, yeshiva circles, and out-and-out Misnagdim. They came out of deference to a giant of vast scholarship, who had symbolized a rare level of personal devotion to G-d as well as a demanding, inspiring leadership of a type that has largely disappeared from the world scene. As Rabbi Yitzchok Hutner (Rosh Yeshiva of Mesivta Rabbi Chaim Berlin — Gur Arye) had said regarding the Satmar Rav on an earlier occasion:

> Noach suffered a maimed leg as punishment for the one time that he was late with the lion's meal in the Ark. It would seem that Noach should have been forgiven this one tardiness. But a lion is king of the beasts, and is worthy of service in a manner that is in keeping with its royal position, without any exceptions — especially this particular lion, which was the last of its kind ... The same, said the Rosh Yeshiva, may be said of the Satmar Rav. "I'm here to honor him because he's the last of the lions."

A great many of those present at his funeral were paying tribute to "the last lion" — the last leader of his kind in our midst.

◄§ The Purity of Another Era

> □ They had heard of the Sigheter Rav's "wonder sons" who were only little children, ninety long years ago. It was said that "Yoilish," the younger child, refrained from unnecessarily touching covered parts of his body, so he could always be prepared to study Torah. A visiting Rabbi asked the Sigheter Rav if it were so. "Come," said the Rav, leading the visitor to the bedroom where his three-year-old Yoel was fast asleep. He lifted his tzitzis-fringes over the child's head and tickled his ear. The sleeping boy slipped his sleeve over his fingers and raised his covered hand to scratch his itchy head.

From the time of his Bar Mitzvah until the outbreak of World War II — a period of forty years — Reb Yoel never slept on a bed, except for *Shabbosos* — studying Torah, on his feet, by day and by night ... In the internment camp in Bergen-Belsen, not only did he eat nothing that might have been un-kosher, subsisting mostly on potatoes, but he fasted as often as four times a week.

He continued this procedure until his last days; and even when he did eat, his first meal usually was a cup of coffee at 3 or 4 in the afternoon ... "Do I want to eat now? A Jew doesn't eat because he *wants* to. He eats because he *must.*"

While he encouraged his followers to work and earn well,

spend on themselves as necessary and give charity lavishly, he avoided spending on himself. Any time he was presented with a new garment, his first reaction was: "Who needs it?"

The Rebbe was fastidious about his personal cleanliness, and would not tolerate a hint of uncleanliness. In part, this was to be fit for prayer and Torah study. In fact, he thought nothing of changing clothes several times during the day if he found them unclean. Even in Bergen-Belsen, he had bartered food for tissues ...

Unknown to many, he was also meticulous about precision in time and manner of performance of *mitzvos*. Only his *Shacharis* was invariably late because of his personal preparations ... On occasion, he could not begin his Pesach Seder until after 11 o'clock because of ill health. This did not deter him from eating the *afikomen* before midnight, as is required by halachah, according to many ... He also consulted an authority present at his Pesach Seder regarding the precise size of his matzos and *marror*, as is required by halacha for the *mitzvos* ...

He took pains to shield his knowledge of *Kabbalah* from the curious. The Rebbe was always surrounded by people — indeed, he enjoyed company; but he was sensitive to prying eyes. He made light of references to *mofsim* (miracles) or kabbalistic involvement in our times. Yet his conduct at meals — the ways he picked at his food, and his deep concentration in *tefillah*, bespoke hidden motives, meaning-laden cryptic gestures.

While he made himself available to people without hesitation, and seemed to enjoy conversing with all his visitors, the Rebbe had a distinctly regal bearing. When walking down Bedford Avenue from his home to the *bais hamidrash*, the sidewalk would clear well in advance of his coming. Not that there was anything forbidding about his appearance. But, until his very last years, a vitality seemed to shine through his smooth, translucent face that bespoke a purity that defied the passage of time, and inspired others to move back in awe.

⤳ The Vast Sea of His Knowledge

It seemed as though he never had to prepare for a lecture, *drashah*, or *shiur*. In Europe the custom had been for someone to open a *Midrash Rabba* at *Shalosh Seudos*, and read three passages at random — giving the Rebbe material for his dissertation. He would then expound at length, quoting passages from the Midrash verbatim ... In America, he would enter the yeshiva's *bais hamidrash*, ask where the *bachurim* were up to in their studies, open the *Gemara* and begin a long, involved lecture without further notice.

□ *Rabbi Yaakov Breish of Zurich had spent years on the section of his* sefer Chelkas Yaakov *that deals with the complicated laws of ribbis (usury). When visiting the United States, he visited the Satmar Rav and spent several hours discussing in detail several difficult topics in his sefer. He later expressed wonder at how thorough the Rebbe's mastery of this topic had been, even though his visit had been unannounced, giving the Rebbe no time for preparation.*

The Rebbe would write his Torah commentaries at two or three o'clock in the morning, relishing every minute. He once remarked, "I could see myself doing this the rest of my life, but I have a directive from my father that one must be prepared to give away his own Torah, if necessary, to help a fellow Jew."

Notwithstanding his round-the-clock involvement in *chessed*, his treasure house of Torah knowledge was vast. Perhaps *Klal Yisrael* was deprived of the greater riches that would have been theirs had he been allowed the luxury of extending the full measure of the *hasmadah* of his youth into his later years, and not suffered the distraction of being father to his community. But then, *Klal Yisroel* would not have had a Satmar Rav, and we would have been infinitely poorer for that loss.

✦§ Father to His Community

A large number of those at his funeral had come as children mourning a very personal loss, many of them ripping their garments in *kriyah* for the loss of a father who had cared for their every need, both spiritual and material. It is extremely difficult to comprehend how so many thousands could experience such an intense relationship with one man. And yet, how else can one explain the phenomenal growth of the Satmar community from several scores of families in the late 40's to so many thousands of followers today — especially when the external trappings of the group's lifestyle is in direct conflict with modern Western culture? To be sure, the explanation for this growth lies in part in the large families generally prevalent in the Torah community. But it also must be attributed to the exceedingly low defection rate among Satmar Chassidim — a phenomenon in which the Rebbe played a pivotal role.

□ *Shortly after he had arrived in America, a young Chassid was discussing the naming of his newly born son with the Satmar Rav, in the presence of another rabbi. "My grandfather was a very good Jew," he said.*

"His name would be a fine choice for your son," commented the Rebbe.

"But several of my nephews and cousins already carry his name. On the other hand, my father-in-law has no one named after him."

"That should certainly be taken into consideration."
"However ... "

And so it continued. After the young father left, the other visitor asked the Rebbe why he permitted himself to become so involved with trivia.

"In the old country, I was a father at home, and could be a Rebbe in the city. But here," the Rebbe sighed, "this is simply not suitable. I have to be a father to my community, and a Rebbe at home."

As visitors streamed into his room, the Rebbe asked questions and listened carefully, seemed to bend his shoulder to carry the load of others, and was *mispallel* (prayed) for their needs.

His manner of closely examining a *kvittel*, looking for clues — and, amazingly, "discovering" errors in the writing of the name of a total stranger ("You write 'Binyamin ben Leah' — isn't there more to the mother's name? — You say 'ben Leah *Esther*'? You should have written it so!") — and the encouraging word he invariably offered, comforting the petitioner ... Stories are legion about occasions when — after hearing the details of a person's problems — the Rebbe swept his table clean of the day's accumulation of *pidyon gelt* (monies for charity, given to the Rebbe by people petitioning for his help and prayers) to give to a needy visitor ... Nor did he limit his compassion and sharing of joys and sorrows to his own immediate group:

The Latin American lady not at all dressed in Satmar tradition, who needed money for her son's hospitalization and left with the full amount ... The man who wept bitterly for all his suffering, and walked out with the entire day's proceeds. Then the Rebbe was informed that the man was a fraud. "*Baruch Hashem!*" exclaimed the Rebbe, "I'm so relieved that he's not in such terrible straits!" ... The editor of an Israeli journal that had slandered — even ridiculed — the Rebbe, was in his room, sobbing for his daughter's terrible personal plight — she was engaged to be married but lacked sufficient funds to purchase an apartment. After the Rebbe had given him a large sum of money, someone whispered into his ear, "Don't you know who that was?" "Of course I do," replied the Rebbe, and then — after a moment's hesitation — called back the editor and gave him even more ...

☐ *An alumnus of a Lithuanian-type yeshiva in Israel sat near the Rebbe at his Pesach Seder. The Rebbe was amused at his guest's pompous measuring of the precise portion of food and drinks required for the rituals (even though the Rebbe himself was no less fastidious). As the guest prepared his matzos, the Rebbe asked him, "Are you sure it's the right shiyur (required amount)?" Similarly, after he ate the marror, and later when he eyed his afikomen before consuming it, the Rebbe smilingly asked, "Is it the shiyur?"*

Finally, the fellow put down his matzah and said, "Rebbe I'm not sure. But isn't it the shiyur of tcheppen (teasing)?"

The Rebbe was deeply disturbed that he had actually offended the man with remarks that he had only meant as a friendly exchange. He begged his forgiveness again and again, as was his habit when he felt he had mistreated someone. Finally he asked him, "Please see me right after Yom Tov."

When the man reported to the Rebbe, he asked, "Why are you here? Why did you come to America?"

"I'm here because I must raise five to six thousand dollars to marry off my daughter."

"I'll get the money for you. And please — any children that you will be marrying off in the future — come here and I'll take care of your financial needs."

The Satmar Rav was not satisfied until he had financed the weddings of the man's four daughters.

⋘§ Builder of a Community

While the Rebbe's personal warm concern for each individual was surely a key factor in the unusually low drop-out rate among his *kehillah's* members, there are additional factors in his leadership that also account for this phenomenon.

When he settled in Williamsburg shortly after arriving in the

United States, he found a handful of his followers in a *bais hamidrash* all day, saying *Tehillim*, learning *Chok* — and spending their time in "the Rebbe's Court". He summoned them to him and insisted that they find jobs to support their families. "If I had the strength (he was in his sixties at the time) I'd also go to work." ... He felt that he could not be oblivious to the stress on material well-being that marks American society. Here, especially, one had to be mindful of the dictum: "Poverty can sway a man from loyalty to his Creator." Moreover, a viable community could only take shape if it is self-supporting on a level comparable to that of the surrounding society. By the same token, he guided his followers to give *tzeddakah* expansively — not to shy away from a sweeping gesture of generosity. Today, members of the Satmar community are active in all phases of business and commerce, as well as in a wide spectrum of occupations, ranging from grocers to computer programmers. And the community itself supports a host of social services, most notably its *bikur-cholim* program — administering to the sick, with fleets of cars and vans carrying hundreds of volunteers to hospitals all over New York, throughout the day.

⋙ A Klal-Yisrael Curriculum

The Rebbe founded the Yeshiva Yetev Lev and the Bais Rochel School for girls, both adhering to the syllabus of pre-World War II Satmar. The Yeshiva emphasizes a rapid pace of study, familiarity with a broad range of topics, and an eye on practical application, through halachah. The girls' school follows a strictly prescribed Hebrew curriculum. Yet the Rebbe was keenly aware of the surrounding yeshiva scene. In fact, shortly after his arrival in the States he delivered *shiurim* in the bais hamidrash of both Mesivta Torah Vodaath in Brooklyn and the Telshe Yeshiva in Cleveland, in response to invitations from the yeshivos' respective leaders.

On a visit to Bais Medrash Elyon in Monsey, the *mashgiach*, Rabbi Yisroel Chaim Kaplan, who took great pride in his Kollel, asked the Rebbe why his *kehillah* does not include one. He replied, "You are raising an elite of *gedolei Yisrael*. I hope to establish a broad *Klal Yisroel*. I dare not sacrifice the average students for the sake of the isolated individual of rare promise."

Nonetheless, the Satmar Rav did recognize the necessity of grooming a leadership of expert *talmidei chachamim*, and from the modest beginnings of several young men studying privately in his home, he eventually founded a full-fledged kollel, with emphasis on *psak halachah.*

Before the kollel's formal opening, it was announced that the Rebbe himself would screen prospective members — but not until after their wedding. The first candidate came in, nervously anticipating a grueling test on Talmud and commentaries ... "How many people did you invite to your wedding?" asked the Rebbe. "At how much per couple? ... What did your furniture cost? ... So much? And you want the community to support you? Forget about it. Kollel is not for you."

As exacting as he was in choosing kollel members, he was forgiving in dealing with his yeshiva students, never expelling a boy from his schools — for how does one expel someone from the Jewish community?

⦿§ The Festivals in Satmar

The Satmar sense of community was especially apparent when the *Yomim Noraim* Season began — first *Slichos*, with the Rebbe leading with his frail voice, precise in *nusach*, heart-rending in emotion ... his pouring forth of soul on Rosh Hashana, and then on Yom Kippur, crowned by his *Ne'ilah* ... Then *Hoshana Rabbah*, when thousands — literally thousands — would crowd the Satmar bais hamidrash to be with the Rebbe, with hundreds of "outsiders" who joined the *mispallelim* to watch as the Rebbe sang the *Hallel*, and waved his *lulav*, cuing thousands to follow his lead — southward, northward, eastward, up, down, westward — "*Hodu* — let us praise G-d" — "*Anna Hashem* — Please G-d, help us, save us!" Waving to and fro, as if the Rebbe were himself waving a thousand *lulavim* — not *lulavim*, but waving a thousand souls in praise and supplication ... Watching as he led his Chassidim in the *Hoshanos*, weeping, and pleading with them to strive for personal improvement, for sanctity — urging them in his moving address, to join him in calling to G-d to "Help us *lema'ancho* — for Your Sake!" ... Then Simchas Torah, when the sea of humanity compressed into his *bais hamidrash* would split, opening a path for the Rebbe, carrying his diminutive Sefer Torah; voices rising and falling in song like breakers on a shore; his *tallis* draped over his head, shielding his eyes, swaying for a moment, and then running — or dancing — or floating — it's difficult to say which ... somehow he seemed to be borne aloft by the swell of voices. How else could he stay on his frail, suffering feet for six hours on end?

And then, after Yom Tov, the triumphant torchlit march accompanying the Rebbe home, closing the season.

◄§ One Man Alone

☐ *The patriarch Avraham was also known as "Avraham HaIvri," because he came to Canaan from Eiver LaNohor, the other side of the river. This title has also been explained to refer to his position as one man against the world — "Avraham be'eiver echad — one man alone on his side," believing in monotheism, while the entire world was on the other side of the issue.*

This one trait assumed major significance: When any of Avraham's contemporaries was asked about his beliefs, he would reply, "Of course, I am an idol-worshiper." Then, even though he well could have ignored monotheism, since Avraham was its only exponent, and idolatry was the universally accepted belief of millions, he would add: "There is another approach: the monotheism of Avraham."

That Avraham could single-handedly invade the consciousness of the entire world and create in their minds the possibility of "another approach" was most noteworthy. Thus, it was perpetuated in his name — "Avraham HaIvri."

The same may be said about the Satmar Rav. Most of world Jewry had accepted the Zionist dream. And even many among those who had rejected its limited, secular definition of Jewishness were excited by the emergence of the State of Israel, and the miraculous victories in '48, '56 and '67. The Satmar Rav was often alone in consistently condemning the State as the pure embodiment of a secular ideal, a *ma'ase Sattan*: dismissing victories on the battlefield as an ideological minefield; opposing mass *aliyah* as a violation of the Three Vows* for settling the country in defiance of world opinion; and participation in the government in any form — even voting in national elections — as strengthening a reprehensible concept by implied recognition. Like some other schools, those of the *Eida Hachreidis*, which is in the Satmar orbit, do not accept funding from the Israeli government.

☐ *Advisors had begged the Rebbe to omit from his writings his directives against going to the Kosel, as being too dif-*

---

* T.B. *Kesubos* 11a: Binding Jewry not to force its way into *Eretz Yisrael*, nor to rebel against the nations, and the nations not to subjugate the Jews excessively.

*ficult to accept, sure to result in the alienation of many of his
followers. He commented, "I don't care if I'm left with only
one minyan of adherents. I'll not refrain from expressing my
beliefs."*

He was once advised by a close associate, "Don't let yourself
get so upset!" The Rebbe replied, "There are a thousand reasons
not to reveal the *Emes*. If one gets upset, he can forget himself for
a moment, and then at least a bit of *Emes* comes through."

The mainstream of the Torah leadership did not subscribe to
his approach toward dealing with the Israeli government. Even
those most strongly opposed to the State's philosophy accepted
its existence and, at worst, felt compelled to deal with it as they
would with any government that ruled a land where Jews lived.
At times they were deeply upset with his unyielding approach —
such as Rabbi Aharon Kotler's vexation with the Rebbe for
"publicly opposing the Chazon Ish, Reb Isser Zalman Meltzer,
the Belzer Rebbe and the Tchebiner Rav — all of whom held that
voting in Israeli national elections was an obligation on every
Torah Jew who took the needs of the *Yishuv* to heart."
Nonetheless, they were always aware of the Satmar position and
often measured their stance against the extremes of the Satmar-
Neturei Karta ideology. And even the most rabid, anti-religious
secularist was aware of the "on the other hand," represented by
this one man's uncompromising stance.

His ideology is represented by his two *seforim VaYoel
Moshe* and *Al Hage'ulah V'al Hatemurah*, written with vast
scholarship and great care — as well as by his spoken word on
numerous occasions.

In spite of the difference between them, a current of admiration flowed between the Satmar Rav and the heads of American
Yeshivos. Said Reb Aharon Kotler: "The Satmar Rav and I do not
have the same approach — neither in Torah study nor in political
matters — but I must say, he is a giant in Torah and a giant in
midos." The Satmar Rav, in turn, spoke at Reb Aharon's funeral,
weeping, quoting *Rashi* (in *Be'haaloscha*): " 'The praise of
Aharon is that he did not deviate' — Reb Aharon remained ever
faithful to his tradition, never deviating."

Similarly, Rabbi Reuvain Grozovsky, the late Rosh Yeshiva
of Mesivta Torah Vodaath and Bais Medrash Elyon, who had
headed the Moetzes Gedolei HaTorah (Council of Torah Sages) of
Agudath Israel, had made it a policy of never responding to
criticisms "from the right" because its adherents are G-d-fearing

Jews, and there may well be some elements of truth in their approach (*Beiyos Hazman* pp. 69-71)....Indeed, Reb Reuvain had often cited a statement by his father-in-law, Rabbi Boruch Ber Lebowitz, a leading Rosh Yeshiva in pre World-War II Europe: "The Satmar Rav was *the* person to contact whenever the Polish and Lithuanian leadership had need to communicate with Hungarian Jewry." When the Satmar Rav visited Reb Reuvain when he was ill from the stroke that had partially paralyzed him, the Rebbe wished the Rosh Yeshiva: "A *refuah sheleimah* — a complete recovery, so we can battle each other once again." . . . Several years later, when he returned home from Reb Reuvain's funeral, the Rebbe seemed unusally depressed. To his Rebbetzin's question as to why he was so troubled, he replied, "The world has lost an *Ish Ha'emes* — a man of rare integrity."

It was not only in regard to its extreme anti-Zionism that the Satmar Rav had molded his community as "a group apart," in the manner of *Avraham Halvri*. He also guided it to being distinguished in its total lack of compromise in mode of dress — not yielding to American pressures, neither in style nor in lack of modesty. If anything, the newer generations have reinforced their dedication to the standards of "Jewishness in dress" that had prevailed in Satmar of old making it much easier, one might add, for the American yeshiva community to adhere to its own standards of propriety without developing a sense of being at the outer edge of society.

Thus, the Satmar Rav's relentless demands for the highest religious standards proved to be an important contribution toward changing the complexion of a significant segment of Orthodox life in America. Witness: Holocaust survivors and their American-born grandchildren — *dayanim* (rabbinical judges), *rabbanim*, diamond polishers, computer technicians, and gas-pump attendants among them — who proudly walk the streets of the New World in traditional garb, making the *shtreimel* an everyweek feature of many communities.

For evidence of the living legacy of the late Satmar Rav, we tend to look at the self-contained communities of his followers that crowd this or that old-world corner of various urban centers; or that are found in unlikely suburban locations, such as New York's Monroe township or Rockland County. But, in many respects, his influence has extended beyond the confines of his immediate following, for those whose compass is set by other stars cannot help but have had their own awareness sharpened by the perspectives of the Satmar Rav.

After all, who can live in the same community as a *tzaddik* — or even in his time — and not be affected by his presence?

When Rabbi Yaakov Kamenetzky spoke at the unveiling of the *matzeivah* (monument) at the gravesite of the Satmar Rav, one week after his passing, he commented on the special gift G-d had bequeathed on our generation through the presence of the Satmar Rav for over nine decades:

"When an era closes, there is always a danger that the succeeding generations will be oblivious to the values and special character of their predecessors. Thus G-d often grants one exemplary member of the preceding era longevity, to permit him to teach the next generation how the old generation lived — by his mere presence. Thus did Rabbi Yehudah Hanassi — who closed the era of the Tannaim by writing the Mishnah — continue to 'frequent his home' for decades after his passing; and Rabbi Yochanan, who compiled the Jerusalem Talmud, lived for hundreds of years...; and thus did the Satmar Rav grace our generation with a greatness in scholarship and piety that had been identified with the glory of days gone by."

Remembering Reb Itzikel

*venerated
tzaddik of
post-war
Europe*

Rabbi Moshe Yitzchok Gerwirczman זצ"ל
5642/1882-5736/1976

BEFORE the devastating *churban* of World War II there were
about one million *Chassidim* in Europe, with hundreds of
tzaddikim to guide them. After the destructon, when new centers
developed in *Eretz Yisrael* and America, only one major haven of
Chassidus remained on the European continent — namely in
Antwerp, Belgium.

The *tzaddik* at the helm was Rabbi Moshe Yitzchok
Gewirczman, a man of few words and profuse deeds. He was a
descendant and spiritual heir of the renowned *Noam Elimelech*
and inherited the *derech* (ways of service) of Shiniv, Tshechenov
and Stropkov, all off-shoots of Sanz from which he absorbed
kedushah that accompanied him throughout his life.

The significance of his presence in Europe was that, without
intending to establish any movement or dynasty, he attracted
many hundreds of followers from that continent and beyond.
Forty or fifty visitors for *Rosh HaShanah* or *Shavuos* was
routine, a Shabbos without guests was unknown. They would not
only come to taste the sweetness of his Shabbos and the joy of his
Yom Tov; they would frequently come to find a sympathetic ear
and consolation in times of distress. It is in this field that he

became legendary — a *baal mofes* (miracle worker) of the old school.

The leading Rebbes of our day had enormous regard for him. During the Six Day War the Gerer Rebbe sent a request to Reb Itzikel that, "since his *tefillos* are known to be effective," he should spare no effort in pleading for his brethren endangered in the battle-torn *Yishuv*. He, in turn, had tremendous regard for them. The writer was privileged to be present when Reb Itzikel, having held a *tisch* with a large group of followers one Friday night in London in the 1960's, made his way to the *tisch* of the Satmar Rav, who was then visiting London. Reb Itzikel sat there, gazing at the Satmar Rav as a little boy gazes at his father.

He would speak of *Rebbes* he remembered from his youth with such humility that one would almost forget that he was a *Rebbe* of consequence himself.

◄§ At the Tisch

וראו כל עמי הארץ כי שם ה' נקרא עליך ויראו ממך *"And all the people — even the simple folk — will see that the Name of Hashem rests upon you" (Deut. 28:10)* — *Kedushah* surrounds you and reaches all those who come into contact with you. And thus they will learn to respect you.

It is this intangible, electrifying spiritual force, which defies analysis and description, that attracts people to a *tzaddik* and enables them to benefit from his company. It is a very subtle form of spiritual energy — not necessarily generated by eloquent *mussar* discourses or visible acts of *mesiras nefesh*. The influence of *tzaddikei-emes* is entirely spiritual, detached from plain words and deeds, highly sensitive and unlike the usual methods of *chinuch* known to all of us.

Those who ever had the *zechus* to find themselves at Mercatorstraat 56, Antwerpen, when the Rebbe was present, could not but feel the atmosphere of elevation, of *Shechinah*[1] that prevailed in his *bais hamidrash*. They could not explain what they felt, they could hardly understand it, but it was absolutely clear that they were standing in the presence of one of the spiritual giants of the generation — in fact of the last two generations. It is impossible to describe what was so impressive about his placid, careful movements, the external simplicity of his *tefillah* and the

1. Reb Avrohom Chaim of Plantsch (father-in-law of the Satmar Rav) saw Reb Itzikel in Shiniv (where the latter became acquainted with the Shiniver Rov, son of the Sanzer Rov) and said, "The *Shechinah* accompanies this young man"

profound look of *dveikus* (cleaving to G-d) on his face — it is un-important to define all that. We knew that he was a genius at con-cealing his true *gadlus* (greatness) — a *tzaddik nistar*[2] (secretive saint) in all that term implies — yet known and loved by thou-sands of admirers, recognized by the *tzaddikim* of the past and present generations as unique in every way. Few knew of his knowledge of *Shas* by heart[3]; no one knew what he added quietly before *Kiddush* every Friday night or what he was saying quietly throughout the Shabbos *tisch*[4]; but we all knew, without the slightest doubt, that here stood a man whose constant *dvaikus* (cleavage to G-d) was part of his personality.

The wealthy man, who has prepared generously for Shab-bos, invites the less fortunate, who cannot afford their own Shab-bos meals, to join him at his table and to partake of his *seudah*. The possessor of spiritual wealth acts likewise, explained the Koznitzer Maggid.[5] Prepared to receive the Shabbos appropriate-ly, he welcomes those who are unable to perfect their own spiritual preparation to join him and thus they can benefit from his superior *avodah*.

This is exactly what we experienced in Antwerp at the *Shab-bos tischen*, where the unspoilt spirit of the day of rest reigned supreme[6] as we sat, unable to take our eyes off the Rebbe's radiant countenance. His house was as open as that of the Patriarch Abraham, offering hospitality to visitors from far and near. On the one hand it was left *hefker* to the needy; on the other hand everyone recognized and revered the master of the household — a master of *tzeddakah* and *chessed* from his earliest youth till his very last days. In his usual discreet and quiet way, he provided for countless poor families and helped hundreds of young men to establish themselves as self-respecting bread-winners.

Incredible amounts of funds passed through his hands — to

2. It is said that the "36 hidden *Tzaddikim*" could well be amongst those we know, since most of their greatness is concealed.

3. His *Rebbe*, Reb Simcha Yissochor Ber of Tshechenov, recommended him to adopt the *Gemara* as a *chaver*. At the time, Reb Itzikel learnt vast amounts of *Gemara* by heart and was known as an *Illuy*.

4. When Reb Chone Halberstam of Koloshitz — a contemporary who perished under the Nazis — inquired about this, Reb Itzikel refused to comment.

5. *Avodas Yisroel, Sidra Mishpatim:* on Chap. 23,12.

6. Standing amongst the large crowd before the burial, the Yashlisker Rav commented "In my youth I visited many great *Rebbes* and felt the richness of the spirit of Shabbos, but the *Neshama-Yeseirah* I experienced together with my father-in-law was unique."(The author was present.)

him a coin was a *mitzvah* artifact just like an *esrog* or *tefillin*[7]. Yet, for himself the *Rebbe* kept nothing, living on the basic minimum and deriving no benefit from *Olam Hazeh* (this world) at all.

Despite all this, a *tzaddik* of this calibre cannot be described in a few lines of writing. An essay cannot do justice to his true essence. Appreciation of *tzaddikim* is a תורה שבע"פ — Oral Law — in that it cannot be committed to writing. It is not for nothing that people with shelves upon shelves of *sefarim* at home, wander across continents and oceans in order to spend a *Shabbos* or *Yom Tov* with a *tzaddik*.

❀ ❀ ❀

Despite his very advanced age of almost 95, people were stunned at the sad news; they found it difficult to believe that a man whose existence had been above natural forces for so many years, had left this life for good. Never again will we be able to watch *Reb Itzikel* kissing the *mezuzah* with that determined look of *dveikus* on his face as he walks humbly and slowly from his small room into his *bais hamidrash*, ready to pierce the heavens with his silent *tefillah*. Never again will we be able to sit quietly around his table, elevated to another world, as the Rebbe sits peacefully partaking of his *seudah*: with tightly closed eyes, as if to say *My soul thirsts for You (Psalms 63:2). Reb Itzikel's* living example of visible and invisible *tzidkus* will be sorely missed by all who knew him.

7. Mentioned by Rabbi E. Halpern in his *hesped* before the funeral.

ᥣᥱ The Sephardi Gadol

*Two examples of towering figures
who led the Eastern Communities*

The Ben Ish Chai

*an outstanding
Sephardic leader
of the past
century*

Chacham Yoseif Chaim זצ״ל
5592/1832-5669/1909

IT IS perhaps to our benefit that many of Chacham Yoseif
Chaim's works contain a photograph, taken in his twenty-sixth
year. This was the year following the death of his father, Rav
Eliyahu; the year Rabbi Yoseif Chaim took his father's place as
Rav of Baghdad. Even those unfamiliar with the art of reading
human features cannot fail to be struck by the inner power, yet
calmness, nobility, and depth that his countenance reveals — truly
reflecting him as a *tzaddik* and *gadol baTorah*.

Today Chacham Yoseif Chaim, known also as the Ben Ish
Chai, is one of the great lights of the international Sephardic community, alongside the Chacham Chaim Yoseif David Azulai (the
Chida) and the Sar Shalom Shar' abi. His place in the lives and
hearts of Sephardim throughout the world is analogous to that of
the Vilna Gaon or the Ba'al Shem Tov in those of Ashkenazim —
and the number of his followers is continually growing.

The *shitah* — the approach in halachic decisions and customs
— of the Ben Ish Chai is followed by thousands from all communities — Persians, Ladino-speaking Sephardim, Moroccans,
Kurdistanis. Although it is one of the most *machmir* (stringent) in

the Sephardic world, its followers only sense its beauty, seemingly unaware of its strictness.

◆§ A Family of Chachamim

Chacham Yoseif Chaim was born in 1832 to a line of great *chachamim* who influenced the moral and spiritual development of Baghdad, proving himself another link in that chain at an early age.

As a boy, he could always be found studying contentedly in his father's vast library. It is told that when he was fourteen he answered one of the questions sent to his father by the sages of Jerusalem. His father, busy at the time, could not tend to it until a day or so later. By the time Rabbi Eliyahu managed to send his reply, young Yoseif's answer had already reached Jerusalem and was found most acceptable. Rabbi Eliyahu received a message from Jerusalem, which included the words: "Your son, dear to your soul, has already preceded you and decided this case. May his father rejoice in him ... "

Rabbi Yoseif Chaim set aside a special room for seclusion where day and night he studied all aspects of Torah — *Shas* ... *halachah, aggadah* and *kabbalah*. He worked tirelessly at his own spiritual perfection, aiming to purify and elevate his body to be attuned to his soul in the service of *Hashem.* He rose every midnight to recite the *Tikun Chatzot* and would say the morning prayers at sunrise. He continued this practice even after his appointment as Rav of Baghdad. He fasted the entire day for six consecutive years, only tasting food at night, to dull his sensual drives ... He had a well dug in his home so that he could have a *Mikvah* available for ablutions whenever he so desired ... The dean of Kabbalists of Jerusalem, Rabbi Chaim Shaul Dowek, testified: "All the Ben Ish Chai's words were ultimately based on inferences from the writings of the *ARIzal...*" and that "the pathways of the heavens were clear to him."

☐ *Every Saturday night immediately following havdalah, the Ben Ish Chai would ascend to the attic of his house to study, permitting no one to disturb him. It was rumored that on these occasions, Eliyahu HaNavi would appear to him to teach him Torah. The young men of his bais hamidrash, Bais Midrash Zilcha, wanted to test the veracity of this report. So they dispatched one of their ranks, Rabbi Yehoshua Sarboni, to ... "rush up the steps and enter the Ben Ish Chai's attic room without knocking, on the pretext of posing a specific* question to him. Then you will see for us whether or not Eliyahu is there."

No sooner was Shabbos over than Rabbi Yehoshua did as he was told. Half-way up the stairs, he met Rabbi Yoseif Chaim descending, who stopped to say: "My wise Yehoshua, in the bais hamidrash are they debating this perplexing problem ...? Go down and tell them that the explanation is as follows ... "

□ Rabbi Yoseif Chaim's nephew, Rabbi Binyamin Ben-Moshe, recounts once entering his uncle's home on a Friday afternoon, finding him sitting and weeping: "I asked him, 'Why are you crying? Are you in pain ...?'

"He replied, 'Nothing hurts me. But just a short while ago the caretaker, who cleans the trash from the yard, passed my door. Someone invited him in to taste one of the Shabbos delicacies, and the man refused, saying that all his life he has been careful never to enjoy something belonging to others. I am full of envy: Here is a man so simple, and yet so much greater than me. Doesn't the Gemara tell us: Greater is he that sustains himself with his own efforts than one who fears heaven? — This is why I am crying.' "

⋖§ His Works

After his father, Rabbi Eliyahu, passed away and Rabbi Yoseif Chaim was only 25 years old, the Jews of Baghdad accepted him as their Rabbi. They followed his halachic decisions and general advice with such complete faith that his disciple, Rabbi Ben Zion Chazon commented: "If the Jews of old would have followed the directives of the prophets in their day as the Jews of Baghdad listen to Rabbi Yoseif Chaim, the Bais HaMikdash would not have been destroyed."

While every Shabbos he would deliver his sermon in the Tsallat L'ziri (the Small Synagogue), on four Shabbosos during the year Rabbi Yoseif Chaim, as the sole preacher that week, would speak in the Tsallat L'ch'biri (the Large Synagogue) ... according to Baghdadian tradition, this shul was built at the outset of the Babylonian exile by Yehoyachin, King of Judah, with earth carried from Eretz Yisrael.

The Ben Ish Chai delivered a drashah every morning for fifty years, from his appointment until his death. He also gave a shiur (lecture) in halachah and aggadah. The latter became the basis of two of his works on the non-halachic portions of Talmud: the five-volume *Ben Yehoyada*, and *Mekabtziel*, a complementary version of *Ben Yehoyada*. In these works on *aggadah*, the Ben Ish Chai always incorporated the thoughts of the *kabbalah* according to the *ARIzal*, including many *gematriot* and an occasional story.

One of these stories concerns an Arab sheikh who, through his humility and awe before the *Sheim Hashem* (the Tetragrammaton), merited a degree of *ruach hakodesh*. This demonstrates the idea expressed in the *Tana Devei Eliyahu* and the Talmud that "It matters not one's background or sex; the *Shechinah* rests on everyone according to the level of his actions."

The four-volume responsa *Rav Pe'alim* and *Torah Lishmah* are works on *halachah*, written under the *nom de plume* "Yechezkiel Kahali." Both include questions from great and small, ranging from the deepest queries on the *Shulchan Aruch* and requests for clarification of kabbalistic concepts, to questions such as "May one name one's child after a letter of the alphabet, especially one which is in the name of Hashem?" (The answer is "yes", as we find in *Pirkei Avot*, ben Hey Hey, as well as Rav Yud, an *Amora* mentioned in Tractate *Ta'anis*.)

The first question in *Rav Pe'alim* is particularly significant to our generation, where emotions assume such a strong role. Rabbi Yoseif Chaim was asked if one should say the *Tikun Chatzot* prayers, in mourning for the destruction of the *Bais HaMikdash*, if one does not feel them in his heart. The answer is, emphatically, to say the prayers: and the Ben Ish Chai cites *Nefesh HaChaim* by Rabbi Chaim Volozhin, the disciple of the Vilna Gaon, to show why every level of prayer is necessary; even deep, heartfelt *kavanah* cannot begin to ascend to heaven without the rock-bottom level of physical utterance of the prayers.

Due to the custom among even unlearned Oriental Jews to read works of *Kabbalah*, the Ben Ish Chai edited a new, voweled edition of the *Zohar*. He added a short commentary of the *Chida* to enable laymen to learn basic teachings and gain inspiration. Before his edition of the *Zohar* had appeared, copies had to be ordered from Poland.

In addition, Rabbi Yoseif Chaim composed many *pizmonim* and *piyutim* (religious poetry) for various occasions, one of the most widely known being "*Va'amartem Ko L'Chai*" in honor of the *tanna* bar Yochai and Lag b'Omer.

ঙ Approach to Halachah

Despite his greatness in tracing halachic problems directly to Talmudic sources (as shown in his *Teshuvos Torah Lishmah*), the Ben Ish Chai always took into account the opinions of Oriental, Sephardic and North European *Acharonim* (later commentaries, from the 16th Century onward). The *Sha'ul Umeishiv*, the Gaon of Vilna, Rabbi Akiva Eiger, the *Shulchan Aruch Harav*, *Chayei Adam* and *Divrei Chayim* are among those often mentioned in his works.

In his introduction to *Rav Pe'alim*, Chacham Yoseif Chaim decries the tendency among some to ignore or even spurn contemporaries or *acharonim*. He also felt that every *posek*, regardless of stature, should take care to write with respect regarding others even when disproving their thinking, for failure to do in the past had resulted in some classic *gedolim* of *halachah* being ignored and even forgotten.

ঙ Halachah and Oriental Minhag

Rabbi Yoseif Chaim's three-hour *Shabbos drashos* were the basic for his most famous work, the *Ben Ish Chai*. His talks opened with an explanation of the week's *Parshah* (Torah reading) in the light of the *kabbalah*, followed by practical *halachah* on a given subject.

This book is considered to be the "Sephardic Kitzur Shulchan Aruch" — the standard reference book in all religious Sephardic homes — and is used in Sephardic yeshivos and religious schools in Israel to teach *halachah*.

The *Ben Ish Chai* gives a vivid insight into the environment and circumstances in which Rabbi Yoseif Chaim and his flock lived:

> The time for havdalah *is given as "twenty minutes after the Moslem call to prayer"* (Ben Ish Chai Toldos Paragraph 2).

Moslem law provides for five prayer periods during a 24-hour day. These prayer periods are very strictly regulated as to time, calculated by the position of the sun, and each prayer period is announced by a *muezzin* singing from atop the minaret of the mosque.

Formerly in all Moslem countries, as in Saudi Arabia today, both men and women observed the extreme in modesty in dress, wearing robes to their ankles, with high necks and long sleeves.

Moslem women wore veils on their heads, and covered their faces, at least the lower part, with a second veil. However, they were accustomed to wearing sandals with no stockings, or went barefoot. Jewish women in those countries wore the same clothes as their Moslem neighbors. Rabbi Yoseif Chaim thus has this to say on *tznius* (personal modesty):

> In European cities, women customarily wear shoes, so their feet are not visible. A guest from a place where women are accustomed to going barefoot must take care to act according to the custom of the place he is visiting, and consider it forbidden to pray before the sight of bare feet (Chapter 21,2).

◄§ The Chacham's Family

Chacham Yoseif Chaim married Rachel, the daughter of Rabbi Yehuda Someich, a relative of his teacher Rabbi Abd-Allah Someich. Rabbi Yoseif Chaim endowed his family life with the same brightness and creativity that he brought to all his endeavors. He frequently took time to discuss Torah and life in general with his wife and children, despite his heavy schedule. He even composed riddles and puzzles for his family, some of which are recorded in the book *Imrei Binah*. The following is a typical teaser from this collection:

> There were two rabbis, one in a small city and one in a large city. A great Gaon wrote letters to each one of them addressing both with the title "Gaon," despite the fact that neither merited this title. His disciples said, regarding each of the rabbis, 'Rabbeinu, so-and-so is not worthy of this.' Regarding both, the Gaon said, 'Hamakom* shall make up for his shortcomings.' What did he mean?"
>
> Answer: "In each case, the title is in proportion to the place. In the small town, even though the rabbi seems unworthy of the title, he is worthy because there was no one else like him in the town. In proportion to the Torah-poverty of the place in which he lived, he is a Gaon.
>
> "In the larger community, the city's size gives the rabbi stature and thus he too merits the title. Therefore, in each case it can be said that 'hamakom' makes up for each persons's shortcomings."

* *Hamakom*, usually a reference to the Deity, literally means "the place."

◁§ Eretz Yisrael

The Ben Ish Chai's strong attachment to *Eretz Yisrael* was evident in many ways. He personally brought a large stone from the Holy Land to be placed at the entrance of the main synagogue (which had soil from *Eretz Yisrael* on its floor) where he gave his *drashos*. All his books were printed only in the Holy Land to help support the *Yishuv* there. Under his influence, one of Baghdad's wealthy Jews donated his entire estate to the building of Yeshivat Porat Yoseif in the Old City of Jerusalem.

During Rabbi Yoseif Chaim's trip to *Eretz HaKodesh* in 1869, he visited various *yishuvim*, stopped at the graves of *tzaddikim*, and met with a number of Kabbalists then in Jerusalem. He was offered the positon of *Rishon LeZion* (Sephardic Chief Rabbi), but, for reasons unknown to us, he did not accept.

◁§ Rabbi Yoseif Chaim and the Community

A Jewish cab driver from Baghdad gave what is probably the most eloquent testimony regarding the Ben Ish Chai's influence on his *kehillah*: even years after Rabbi Yoseif Chaim's death, the average working Jew in Baghdad spent four hours of his day at work, the rest of the time studying Torah.

Rabbi Yoseif Chaim's *takanot* (ordinances) had included the excommunication of any violator of the *Shabbos*, however slight his offense ... Even those who came late for prayer never repeated their error.

□ *Throughout his life no man dared defy the Ben Ish Chai, with one well-known exception. In 1876, a Viennese teacher, Jacob Obermeyer, came to Baghdad and attempted to introduce a number of leniencies in Jewish law. Rabbi Yoseif Chaim forcefully condemned these innovations, but Mr. Obermeyer was not fazed. He sent letters to Hamagid (a weekly organ of the Maskillim) attacking the positon of the Chacham. When copies of the newspaper reached Baghdad, the communal leaders were shocked, and united in putting Mr. Obermeyer into cherem (excommunication). The book Todlos Yehudei Bavel (History of Iraqi Jewry) records that a sharp rebuttal, signed by twenty-seven leading rabbis and scholars, was sent to Hamagid, and that the cherem-proclamation was read aloud in all synagogues in Baghdad. It was even sent to Jerusalem, where it was published in a special edition of the Orthodox journal Halevanon (5636).*

A short time later, Mr. Obermeyer was informed by telegram that his mother died — which local rabbis interpreted as a result of his defiance of the Ben Ish Chai. When he sought to have a minyan meet in his home during the week of mourning, no Baghdadian Jew would cross his threshold — until he retractd his criticisms of the Ben Ish Chai, and begged for his forgiveness.

◆§ His Legacy

Rabbi Yoseif Chaim died in 1909. He left a daughter and a son, Rabbi Yaakov, a *gadol* whose opinions and explanations the Ben Ish Chai incorporated into many of his works. Rabbi Yaakov later took his father's place as Rav and *Maggid* of the community of Baghdad and wrote works of his own.

The aura of Rabbi Yoseif Chaim shines far beyond the borders of Iraq. His spirit and warmth and inspiration are everywhere, conspicuous in hundreds of ways. One can see families gathered around the holiday table, lovingly and joyously following the order of the *se'udah* (festival meals) recommended in *Tefilat Yesharim*, the Ben Ish Chai's *Machzor*. His books are "religious bestsellers," not only to the Sephardic public. In Jerusalem alone one can see several small yeshivos and Talmud Torahs that bear his name, as well as others that follow his *shitah*. During the last three years, two new Sephardic schools that teach Rabbi Yoseif Chaim's *shitah* have been established in Jerusalem, one of which was founded by Rabbi Menachem Basri, one of his descendants.

An appropriate ending to a biographical sketch of Rabbi Yoseif Chaim might be the title of one of his books: עוד יוסף חי "Yoseif Still Lives."

The "MeAm Loez"

champion of the common man

Rabbi Yaakov Culi זצ״ל
5449/1689-5492/1732

"IT MAKES you feel like becoming a better Jew."
This was the first reaction of a friend after examining several chapters of *MeAm Loez*, which I had recently begun to translate into English. His words did not surprise me. While working on the book, I too had felt tugs at my heartstrings, and I found myself saying blessings with more feeling, being just a bit more careful of my religious obligations. The *sefer* is indeed like a magnet, drawing a person closer to Torah.

For close to 200 years, *MeAm Loez* enjoyed unparalleled popularity among the common folk of Sephardic Jewry. A large and expensive set was often given as a gift to a new son-in-law, much as a *Shas* (set of the Talmud) is today. In many synagogues, the regular evening Torah-study session between *Minchah* and *Maariv* centered on this book, and a number of groups were formed for the express purpose of studying it. It is said that Rabbi Chaim Medini, famous as the author of the encyclopedic work *Sedei Chemed*, would join such groups, so greatly did he value its wisdom.

Nowadays *MeAm Loez* in Hebrew has become a popular Bar Mitzvah gift. Nevertheless, many yeshiva students seem to shun it, as part of a common prejudice against anything written in the vernacular — for the *MeAm Loez* was originally written in Ladino.

True enough, this work was specifically written for the common man. Far from talking down to the common man, however, the author uplifts the reader with a rich anthology of Torah thoughts from the Talmud, Midrash, *Zohar*, halachic literature, and philosophy, together with in-depth discussions and analysis.

The Author

The author of *MeAm Loez*, Rabbi Yaakov Culi, had enjoyed a reputation as one of the giants of his generation. He was born in Jerusalem in 1689 to Rabbi Machir Culi (1638-1728), a well known scholar and saint who was a scion of one of the leading Jewish families of Crete (Candai). Crete had belonged to Venice, but in 1645 the Turks invaded this island and laid siege to its capital and chief cities. This siege lasted for twenty-five years, one of the longest in modern history, and resulted in almost two hundred thousand casualties.

When the Turks were finally victorious in 1689, the island's economy was in shambles, with the Jews suffering most of all. Fleeing with his remaining wealth, Rabbi Machir eventually settled in Jerusalem around 1688. Here he found a city of scholars, boasting such luminaries as Rabbi Chezkiel di Silva (author of *Pri Chadash*) and Rabbi Ephraim Navon (author of *Machaneh Ephraim*). Leading the community was Rabbi Moshe Galanti, who had been appointed as the first Rishon LeTzion, Chief Rabbi of the Sephardic Jews, in 1668. Rabbi Machir was drawn to another prominent sage, Rabbi Moshe ibn Chabib, and soon married his daughter.

Their first son, Yaakov, was born in 1689, a time of great upheaval in Jerusalem. It began with one of the worst famines in memory, causing many to flee to other locales. A second, even more severe blow to the Jewish community was the death of the illustrious Rabbi Moshe Galanti. This Torah giant had been the undisputed leader for twenty years, and his passing left a great void in the community. His place was filled by Rabbi Yaakov's maternal grandfather, Rabbi Moshe ibn Chabib.

His Grandfather's Legacy

As a child, Rabbi Yaakov showed great promise, rapidly gaining reputation as a prodigy. He was raised on his grandfather's knee, and by his sixth year was questioning some of his Talmudic interpretations. Although he was only seven when Rabbi Moshe ibn Chabib died, the memory of his grandfather deeply impressed him for the rest of his life.

A year later, tragedy struck again when his mother died. His father soon remarried and the family moved to Hebron, and then to Safed. Here the young genius advanced rapidly in his studies, and began the major task of editing his grandfather's numerous writings. Probing his father and other local rabbis for information, he became aware of the gigantic stature of Rabbi Moshe ibn Chabib.

Among the things that he learned was that his grandfather had been born in Salonica in 1654, descending from a famed family with origins in Spain. Among his ancestors were Rabbi Yosef Chabiba (circa 1400) — the *Nimukei Yosef*, and Rabbi Yaakov ibn Chabib (1459-1516) — the *Ein Yaakov*. His grandfather had lived in Constantinople for a while, and then came to Jerusalem at the age of sixteen. In 1688, when but thirty-four, he was appointed head of the great Yeshiva founded by Moshe ibn Yeush, a philanthropist friend from Constantinople. When Rabbi Moshe ibn Chabib died at 42, he had already earned a reputation as one of the greatest sages of his time.

◄§ The Constantinople Venture

Rabbi Yaakov was determined to publish his grandfather's works. Since adequate printing facilities did not exist in the Holy Land at the time, he went to Constantinople, where he had hoped to find financial backing for this task. He arrived in the capital of the Ottoman empire in 1714.

A sensitive young man of 24, Rabbi Yaakov was aghast at conditions in Constantinople. True, the city had many sages who toiled day and night to uplift the community, as well as a great Kolel (institute of advanced study), known as The Hesger. But in general, community life was sinking. Constantinople had been a center of Shabbatai Tzvi's false Messianic movement, and more than any other city, it had suffered from this heretical spirit. Jewish education was virtually nonexistent, and most of the populace were barely literate in Hebrew. People did attend synagogues, but beyond this Jewish life was on the verge of total disintegration.

Winning support from a Chaim Alfandri, he began work on his grandfather's classical work *Get Pashut*, a profound treatment of the extremely complex laws governing Jewish divorce. This was finally printed by Yitzchak Alfandri, a relative of Chaim, in 1719 in Ortokoi, a suburb of Constantinople. (The only other *sefer* I know of published in Ortokoi is *Bnei Chayay*, in 1717.)

◄§ Disciple of the "Mishneh LaMelech"

At this time, the undisputed leader of Sephardic Jewry was Constantinople's Chief Rabbi, Rabbi Yehuda Rosanes (1658-

1727). He learned of the brilliant scholar who had come to town, and before long, had appointed him to his *bais din* (rabbinical court) — no mean accomplishment for so young a man. Rabbi Yaakov Culi soon became the prime disciple of this leader of world Jewry.

Rabbi Yaakov had just finished printing his grandfather's *Shemos BeAretz*, when tragedy struck the Jewish community. His great master, Rabbi Yehuda Rosanes, passed away on 22 Nissan (April 13), 1727. During the mourning period, the sage's house was looted, and a number of his manuscripts were stolen. The rest were left in a shambles, scattered all over the house. Assuming authority rare for a man of his youth, Rabbi Yaakov Culi undertook the responsibility of reassembling these important writings and editing them for publication.

During the first year, he completed work on *Perashas Derachim*, a collection of Rabbi Yehuda's homilies. In his introduction to this book, Rabbi Yaakov Culi mourns the loss of his great master ... But his main work had just begun: Rabbi Yehuda had left one of the most significant commentaries ever written on the Rambam's *Mishneh Torah*, the monumental *Mishneh LaMelech*.

Rabbi Yaakov spent three years carefully assembling and editing this manuscript. Contemporary scholars struggle through the lengthy, profound sequences of logic found in this commentary; to be sure, the editor was in perfect command of every one of these discussions. Where certain points were ambiguous, or where additional explanations were required, Rabbi Yaakov added his own comments in brackets. In 1731, the work was completed and printed as a separate volume. Just eight years later, it was reprinted with the *Mishneh Torah* — below the *Rambam's* text, on the same page — one of a half dozen commentaries accorded this singular distinction.

Today, the *Mishneh LaMelech* is included in all major editions of the *Rambam's* code. Studying it, one also sees Rabbi Yaakov Culi's bracketed commentaries and notes. At the beginning of every printed *Rambam*, one can find his introduction to this work. Thus, at the age of forty, he had already won renown as a leading scholar of his time.

◄§ His Own Life Work

Having completed the publication of the works of both his grandfather and his master, Rabbi Yaakov began to search for a project that would be his own life work. There is no question that he could have chosen to write a most profound scholarly work, joining the ranks of so many of his contemporaries. Instead, he decided to write a commentary on the Torah for the unlettered Jew. As he writes in his preface: *This might strike many of his colleagues as strange. Why would he, a scholar of the first water, write a work for the masses? Surely, one of his stature should address himself to the scholarly community.* But apparently he was otherwise motivated: *How could he engage in scholarship when he saw Jewish life disintegrating all around him? How could he close his eyes to the thousands of souls, crying out for access to the Torah?*

⋖§ Ladino — The Language of his Work

As his vehicle of expression, Rabbi Yaakov chose Ladino, the common language spoken by Sephardic Jews. Ladino is to Spanish as Yiddish is to German. Written with Hebrew letters, it looks very strange to the untrained eye; but with a little experience and a good Spanish dictionary, it rapidly becomes comprehensible.

Ladino was developed among the Jews of Spain. As long as the Jewish community flourished there, Ladino was written with the Spanish alphabet, with a liberal sprinkling of Hebrew thrown in. In concept, it was not very different from the language used in much of today's Torah literature, where Hebrew is intermingled with English.

After the Jews were expelled from Spain, they gradually dropped use of the Spanish alphabet, and began writing Ladino with Hebrew letters, which they knew from their prayers. At first there was no literature in this language; it was used primarily in correspondence and business records. The first books in Ladino appeared in Constantinople — a translation of the Psalms in 1540, and one of the Torah in 1547. A few years later, the first original work was published in this language, *Regimiento de la Vida* (Regimen of Life), by Rabbi Moshe Almosnino.

While a few other classics, such as *Chovos HaLevavos* (Duties of the Heart) and the *Shulchan Aruch* had been translated into Ladino, the amount of Torah literature available to those who did not understand Hebrew was extremely sparse. It was this vacuum that Rabbi Yaakov Culi decided to fill. As he points out, even such major works as the *Rambam's Commentary to the Mishnah*, and Saadiah Gaon's *Emunos VeDayos* (Doctrines and

Beliefs) had been written in Arabic, the vernacular in their time. But no work of this scope had ever been attempted in the vernacular.

◄§ The Scope of "MeAm Loez"

What Rabbi Yaakov had planned was nothing less than a commentary on the entire Bible, explaining it from countless approaches. Where the Scripture touched on practical application of the Law, it would be discussed in length, with all pertinent details needed for its proper fulfillment. Thus, for example, when dealing with the verse "Be fruitful and multiply", the author devotes some fifty pages to a discussion of the laws of marriage, including one of the clearest elucidations of the rules of family purity ever published in any language.

Then, as now, considerable money could be gained in publishing a successful book. Here the saintliness of the author comes to the fore. In a written contract, he specified that all the profits realized from sales of the book were to be distributed to the yeshivos in the Holy Land, as well as the *Hesger Kolel* in Constantinople. He would only retain for himself the standard commission given to charity collectors.

The work was originally planned to consist of seven volumes, encompassing all the books of the Bible. In the two years that the author worked on it, he completed all of the book of Genesis *(Bereishis)*, and two-thirds of Exodus *(Shemos)*, a total of over eleven hundred large printed pages. (In the current Hebrew translation, this fills over 1800 pages.) Then, at the age of 42, on 19 Av (August 9), 1732, Rabbi Yaakov Culi passed away, leaving his work unfinished.

The contemporary Sephardic sages saw the strong positive effect *MeAm Loez* was having on the community, and thus sought others to complete the work. Rabbi Yaakov had left over voluminous notes, and these would be incorporated into the continuation. The first one to take on this task was Rabbi Yitzchak Magriso, who completed Exodus in 1746, Leviticus in 1753, and Numbers in 1764. Deuteronomy was finished by Rabbi Yitzchak Bechor Agruiti in 1772. These latter sages followed Rabbi Culi's style so closely, that the entire set can be considered a single integral work.

Never before had a work achieved such instant popularity. But even greater than its popularity was its impact. Thousands of readers who had been almost totally irreligious suddenly started to become observant. A new spirit swept through Sephardic communities, similar to that engendered by the Chassidic movement in Eastern Europe a half century later. Very few *sefarim* in modern times have had such a great impact on their milieu.

◂§ Reprints and Translations

The *MeAm Loez* was reprinted at least eight times, in cities around the Mediterranean region. The volumes were so heavily used, that few copies of the older editions are existent — they were literally worn out, just like a *Siddur* or *Chumash*. An Arabic translation published under the name of *Pis'shagen HaKasav*, was prepared by Rabbi Avraham Lersi, and was published in various cities in North Africa between 1886 and 1904. An edition of *Bereishis*, transliterated into Spanish letters, was published in 1967 by the Ibn Tibbon Institute at the University of Grenada, Spain.

Although this was one of the most popular volumes in Sephardic countries, it had been virtually unknown to Ashkenazim, who generally do not read Ladino. With the destruction of most Ladino-speaking communities in World War II, the number of people who could read the *MeAm Loez* in the original diminished. Translation of the entire set into Hebrew in the late 1960's finally brought it to the attention of the contemporary Torah world. Although the original name of the *Sefer* was *MeAm Loez*, in the Hebrew edition the word *"Yalkut"* (Anthology) was added. One reason for this was the fact that certain portions, which the translator felt were not pertinent to our times, were omitted.

In naming his work, Rabbi Yaakov Culi based the title on the verse, "When Israel went out of Egypt, the house of Jacob from a strange-speaking people *(MeAm Loez)*, Yehudah became His holy one, Israel His kingdom" *(Psalms* 114:1). Through the medium of this book, he had hoped that his people would emerge from the shackles of ignorance. Yehudah in Rabbi Culi's reference alludes to Yehudah Mizrach, a Constantinople philanthropist, who underwrote the costs of the printing of the first edition. His reference to the last phrase in this verse was then meant to be a prayer that this work would bring Israel to once again become part of "His kingdom."

He succeeded, perhaps beyond his fondest dreams. A half century after his death, Rabbi Chaim Yosef David Azzulai (the *Chida)* wrote of him, "He was expert in the Talmud, codes and commentaries, as we can readily see from his book *MeAm Loez*, which he wrote to bring merit to the multitudes. Fortunate is he and fortunate is his portion."

ఆ The American Experience

The struggle to transplant
Old World standards of religious fidelity
to the hostile terrain of America

The Chacham for the Colonies

*he came from
Hebron to the
New World to
serve*

Rabbi Raphael Chaim Yitzchak Karigal זצ״ל
5492/1732—5537/1777

THERE is endless fascination with the American colonial era as the formative years of a leading world civilization. No less intriguing is the story of the origins and early struggles of the Jewish *kehillos* of this country in that period. These tiny communities began from nothing and set the stage for what has eventually become a leading world Jewish center.

Contrary to popular opinion, there *was* an active Jewish life in colonial America. While the early American *kehillos* could not compare with any of their Old World counterparts, neither in numbers nor in Torah scholarship, a handful of loyal Jews did struggle heroically to maintain and perpetuate their Torah heritage. During the colonial epoch, these struggles were only marginally successful, but until the beginning of the nineteenth century at least all official expressions of organized Judaism in the country were faithful to Torah tradition. "Emancipation" was unnecessary, "enlightenment" was unknown, and it was only later, when abandonment of Jewish heritage became more obvious, that the United States became worthy of characterization as a "*treifah medinah.*"

During the colonial period, a number of individuals were in

the front rank of Torah leadership in this country. Perhaps the greatest scholar among them, and certainly a most interesting personality, was Rabbi Raphael Chaim Yitzchak Karigal. Rabbi Karigal was a most rare combination — a typical Sephardi *Chacham* from *Eretz Yisrael* who spent a number of years in 18th century America. His turbulent life story and far reaching travels provide us with a bird's-eye view of contemporary Jewish life in many parts of the world.

◆§ Rabbi Karigal's Hebron

Rabbi Raphael Chaim Karigal was born in 1732 in the ancient Sephardi *kehillah* of Hebron in *Eretz Yisrael*. The Jewish *Yishuv* in Palestine was then concentrated in the four *arei hakodesh* (holy cities): Jerusalem, Hebron, Safed, and Tiberias. The remainder of the land was mostly desolate wilderness. Even these four "cities" were ancient, unhealthy, and decaying towns in which small, oppressed, and persecuted Jewish minorities lived under the uncivilized, brutal rule of Turkish pashas.

The major bright spot in Jewish life in *Eretz Yisrael* was the people's absorption in and devotion to Torah study. From the time of the Spanish expulsion, *Eretz Yisrael* had developed into a great Torah center, especially for Sephardic Jewry. It was the home of the great yeshivos of the Sephardi world, and the source of the majority of the Sephardic rabbis and spiritual leaders of the Diaspora. Indeed, at this time Palestine was almost totally a community of scholars, with the exception of a handful of laborers. The *talmidei chachamim*, both native and foreign born, were supported by donations from Jews the world over. Indeed, it was this situation which led *Eretz Yisrael* to its position as a spiritual and intellectual center of the Sephardi Diaspora.

Each of the four *kehillos* took pride in its own scholars and yeshivos, and each enjoyed its own period of prominence over the others. During the mid-1700's, Hebron was second only to Jerusalem, the leading Palestinian community. Among Hebron's great scholars in the mid-eighteenth century was the world famous *Chida*, Rabbi Chaim Yosef David Azulai (1724-1806), the leading Sephardi authority after the time of Rabbi Joseph Karo (1498-1566).

It was into this community that Raphael Karigal was born. He studied at a local Hebron yeshiva, Chesed L'Avraham V'emes LeYaakov. This school had been founded in 1659 by the Amsterdam Sephardi millionaire, Avraham Israel Pereira, a Marrano who had escaped from Portugal to Amsterdam and became a leader of its *kehillah.* His son, Jacob Pereira, continued to support this yeshiva after his father's death, underwriting not only the Yeshiva's budget, but also all the living expenses of its scholars.

Rabbi Karigal's teachers included Rabbi Mordechai Ze'evi, Rabbi Meir Gedaliah, and Rabbi David Melamed, who conferred *semichah* on him in 1750. Rabbi Karigal then went to Jerusalem where he continued his studies. Among the leading Jerusalem scholars with whom he studied was Rabbi Jonah Navon (1713-1760) author of *"Nechpa Bakesef."*

ৰ§ The "Shliach": Hebron's Torah Ambassador at Large

As a measure of his contemporaries' favorable opinion of him, Rabbi Karigal was appointed to be a *shliach* of Hebron in 1754, when he was only twenty-one. While it was understood that his mission was basically to travel to the Diaspora to raise money for his community's scholars, a *shliach* was much more than a fund raiser. He would also bring the fruits of the Holy Land's Torah study to the Diaspora. While on his travels, he would be asked difficult questions of *halachah,* and be requested to resolve communal disputes and problems. He would also check into the health of the local Torah institutions, suggesting improvements in them. Thus, a prominent scholar would be selected as a *shliach* ... As a case in point, the *Chida* had spent much of his career traveling the world as a *shliach* of *Eretz Yisrael.*

On Rabbi Karigal's initial trip as a *shliach,* he toured the Jewish communities of nearby Egypt for three months. He then left by ship for Izmir, Turkey, continuing on to the leading *kehillos* of Constantinople, Salonika, and Adrianople; traveling on to the east, to the *kehillos* of Syria, Iraq, and Persia. In Persia his last stop was the large community of Isfahan. This trip, under the difficult travel conditions of the time, lasted two years, after which he returned to Hebron.

In 1757, the Hebron *kehillah* dispatched Rabbi Karigal on a second, even more difficult and far-reaching trip — to Western Europe. Rabbi Karigal first sailed to Italy. He spent much time in the various *kehillos* of Italy, where he was highly regarded and his opinion was eagerly sought. The famous controversy was then raging over the writings of Rabbi Moshe Chaim Luzzato (author of *Mesilas Yesharim)* and their delvings into the doctrines of *Kabbalah.* Rabbi Karigal was invited to help mediate this dispute and actively sought to resolve it.

Rabbi Karigal then traveled north to Vienna, Prague, and a number of German communities. After visiting the wealthy Sephardi *kehillos* of London and Amsterdam, in 1762, Rabbi Karigal prepared to return to Hebron. Just at that time, the *parneisim* (community leaders) of the Amsterdam *kehillah* learned of the death of Rabbi Raphael Mendes de Sola, Rav of the Sephardi community of the Caribbean island of Curacao. Curacao, a Dutch colony, was under the influence of the Amsterdam *kehillah* and turned to it for guidance. Rabbi Karigal had won the admiration of the *parneisim* of Amsterdam and they urged him to accept the newly vacated position. Rabbi Karigal accepted this appointment and left for Curacao.

The Curacao *kehillah* of this period consisted of rich international Sephardi merchants. An idea of their wealth can be gained from the salary paid to their new Rav: 750 pesos a year — a huge sum, exceeding the salary of Rabbi Shlomo Shalem, the *Chacham* of the world famous Amsterdam *kehillah*.

Rabbi Karigal remained in Curacao for only two years. One might assume that his longing to return to *Eretz Yisrael* impelled him to leave. While there, however, he established a local yeshiva where he taught a number of students. In 1764, he returned to Amsterdam and traveled on to *Eretz Yisrael* and Hebron.

In 1768, Rabbi Karigal again left Hebron. Difficulties in making a living and supporting his growing family forced him to accept another *shlichus* abroad. He went to Marseilles and Paris, eventually settling in London. During his two-and-a half years in London, he taught at the Sephardi *bais hamidrash* there. In 1772, he left England for the Caribbean island of Jamaica, which boasted an active Sephardi community. A year later, he set sail for the North American continent to visit its Jewish *kehillos* for the first time. Thus, in 1771 Rabbi Karigal arrived in Philadelphia, whose tiny local *kehillah* received him with great honor. After a month, he left for the much larger Jewish community of New York.

For some reason his stay in New York was a brief one, and after a few months Rabbi Karigal left for Newport, Rhode Island, a major Jewish community.

As the Northern apex of the famous triangular trade with Africa and the West Indies, it was an important center of international commerce. These trade opportunities attracted Jewish settlers. In addition, Rhode Island had been founded by Roger

Williams with the guarantee of religious freedom, which made it possible to carry on an organized and active Jewish life.

The Newport *kehillah* — "Khal Kadosh Yeshuat Yisrael" — had been founded in 1658, the second Jewish community to be established in North America. (New York had been the first, in 1654.) Like all colonial *kehillos*, it followed Sephardic practices in both *minhag* and organizational structure. The beautiful Touro Synagogue, which was constructed by the *kehillah* in 1763, is still standing. It is a National Historical Site and the oldest synagogue extant in the United States. The outstanding beauty of its architectural lines is still impressive today.

◆§ The Newport Welcome

In Newport, Rabbi Karigal was received with great honor, as the most outstanding *talmid chacham* to have visited the town until then. He served the *kehillah* there as their unofficial Rav during his stay, as he had in New York and Philadelphia. While his visit to Newport was a relatively short one, his strong influence remained long after his departure. Undoubtedly his presence in Newport contributed to its standing as America's leading, most active Jewish community until after the Revolution.

While in Newport, Rabbi Karigal came into contact with one of the leading non-Jewish intellectuals of colonial life, Rev. Ezra Stiles. Stiles was president of Yale College and a famous Protestant minister. He was very impressed with the demeanor and bearing of Rabbi Karigal and left detailed descriptions of Rabbi Karigal and his actions in his letters and diary. The character and learning of a true *talmid chacham* were so unusual in eighteenth century America that Stiles became one of Rabbi Karigal's greatest admirers. He asked him many questions concerning the Jewish religion and the Hebrew language and carefully recorded the answers he received. Stiles wrote a number of Hebrew letters to Rabbi Karigal, which were preserved. He went so far as to minutely describe the physical appearance and costume of Rabbi Karigal. Indeed, Stiles commissioned the painting of a picture of the Chacham as a remembrance. It is this portrait that we have today.

We quote from the diary of Reverend Ezra Stiles (preserving his spelling, syntax, etc.):

> (March 30th, pp. 357-8)
> This Afternoon the Rabbi came to visit me in Company with Mr. Lopez. We conversed largely on the Gemara, the 2

Talmuds (of which he preferred the Babylonish), the
Changes of the Hebrew Language in different Ages ...

The Rabbi's Dress or Aparrel: Common English Shoes,
black Leather, Silver flowered Buckles, White Stockings. His
general Habit was Turkish. A green Silk Vest or long under
Garment reaching down more than half way the Legs ... (A
description of unusual detail followed, culminated with a
depiction of the classical Turkish Tallis.) When he came into
the Synagogue he put over all, the usual Alb or white
Surplice, which was like that of other Jews, except that its
Edge was striped with Blue straiks, and had more Fringe. He
had a White Cravat round his Neck. He had a long black
Beard, the upper Lip partly shaven — his Head shaved all
over. On his Head a high Fur (Sable) Cap, exactly like a
Woman's Muff, and about 9 or 10 Inches high, the Aperture
atop was closed with green cloth. He behaved modestly and
reverently.

... Whether Moses Wrote All the Pentateuch
(April 22nd & 23rd, p.368)
I visited the Rabbi. I asked him whether Moses wrote all
the Pentateuch, particularly the Account of his own Death?
also Gen. 36,31? — he answered, yes; that he wrote of
Things future and present, as Isaiah wrote of Cyrus. He
spake with the deliberate Confidence of Demonstration —
and he is a Man of great Modesty and Candor, and most
remote from a disposition to obtrude his own Assertions
without being ready to offer the Reasons.

(July 15th)
Spent the Afternoon with the Rabbi ... I asked him
whether the Rabbins of this Age thought themselves to have
any particular Reasons for expecting the Messiah im-
mediately? He said not; but he thought it was high Time for
him to come.

While in Newport Rabbi Karigal busied himself, as he had
on his other travels, with strengthening local Jewish life. Thus, he
spoke regularly to the *kehillah* on Shabbos and *Yom Tov*, inspiring this small isolated community to be loyal and faithful to their
Torah heritage. He was also active in other Jewish matters. He
was in communication by letter with Isaac Pinto, a member of the
New York *kehillah* who was the first known American translator
of parts of the *Siddur* into English. Pinto had requested Rabbi

Karigal's help in translating certain verses of the Torah into English.

On the festival of Shavuos in 1773, Rabbi Karigal gave a spirited sermon in Newport. This address dealt with the lot of the Jewish people in exile and inspiring their faith in the eventual coming of *Moshiach*. Rabbi Karigal was witnessing the deterioration of the local community's Jewish ideology on this score due to the strong Christian influence surrounding them, and therefore felt the need to choose this topic. While his speeches as Hebron *shliach* in Europe and Asia had been given in Hebrew, in Newport he spoke in Spanish which was still the language of the Jews in North America. This was probably due to the relative Jewish ignorance of the community and their inability to follow an involved Hebrew discourse. The *parneisim* of Newport were so impressed with this *drashah* that they had it published in English translation in 1773 — the first Jewish discourse to be published in America.

◄§ Farewell to the New World

Rabbi Karigal left Newport on July 21, 1773, and set sail for the Dutch colony of Surinam, in South America, which had a flourishing Jewish community. In 1774, he was invited to the *kehillah* of the British island of Barbados in the Caribbean. Barbados had had no Rav since the death of the previous occupant of that office twenty-two years before, and its Jews eagerly took advantage of the rare presence of a *talmid chacham* in the Western Hemisphere, electing him as their spiritual leader. Rabbi Karigal accepted this appointment and served as Rav in Barbados until 1777. It was in that year that this intrepid Torah pioneer and traveler ended his voyage in this world and died at the young age of forty-five. He left us with a fascinating and inspiring record of a life spent traveling and working for the growth of Torah and Judaism all over the globe.

A Homegrown Torah Pioneer in America

Gershom Mendes Seixas זצ״ל
5505/1745-5576/1816

*prime religious
authority for the
Jews in early
America*

MAINTAINING Jewish life in Colonial America, which began over a hundred years before the Revolutionary War, was always a struggle. By 1776, only 2,500 Jews were scattered in various settlements dotting the countryside — in New York, Rhode Island, Pennsylvania, South Carolina, and Georgia. Yet out of this handful of pioneers we find a number of fascinating personalities well worth studying — and emulating. Undoubtedly, a leading force behind Torah observance in colonial America was Gershom Mendes Seixas (pronounced *Seishas*). He was *chazan* and general religious functionary in New York City's Kahal Shearith Israel, but his activities on behalf of Torah were spread all over the countryside.

◆§ The Marrano's Son

Gershom Mendes Seixas was born in New York on January 14, 1745. His father, Isaac Mendes Seixas, had lived as a Marrano in Lisbon, Portugal, until he escaped to New York. At that time the various communities of the New World were major places of refuge for Marranos fleeing Spain and Portugal. In New York, Isaac Seixas married the American-born Rachel Levy, daughter of

Moses Levy, a very wealthy German Ashkenazi immigrant, who had become *parnes* (president) of the New York *kehillah*. They came to head a large family that played a major role in the American Jewish world over the following century.

The young Gershom received both his Jewish and secular schooling in New York City. Kahal Shearith Israel, the New York *kehillah*, had for some time maintained a school teaching both religious and general subjects to children, with the *chazan* of the community serving as teacher. No permanent rabbis served Colonial America — perhaps because the *kehillos* had trouble attracting scholars willing to live at what was then, literally, the other end of the earth. True, visiting rabbis, such as Chacham Karigal, occasionally remained for a time to serve temporarily as local Rav. This, however, was rare. Generally, the *chazan* of the community was also teacher, preacher and usually *shochet* (ritual slaughterer) and *mohel* (circumciser) as well. Not having *semichah*, he could not be called "rabbi," but resorted to the title "minister". Many of the *chazanim*, however, were scholars with a deep dedication to Torah observance.

The *chazan* of Shearith Israel at this time was Joseph Jessurun Pinto. He was originally from Amsterdam, where he had studied in the Sephardi yeshiva. When a vacancy occurred in New York in 1758, the officers of the *kehillah* wrote to the Sephardi community in London requesting "a young man of good morals and strictly religious" to serve as their *chazan*. Pinto, 29 at the time, was recommended and accepted the position. He left his fiance in London, commissioning Dayan David de Castro of London to be his *shliach* (proxy) and affiance her in his absence. She later followed her husband to New York.

During Pinto's tenure in New York, he drafted an official Jewish calendar for New York with the local times for the beginning and end of *Shabbos* and holidays. From his letters, which contain numerous quotes from the Talmud and Midrash, it is apparent that he was something of a *talmid chacham*. It was from Pinto that Gershom Seixas learned Torah.

In 1766, Pinto left for Europe ostensibly on family matters, but actually to become *chazan* of the Sephardi community in Hamburg. The New York position remained unfilled until July, 1768, when Gershom Seixas, then only twenty-three, applied for it. He was the only American-born candidate for the position — actually the first American ever to apply for a position as a *klei kodesh* (religious functionary) — competing with several foreign candidates. Seixas' credentials: he had been taught by Pinto, and was fully qualified as *chazan*, *shochet* and *mohel*. Although not a *musmach* (ordained rabbi), he seems to have been well-learned and possessed a strong commitment to Jewish values. Seixas was accepted.

In 1775 he married Elka'la, daughter of Abraham Cohen, an Ashkenazi immigrant. Ten years later, after having borne four children, Elka'la died. Seixas then married Hannah Manuel, who brought nine more children into the Seixas family.

In August, 1776, when it was clear that the British army would occupy New York, Gershom Seixas, a strong supporter of the American Revolution, led the congregation in leaving the city. He took the *sifrei Torah* and other religious objects with him to Stratford, Connecticut, where he remained until 1780. In 1781, he was invited to serve as *chazan* at the Sephardi congregation Mikveh Israel in Philadelphia. He remained in Philadelphia for a number of years and helped the local community grow. In 1782, he led the construction of a new synagogue building there.

When the Revolutionary War ended in 1783, many Jewish refugees from New York returned home and began reconstructing Jewish life there. An exchange of letters between the New York *kahal* and Seixas, asking him to return, revealed many aspects of communal life, some surprisingly similar to our own, including the low salary paid to communal workers.

Seixas returned to New York in 1784 in an agreement that placed the then-*chazan* in New York, Jacob Raphael Cohen, in Seixas' former position in Philadelphia. Seixas remained in New York for the rest of his life, assuming an active role in communal affairs.

◄§ Initiative and Dedication

In 1802, a Jewish stranger who died in New York was buried in Potter's Field. When Seixas learned of this, he was shocked and immediately organized the *"Hebra Hased Va'Amet,"* the first free burial society for the Jewish alien and stranger. In 1798, Seixas had also led the way in founding *"Kalfe Sedaka Mattan Besether"* (Fund for Charity and Anonymous Gifts) to help local poor as well as needy in *Eretz Yisrael*. In an appeal in 1807 for the *Kalfe Sedaka*, he stated "There is not a prophet from Moses to Malachi ... but what takes notice of the remarkable events that have attended us, from the commencement of our general captivity, even unto the present day. Twice have we been redeemed according to the sacred history and we have every reason to expect, the third time is rapidly approaching when we shall be established forever."

Seixas emphasized the imminent coming of *Mashiach* and the end of the Exile in speeches throughout his career. He may have felt that the success of the Revolution, which granted equal rights to Jews, made it essential that he remind his people that they were still in *galus*. Indeed, there was a decline in religious observance and commitment among American Jews following the Revolution. Thus, in 1789, (in a sermon entitled "A Religious Discourse") he pointed out that attainment of civil rights did not signify the end of "the captivity." From 1799 to 1807 a string of sermons reflected a growing religious neglect, for he appealed to his fellow-Jews to return to full Torah observance, and thereby fulfill a condition for redemption. Again, in a Thanksgiving Day sermon given in 1804, he reminded his listeners that "G-d will gather us again from all corners of the earth ... and reinstate us in our former possessions."

Gershom Seixas had continual salary problems with his congregation. His pay was indeed quite meager and he was forced to subsist on a poverty line income. In 1803, his salary was $500 a year while the *shochet* (who had meanwhile been employed separately) received $250, and the *shammas* $125. In 1808, after much effort, his annual salary was raised to $750. He did receive extra income as an occasional *shochet* and *mohel*.

Seixas' dedication to the *mitzvah* of *milah* was indeed exemplary. He was the sole *mohel* not only in New York but throughout the Northeast. He was frequently called to Newport and neighboring cities to perform this *mitzvah*.

Probably his most strenuous trip was undertaken in 1811, when he was sixty-six. He left New York in October on a journey of several weeks to perform a *milah* in Montreal. He then traveled on to Three Rivers, Canada, where he circumcised two more babies. He performed a fourth *milah* in the town of Berthieville, Canada. Seixas finally returned to New York at the end of November. The trip had lasted thirty-four days and had been undertaken for the sake of just four children. We must bear in mind that in those days travel was truly hazardous. There were no roads through the woods and much of the territory was occupied by hostile Indians and infested with wild beasts. Also, kosher food was not readily available along the way. The monetary compensation for *milah* was also quite modest. On one occasion, out of Seixas' fee of twenty-four shillings, twenty-two went for his carriage fare.

◆§ New York's Prime Authority

For many years, Gershom Seixas was New York's prime religious authority. Although American born and educated, he was an acknowledged *talmid chacham*. In his early years, he organized a New York *bais din*, consisting of himself, Abraham Abrahams, a learned immigrant from Brisk, Lithuania, and Isaac Pinto. Pinto translated the first *sefarim* to be printed in English in America: *machzorim* printed in 1761 and 1766. Seixas was later assisted in religious matters by his son-in-law, Isaac Baer Kursheedt, a German immigrant, who had studied in the Frankfurt yeshiva.

We have records of a number of *halachic* questions asked of Gershom Seixas: One was: *Must the Kohen always be called first to the Torah?* to which he replied in the affirmative ... This question still comes up in some American congregations. — Another question dealt with the removal of bodies from the New York cemetery when it was threatened with flooding. The records tell us that in response, Seixas opened the *Shulchan Aruch Yore' De'ah* and read the appropriate chapter to the assembled company.

Gershom Seixas was also active in dealings with non-Jews. He was highly respected in the general community. Indeed, soon after the Revolution he was appointed a trustee of Columbia University, a position he held for a number of years. He was also adept in his dealings with leaders in the Christian world. For example, when George English, a missionary, attempted to engage him in theological correspondence and discussion, Gershom Seixas declined to become involved, yet he remained friendly with him.

Seixas remained in his position in New York for the rest of his life. With advancing age, he became progressively weaker. He fell seriously ill in 1813, lingering on for several years, until July 2, 1816, when he died. His death not only ended an interesting life filled with Jewish devotion, it also brought down the final curtain on the Jewish colonial period in America marked by the *mesiras nefesh* and devotion to Torah demonstrated by Gershom Seixas' own life.

From Germany to Baltimore

*the first Rabbi
to hold a positon
in the United
States*

Rabbi Abraham Joseph Rice צז״ל
5562/1802-5622/1862

WHILE it is generally known that New Amsterdam (New York), the first Jewish settlement in this country, was founded in 1654, the early centuries of Jewish life here show no evidence of Jewish learning or strong religious loyalty. This did not exist on a large scale until the mass immigration of East European Jews to this country, beginning in the 1880's. Nevertheless, there were some exceptions to this overall picture. A number of Jews pioneered for Torah in this country during earlier periods. While their accomplishments may not all have stood the test of time, they still earn our admiration and respect. In the front rank of these personalities stands Rabbi Abraham Rice, the first *musmach* (ordained rabbi) to act as a rabbi in this country.

⤐ The Influx of the Mid-1800's

Jewish life in the United States underwent a radical change in the second quarter of the nineteenth century. Before 1825, only a small number of Jews were here, living in a few tiny communities. After 1825, large numbers of Jews began to emigrate from Germany to America. These Jews had seen the medieval restrictions on their lives first lifted by Napoleon, and then reimposed on them by their victorious German rulers after 1815. In addition, they were undergoing great economic hardships. A stream of immigration to the United States began, and soon became a flood. The population figures indicate the size of this movement: In 1825, there were 6,000 Jews in America; by 1848, there were 50,000; and by 1860, their number reached 150,000. One of the spiritual leaders and pioneers of this migration was Rabbi Rice.

Abraham Joseph Rice was born in Gagsheim, near Wurzburg, Bavaria, in 1802. The small towns and villages of south Germany were still permeated with the old uncompromising pre-Reform devotion to Torah and *mitzvos*. Abraham Joseph Rice first studied under Rabbi Abraham Bing (1752-1841), who was Chief Rabbi of Wurzburg and maintained a yeshiva there. Rabbi Bing had studied under Rabbi Nosson Adler at Frankfurt, together with the Chasam Sofer. Many of the great leaders of German Orthodoxy in the nineteenth century were products of the yeshiva in Wurzburg. These included the renowned Rabbi Jacob Ettlinger of Altona, and the Chacham Isaac Bernays of Hamburg, both of whom later had a strong influence on Rabbi Samson Raphael Hirsch.

Rabbi Rice continued his studies at the yeshiva of Rabbi Wolf Hamburger (1770-1850) in Fuerth. Rabbi Hamburger was the acknowledged Torah authority in the Germany of his time. He was author of two collections of Responsa, *Simlas Binyamin* and *Sha'ar Hazekeinim*, containing *teshuvos* to queries from all over the country. Rabbi Wolf Hamburger bitterly fought the growth of Reform in Germany with uncompromising zeal. Indeed, he was forced to leave Fuerth eventually by the Reformers who succeeded in closing his yeshiva. He strongly influenced his students in their view against Reform. Rabbi Rice became a close *talmid* of Rabbi Hamburger, received *semichah* from him, and corresponded with him even when in the United States. Among the other students at this yeshiva was Rabbi Seligman Baer Bamberger, the future great Wurzburger Rav.

For a short time after leaving Fuerth, Rabbi Rice served as *rosh yeshiva* in the private *bais hamidrash* of a wealthy man in Zell. The rabbis of Germany, however, had become aware of the growing number of Jewish emigrants leaving for America, realizing that they would be facing many challenges to their religion in the new country. Worse, there was no spiritual leadership to help them withstand the temptations of their new environment. Consequently, in 1840 Rabbi Rice was prevailed upon by his

teachers and colleagues to go to America as the country's first ordained rabbi.

⊷§ The New World's Chaos

Rabbi Rice arrived in New York late in 1840, finding total
chaos in his new country. There were no qualified rabbis in the
country at all; yet thousands of Jews were already living in the
United States, and every boat brought new arrivals. It was a
perfect set-up for charlatans. Anyone wanting to make an easy
dollar claimed to be a European rabbi and discharged rabbinical
functions. As Rabbi Rice later wrote: "In this country, men who
have studied neither Bible nor Talmud have assumed the title of
'Rabbi,' donning the rabbinical cap on their heads in the same
way that Napoleon placed the crown on his head."

Rabbi Rice was first advised to go to Newport, Rhode Island,
where, he was told, he would be able to revive that city's once
flourishing colonial Jewish community. He soon felt, however,
that there was no possibility of organizing a Jewish community in
that town. A *landsman* invited him to join him in Baltimore and
become the first Orthodox rabbi there. He quickly accepted this
invitation.

Congregation Nidchei Israel, the first and only *shul* in
Baltimore at that time, had been founded in 1830 by a group of
Bavarian Jewish immigrants. In 1841, Rabbi Rice came to serve as
its Rav.

Rabbi Rice soon became aware of the low state of observance
of Torah and *mitzvos* in the United States of his day. The
overwhelming majority of German immigrants had very little
Torah knowledge. Soon after their arrival, they began to discard
observance of one *mitzvah* after another. The first and most
serious casualty was usually *Shabbos* observance. Others soon
followed.

There was also another serious development. As large-scale
immigration to the United States continued, adherents of the
growing German Reform movement began arriving, including
prominent Reform rabbis such as Max Lilienthal, Isaac Meyer
Wise, and David Einhorn. Under their influence, pressure for
reform in *tefillah* and *mitzvah*-observance began to grow even
among nominally Orthodox Jews.

Rabbi Rice attempted to deal with these developments as
they arose. He received *halachic* questions from all over the
country dealing with a variety of problems. One was the accept-

ability of West Indian *esrogim* for use on Succos. These *esrogim* were suspected of being hybrid with lemons, and hence not kosher. In his response Rabbi Rice showed a high degree of Talmudic scholarship. He concluded: "I think it my duty ... to state that these *esrogim* are kosher; not a word can be found against them in all *poskim, rishonim,* and *acharonim.*"

Another problem he dealt with was the *kashrus* supervision of oil. It was suspected that lard was melted and mixed into oil sold as pure olive oil. Rabbi Rice published notices calling the attention of the Jewish public to this fact, advocating that *mashgichim* (supervisors) be appointed to oversee the production of the oil. When Reform spokesmen answered Rabbi Rice and attempted to show that consumption of such oil even with lard was permissible, they found that they had more than met their match. In a series of scholarly articles, Rabbi Rice completely refuted their position.

As the first rabbi in the United States, Rabbi Rice was also asked to set precedents in the writing of the names of various cities for *gittin* and *kesubos* (documents associated with divorce and marriage), where correct spelling is binding to the document's validity.

When Isaac Leeser began to publish *The Occident* as an Orthodox monthly in English, Rabbi Rice quickly came to his aid. He wrote articles in *The Occident* expounding the Torah point of view on Reform and related matters. When Isaac Meyer Wise, the founder of Reform Judaism in America, published his *History of the Jews* in 1853 in which he denied the historical truth of the Bible, Rabbi Rice responded with a sharp attack in Hebrew in *The Occident.* In this article he refers to Wise as *"ha'ish hamishugah hazeh"* adding *"lo bassi lephalphel im ha'ish hazeh ki d'var Hashem bazah"* ("an insane man...I do not debate such a person, for he reviles the word of G-d").

Rabbi Rice felt that religious apathy and the success of Reform were in good measure due to the lack of any organization in American Jewish life. A national *bais din* with a centralized rabbinical authority could combat Reform much more effectively. Isaac Leeser enthusiastically joined him in this idea. In 1845 Rabbi Rice wrote of "the great importance of selecting a spiritual chief for a *bais din* for the purpose of regulating our spiritual affairs." In another article he explained the necessity to prevent the uninitiated from giving their crude decisions, which are but too well calculated to do permanent injury to our faith." He was obviously referring to the Reform rabbis who were then arriving and assuming positions in America. Unfortunately, nothing was done to bring this plan to realization, and chaos remained the keynote of American Jewish religious life.

⋖§ Farewell to the Pulpit

In spite of all Rabbi Rice's efforts, the rising tide of Reform could not be stemmed. Even within Rabbi Rice's own congregation in Baltimore, demands for changes began to be heard. Rabbi Rice had originally forbidden *aliyos* to be given to Sabbath violators in his congregation. With more and more members desecrating Shabbos, however, Rabbi Rice was forced by congregational demands to allow this measure to be repealed. Nevertheless, in an act of defiance, he announced that, as a matter of *halachah*, when such individuals recited the *brachah* over the Torah, no "*Amein*" was to be answered by the congregation. Needless to say, this caused great hostility towards the Rabbi in the community.

His relations with his congregation were further exacerbated when a prominent member died: the deceased was a Mason, and the rites of that lodge were performed at his funeral. Rabbi Rice denounced these ceremonies as heathen practices, having no place at a Jewish funeral. This brought about further resentment against the Rabbi.

In addition, the congregation began to exert pressure to change the order of *tefillah*. The Rabbi was requested to allow certain *piyutim* to be deleted. Rabbi Rice knew that this was only the beginning. If he gave in on this relatively minor point, more substantial and serious demands would follow. Thus in 1849, rather than compromise his principles, he resigned from his position.

He continued to live in Baltimore and engaged in business to support himself. He first opened a dry goods store and eventually a grocery. In the meantime, he organized a private *minyan*, which was absolutely Orthodox in practice. He served this *minyan* as rabbi without charge.

An idea of his feelings while acting as rabbi in Baltimore can be gained from a letter he wrote to his revered rebbe, Rabbi Wolf Hamburger in Fuerth: "I dwell in complete darkness, without a teacher or companion ... The religious life in this land is on the lowest level. Most people eat foul food and desecrate the Shabbos in public." It is difficult to fully assess the terrible loneliness of this isolated Rav and *talmid chacham* in the spiritual desert of mid-nineteenth century America. Rabbi Rice concluded by saying, "I wonder whether it is even permissible for a Jew to live in this land." Indeed, he seriously considered returning to Europe, but was obviously unable to do so.

Even while engaged in private business, Rabbi Rice did not forsake the *Klal.* He continued to speak and to write against Reform. When Dr. David Einhorn, the radical Reform preacher, set up a temple in Baltimore, Rabbi Rice spoke out. In the pages of *The Occident* he denounced innovations introduced by Einhorn, as contrary to Jewish law. In his article, he attacked the Reform preachers as having no right to the Jewish title of rabbi. "I deem it unbecoming to contend with such men," wrote Rabbi Rice. Again in 1855, he wrote a defense of Orthodoxy in *The Occident:* "The heavens may vanish in smoke, and the earth wear out with old age, and still not one iota will vanish from our religion."

Rabbi Rice was deeply concerned over Jewish education. He opened a school in Baltimore where he tried to bring up an Orthodox young generation. He strongly opposed the use of German by the old generation, claiming that it only alienated children from religion, which was branded by its German-language packaging as an Old World, un-American institution. By increasing the use of English, he also hoped to limit the influence of the Reform Movement, which relied on materials from Germany for texts and documents. He explained his position by writing, "Though the great ocean divides us, the sparks scattered from the conflagration abroad are already kindling a flame in our dwelling."

✑§ A Brief Reprieve

In 1862 Rabbi Rice was invited to return to Congregation Nidchei Israel as rabbi. He accepted after he was assured of strict adherence to Orthodoxy. He was unable to accomplish much for Torah in his new position, however, for his years of struggle had taken their toll. Only a few months after accepting the appointment he passed away, at the age of sixty. His congregation did not remain Orthodox very long. In 1871 an organ was introduced and the Reform prayer book was adopted. Congregation Nidchei Israel became a full-fledged Reform temple. In a short while Rabbi Rice's children became irreligious and alienated from Torah Judaism. Thus ended the career of the first American Rav.

This would appear to be the conclusion to the story of Rabbi

Abraham Joseph Rice of Baltimore — both on the personal level and the communal level. In the first aspect, there is a fascinating postscript related to me by a former resident of Baltimore now living in New York City. While still in Baltimore, this man and his family became acquainted with a young man descended from Rabbi Abraham Rice. Totally irreligious and ignorant of Judaism, he returned through the influence of this person and his family and became a fully religious Jew, joining a Chassidic group. Today he lives in Brooklyn and is indistinguishable from his Chassidic neighbors. Thus, after a number of generations, one can witness "the return of Torah to its former hosts."

It would be equally wrong to conclude that Rabbi Rice's contributions to Torah in America had no lasting impact. Nurturing the growth of Torah life in a country is similar to planting a crop in a field. At first, the hard unworked soil must be broken up by a plow and a hoe. Only then can the seeds be planted and the crop raised. Perhaps the efforts of Rabbi Rice and his colleagues served to plow the hard unbroken soil of America, in preparation for the twentieth century crop of Torah flourishing here. In this way we can all be considered spiritual heirs of Rabbi Rice.

Rabbi of the Confederacy

he came from Pressburg to lead New Orleans' Jews

Rabbi Yissachar Dov Illowy זצ"ל
5574/1814-5631/1871

OUR APPRECIATION of American Jewish history is directed towards personalities who founded institutions where previously none existed. Others no less deserving of admiration, however, are the Torah pioneers who were not so successful. Many of these individuals came to America to face a sweeping spirit of materialism and abandonment of "Old World" values, much to the detriment of the general commitment to Torah Judaism. They fought uphill battles with unusual valor and even though the apparent results were often dismal, their spirit and ingenuity succeeded in serving as sources of inspiration to their contemporaries as well as to us today. Outstanding among these intrepid Torah pioneers was Rabbi Yissachar Dov (Bernard) Illowy, whose struggles form a fascinating chapter in nineteenth century American Jewish history.

๛ A Talmid in Pressburg, a Student in Budapest

Yissachar Dov Illowy was born in Kolin, Bohemia, in 1814. Kolin had been a leading *kehillah* of Central Europe for many centuries, boasting great scholars as its *rabbanim*, such as Rabbi Elazar Kalir, author of *Or Chadash* on the Talmud, and Rabbi

Elazar Fleckles, author of *Teshuvah Me'ahavah*. Rabbi Illowy himself came from a family of distinguished rabbis. His first *rebbe* was his father, a businessman who regularly taught a group of young Torah scholars. After a number of years, Yissachar Illowy enrolled in the world-famous yeshiva in nearby Pressburg, Hungary, where he developed a close relationship with the Chasam Sofer, Rabbi Moshe Sofer, eventually receiving *semichah* (rabbinical ordination) from him. He later enrolled in the University in Budapest where he earned a doctorate.

For a while he earned his livelihood tutoring secular subjects to wealthy men's children in Znaim, Moravia, later becoming a professor in a *Gymnasium* in that city. Before long, however, he changed his life's course. He was unusually well-equipped to lead the battle against the tide of Reform and assimilation that was sweeping Western and Central Europe, and he applied for a number of rabbinical positions in these areas.

He probably would have been successful in his quest had he not been suspected by the Hapsburg regime in Vienna of having been in sympathy with the local revolutionary elements during the upheavals of 1848. Thus the Austrian government forbade any Jewish community in the Empire to accept him as their Rav. Rabbi Illowy then applied for positions in Germany, where the *kehillah* of Cassel wanted to accept him as their Rav and as Chief Rabbi of Hessen as well, but the local government there also vetoed the appointment for similar reasons. Rabbi Illowy then turned to the United States where it was not a liability to favor revolutionary activity. Two rabbinical leaders who had strongly recommended him for the Cassel position were Chief Rabbi Nathan M. Adler of Great Britain and Rabbi Samson R. Hirsch of Frankfurt. Rabbi Illowy was to remain in close personal contact with them throughout the rest of his career.

✑§ U.S.A., 1853: Orthodoxy on the Decline

Rabbi Illowy arrived in America in 1853, when the state of Judaism was markedly on the decline in this country. In 1824, when Isaac Leeser had come here, and even in 1840, when Abraham Joseph Rice had arrived on these shores, Reform Judaism had achieved no wide-spread acceptance in this country. True, non-observance of *mitzvos* had grown and commitment to Torah had weakened, but almost all official expressions of Judaism in the United States were still Orthodox. In the 1840's, however, leading exponents of German Reform had begun to emigrate to the United States, and active opponents of Torah Judaism such as Isaac Mayer Wise and Max Lilienthal emerged as important factors on the American Jewish scene. These "rabbis," many of whom had never seen the inside of a yeshiva, organized Reform congregations all over the country. Ignorant German immigrants of the period — many of weak commitment — followed the lead of these clever impostors. While increasingly more congregations throughout America were turning Reform, Orthodox Judaism lacked spokesmen and able writers to combat the sweeping Reform tide.

Thus Rabbi Illowy had an ample field for work before him when he arrived in New York. As a true *talmid chacham* and an educated university graduate — both in short supply here at the time — he was especially qualified to debunk Reform mythologies, both in their own terms and by Torah criteria. He was soon engaged as Rav by Congregation Shaarei Zedek in New York, then a leading Orthodox synagogue.

Rabbi Illowy weathered a stormy career in the rabbinate. He rarely remained long in one congregation. His unyielding Orthodoxy, expressed in zealous speeches and writings against Reform, was not calculated to win the approval of even the members of Orthodox synagogues of mid-nineteenth century America. The Orthodoxy of many of these individuals was itself quite weak. In less than twenty years, Rabbi Illowy served in seven congregations. Indeed his travels trace a sad portrait of the state of religion in the United States of his time.

After a short tenure in New York, Rabbi Illowy moved on to Philadelphia where he was Rav for a brief period in Congregation Rodef Shalom, followed by service in St. Louis, Syracuse, and Baltimore. His longest stay was in New Orleans, where he served as Rav from 1860 until 1865, during the Civil War. His last *rabbanus* was in Cincinnati, from 1865 until the end of his career.

◆§ Articulate Opponent of Reform

Rabbi Illowy was greatly involved in polemics with the leading Reform figures of the period, primarily through articles in Leeser's Orthodox magazine, *The Occident*. He was gifted with a sharp satirical pen and a keen sense of language, which he used in literary pieces in Hebrew, English, and German, the contemporary Jewish language in America. In all three languages, his style was fluid and elegant, and his writings are still a pleasure to read.

Aside from Rabbi Rice, Rabbi Illowy was the only *talmid chacham* in the country capable of answering the clever and misleading publications of the Reform movement. As a new immigrant, he first agreed to attend Isaac Wise's Reform conference in Cincinnati in 1855, but when he became aware of the nature of the gathering, he quickly removed his name from the list of participants, and he publicized this move in *The Occident*. From that time on, he was a sharp opponent of Wise. In 1856, we find him penning a scholarly letter protesting Wise's attempt to permit a *yevamah* to remarry without *chalitzah*, which is forbidden by Torah law. When a reader of *The Occident* questioned statements from the Talmud that seemed to contradict modern scientific findings, it was Rabbi Illowy who replied, effectively dealing with the alleged difficulties.

Nor did Rabbi Illowy flinch from writing personal reproaches to the major Reform leaders. Upon publication of Wise's *History of the Jews* in 1853, which denies the historical truth of the Bible, Rabbi Illowy responded with a long Hebrew letter in *The Occident* addressed to Wise: "How could your heart entice you thus to outstep all bonds to distort the truth and to shelter under the wings of falsehood, in order to make yourself a name? ... What will you do on that coming day when your Master shall question you, 'I set thee to guard the vineyard but my vineyard thou has not kept!' "

Similarly, in another long Hebrew letter he reproached Lilienthal, formerly an Orthodox rabbi, for his Reform activities in Cincinnati — specifically attacking the Reformers' contention that by reducing the "yoke of *mitzvos*" they were bringing about a renewal of commitment to Judaism: "With all the orations that you have given every Sabbath in an elegant and cultured style, what have you accomplished? ... What have you done to strengthen our faith? Where, then, are the *ba'alei teshuvah* who returned from their evil ways through accepting a new Torah you have given them? Where are those who have stopped their hands from working on the Sabbath day?" This letter closed with a quote from *Rambam's* ninth Principle of Faith: "I believe with perfect faith that this Torah will not be changed and that there will never be any other Torah from the Creator."

In 1856, when the new Temple Emanuel Reform prayer book was published, Rabbi Illowy wrote a brilliant English language attack on it in *The Occident*. In a masterful, scathing analysis of the changes introduced into the *tefillah* by this work,

Rabbi Illowy marshals, point by point, evidence of the *halachic* ignorance displayed by its authors: "Several members of my congregation ... found themselves induced, partly perhaps by the beauty of the binding and fineness of the paper of a prayer book recently published, and partly perhaps by the brevity of its contents, to endeavor to procure its adoption in their respective synagogues" he writes. When asked his *halachic* opinion of this, he answered, "It might be good enough for those Israelites who have no other use for their prayer books than to keep them as an ornament for their parlor tables, but no true Israelite could use it as a prayer book proper." Indeed he writes that he publicly announced in his congregation that any Jew using this book is excluded from the loyal Jewish people, commenting further, "For the omission [from the prayer book] of the verse: אשרי איש שישמע למצוותיך ותורתך ודברך ישים על לבו (Fortunate is the man who harkens to Your commands, and takes Your Torah and Your words to heart), the compiler has his good reasons."

Rabbi Illowy was also an active contributor to the German-Jewish press in Europe. While yet in Europe, Rabbi Illowy had become friendly with Rabbi S.R. Hirsch of Frankfurt. In America he became the local correspondent for Rabbi Hirsch's German magazine *Jeschurun*, often reporting on the American Jewish scene and bemoaning its low religious state. He frequently translated his English language articles against the American Reformers for publication in *Jeschurun*. In one article he describes America as "an unclean land ... many ignorant, yet all are wise and intelligent in their own eyes though they know not the Law." In another communication, he warns European Jews "not to permit themselves to be lured hither by the desire to increase their fortunes ... if they still have a heart for the religion of their fathers." In later years he wrote for *Der Israelit*, the journal founded by the noted Orthodox writer and editor Rabbi Dr. Marcus Lehmann, of Mainz.

In addition to his polemic writings, Rabbi Illowy was very much the traditional, learned Rav. In every city that he served he would compel the local *shochtim* (ritual slaughterers of cattle and fowl) to report to him for testing. They also were required to assure him with *tekias kaf* (a binding handshake) that they would not slaughter on Friday afternoons, which Rabbi Illowy feared could lead to selling kosher meat on the *Shabbos*. In addition, he either founded a Jewish school or strengthened the existing one in every city where he was rabbi.

Rabbi Illowy attempted to influence his congregants to greater observance of Torah and *mitzvos*, invariably achieving some measure of success. When he arrived in New Orleans in 1860, only four or five members of his *shul* were strictly kosher, and there was only one *succah* in the entire city. The following year, there were forty *succos*, and almost every home was kosher. He attempted to establish personal links with his congregants by visiting them in their homes, without compromising his role as the traditional Rav ... A contemporary account describes his study: the small pocket book size *Yore De'ah* always on the desk, next to his chair, for easy reference.

⋖ Halachic Guidelines ... From New Orleans

Many halachic questions were sent to him from all over America: regarding acceptable conversion of gentiles ... the *kashrus* of various *sifrei Torah* ... the use of a gas light for the *mitzvah* of Channuka (Rabbi Illowy forbade it).

While in New Orleans during the Civil War, his congregation was faced with another problem. The Union naval blockade had cut off the south from any source of imported *esrogim* for Succos. While the four species were available, Rabbi Illowy declared the locally, grown *esrogim* to be *pasul* (unfit). Hence, throughout the war, the *arba'ah minim* were taken in New Orleans without a blessing.

When he anticipated resistance from his congregants regarding certain difficult *halachic* questions, Rabbi Illowy frequently turned to European authorities for support. He carried on an extensive *halachic* correspondence with Chief Rabbi Adler of London and his *bais din*. Rabbi Adler was accepted in the Western world as a great *halachic* authority. To a lesser degree, Rabbi Illowy also maintained *halachic* contact with Rabbi S.R. Hirsch and other German rabbis.

Among the questions this correspondence dealt with was whether the children of Jewish fathers and gentile mothers may be circumcised. Rabbi Illowy forbade this, since the circumcision was not followed with immersion in the *mikvah*, leaving the children non-Jews. In addition, he maintained that these children would, in any case, never observe *mitzvos*, hence why circumcise them? His decision, which was subsequently published in *Der Israelit*, was supported by leading German authorities including Rabbi Marcus Lehmann and Rabbi Ezriel Hildesheimer.

Another topic of correspondence was the *kashrus* of the

Muscovy duck, which Jews of New Orleans were eating when Rabbi Illowy had arrived there. Rabbi Illowy found it lacking the halachically required tradition of acceptability, and hence declared it a *treifah* fowl. When the local *shochet* refused to accept his decision, Rabbi Illowy wrote to European scholars for support, noting that no American tradition of acceptability of this fowl was halachically valid, since there had never been a Torah scholar resident in New Orleans. Both Rabbi Adler and Rabbi Hirsch concurred with this opinion.

Rabbi Illowy actively promoted Orthodoxy in deed as well as in word. While in Baltimore in 1859, he was invited to address the Hebrew Benevolent Society dinner. When he was casually informed by one of the organizers that no arrangement had been made for ritual washing of hands before the meal, he refused to attend. This omission had been arranged through the influence of the radical Reform preacher Dr. David Einhorn, then in Baltimore. Rabbi Illowy delivered a sermon denouncing the dinner as having an "intolerant and sinful character" and urged his members to boycott it. Needless to say, the dinner arrangements were changed to conform with *halachah*.

৺ Farewell to the South

The nature of his troubled career is exemplified by the circumstances under which he left New Orleans. At the conclusion of the Civil War in 1865, Jews from other areas of the South flocked to that city. These newcomers joined Rabbi Illowy's congregation, expressing a desire for Reform. Their first demand was for a mixed choir for the High Holy Days. When the trustees refused, an election was held and they were replaced. The new president was a man who publicly stated: "The *sefer Torah* has no more worth for me than another book written in ancient times" (as quoted in a letter from Rabbi Illowy to Rabbi Hirsch). These new officers soon accepted the Reform demands. Rabbi Illowy immediately resigned and left the city. In a bitter article in *Der Israelit* he describes the events: "The enemies of goodness and religion destroyed all, ... my delicate garden devastated."

Fortunately, Rabbi Illowy was then invited to serve as Rav of a newly established Orthodox congregation in Cincinnati. We can sense his joy in his description (in a letter to a friend) of the synagogue as strictly Orthodox, having prayers three times a day in accordance with Jewish tradition.

Unfortunately, he was not to serve in this position for long.

His years of struggle had worn him out and, ill with chronic dyspepsia, he was forced to retire, after a short time, to a farm outside of Cincinnati. However, he remained active in Jewish affairs until the last. During these years, he published an article attacking the recently arrived Marcus Jastrow as being a hypocrite. Jastrow was an advocate of the Historical Judaism school of Frankel, which was the forerunner of Conservatism in this country. Rabbi Illowy sensed the danger in this approach and asked Jastrow in his article to openly declare whether or not he accepted the doctrine of the Divine revelation of the entire Torah. This was a commitment carefully avoided by most members of this group, for their basic approach was one of blurring the boundaries between Orthodoxy and Reform.

Rabbi Illowy did not remain in retirement for long. Worn out by his increasingly painful illness, he died on his farm in June, 1871. He left behind him the record of a lifetime spent in the struggle for Torah Judaism in this country. Viewed from the standpoint of tangible achievements, the story of his life may seem a total failure. However, the courage and determination exhibited by Rabbi Illowy in his lonely battle for Torah supremacy in this country over a century ago surely inspired many of his contemporaries, and should equally serve as an inspiration to us all.

Teacher of New York City Jews

Samuel Myer Isaacs זצ"ל
5564/1804—5638/1878

*battler for
orthodox
integrity in
Nineteenth
Century
America.*

THE CONTEMPORARY Torah world with its high standards of scholarship, *kashrus*, *mitzvah*-observance and *hashkafah* is truly a phenomenon of the very recent past. Certainly nothing resembling it ever existed previously in this country. Nevertheless, study of American Jewish history of the more distant past is of inspirational value. While it does not reveal great Torah success stories, it does bring to light tales of noble endeavors on behalf of Torah Judaism, and illustrates that there were early fighters for Torah on the continent, who did succeed to some degree.

Among the greatest Torah pioneers of the last century was Samuel Myer Isaacs, an important figure in Orthodox Jewish circles in New York for over thirty-five years. Isaacs was born in Leeuwarden, Holland, on January 4, 1804. His father, a wealthy banker, fled to England in 1814 from Napoleon's invading armies. The London where Isaacs was brought up possessed a number of noteworthy Torah personalities, especially the Chief Rabbi Solomon Hirschell (1762-1842), son of Rabbi Hirschell Levin of Berlin and great-grandson of the Chacham Zvi. Rabbi

Hirschell was responsible for issuing the famous *cherem* against the Reformers in London in 1842. As a boy, Isaacs was close to Rabbi Hirschell, and it was from him as well as the various *dayanim* of the *bais din* (among whom were disciples of Rabbi Yaakov of Lisa and Rabbi Akiva Eiger) that he acquired a good measure of Talmudic learning, although he never studied for or received *semichah* (rabbinic ordination).

Rabbi Hirschell was aware of the scholastic and oratorical talents of young Isaacs and had him appointed principal of the London Neveh Zedek Jews' Orphan Asylum, where he supervised the religious and secular education of the children. Samuel Isaacs was fit for larger responsibilities, however, and his opportunity for service soon came.

◄§ America — a British Spiritual Colony

During the early nineteenth century, a relatively large stream of emigration began to move from London to various new English-connected areas of settlement, including Australia, South Africa and Canada, with the largest group heading to America. This resulted in the establishment of the first Ashkenazic congregation in New York — Bnai Jeshurun, in 1825. This synagogue was formed primarily by English Ashkenazim, some who had previously been members of New York's only congregation — the Sephardic Spanish and Portuguese Shearith Israel — and others who were new arrivals from London. Apparently, by 1825 there were enough Ashkenazim in New York interested in supporting their own *kehillah*. The new-formed congregation bound itself to the *minhag* of London and referred its religious questions to the Chief Rabbi and *bais din* in England.

Not only the newly-formed Bnai Jeshurun looked to Rabbi Hirschell for guidance. Since there were no rabbis and very few knowledgeable laymen in America, congregations all over the country turned to the London rabbi and *bais din* — the closest religious authority to the United States and the one easiest to communicate with for guidance, conferring them with a sort of informal recognition. This can be seen from the numerous halachic queries and answers related to American problems found in the records of Rabbi Hirschell's *bais din*.

In view of the terrible spiritual void existing in America, Rabbi Hirschell encouraged Samuel Isaacs to leave London and accept the position of *Chazan* and preacher at Bnai Jeshurun in 1839. Isaacs expressly promised his teacher before leaving that he would do everything in his power to oppose anti-Torah forces in the New World.

Isaacs was engaged at Bnai Jeshurun "to give lectures on *Shabbos HaGadol*, on *Shabbos Teshuvah*, and on every Shabbos preceding *Rosh Chodesh* and at other times when the *parnes* and trustees may so direct." He was the first to introduce regular English sermons into the American synagogue. His sermons are masterpieces of oratory, many of which are still applicable today. They are all dedicated to strengthening Torah observance among the congregants, and exhibit a high degree of learning by the author.

~§ Filling the Void

Isaacs' main efforts were in education, for he was fully aware that setting up Jewish schools offered the only way to ensure a future for Orthodoxy in this country. In 1842 he reorganized the afternoon Hebrew school of Bnai Jeshurun, converting it into an all-day Hebrew and English school for boys, known as the New York Talmud Torah and Hebrew Institute. By the next year, there were eighty pupils in the school, which had a budget of $1,500 — a substantial sum in those days. In 1845, the highest class, which consisted of two boys, was able to translate and understand Rashi, an unheard-of accomplishment in America at the time.

The success of the school was shortlived, however, for it soon ran into financial difficulties. Bnai Jeshurun was unable to support it alone and Isaacs tried to make it into a community project. He asked the various synagogues that had begun to form in the city to send delegates to a meeting to support the school. They, however, refused. Rich Jews were unwilling to send their children to the school and the poor Jews could not afford to. After a valiant struggle, the Talmud Torah closed its doors in 1847.

Other congregations in New York continued to maintain their own elementary day schools throughout the 1840's and 1850's, but there was no Jewish high school anywhere in the country. Isaacs expressed concern about this in an article he wrote in 1857 urging the founding of such a school "in which anyone who pleases can be taught the truths contained in the Bible and the commentaries on the Law." He continued: "We cannot afford to lose a day. תלמוד תורה כנגד כולם (Torah study ranks supreme)." Finally, in the late 1850's, Isaacs convinced the New York congregation to open a private Hebrew high school for Jewish students, enrolling boys from all the various New York synagogues. Isaacs himself taught the Hebrew subjects, which reached quite a high level for the time, including the study of *Mishnah*. After some years, financial difficulties also closed this school.

In addition to fighting for Jewish education, Isaacs was very concerned about safeguarding *mitzvah*-observance. The *mitzvah* most neglected by immigrants to America at the time, and indeed, subsequently until our own time, was *Shabbos* observance. Upon his arrival in New York, Isaacs attempted to exclude Sabbath violators from membership on every board at Bnai Jeshurun. He received no congregational backing in this, however, and failed.

The Sabbath issue eventually led Isaacs to leave his pulpit at Bnai Jeshurun. A group of members inspired by Isaacs became disgusted with the lenient attitude towards Sabbath violation in the officially Orthodox congregation — such as the practice of giving synagogue honors to Sabbath violators — and seceded in 1845, founding Congregation Shaarei Tefila "on pure orthodox principles."

Isaacs assumed the pulpit there in 1847, remaining until his death. At the time, he expressed his feelings about Sabbath observance in Leeser's *Occident:* "In the days of yore violators were ... stoned to death ... but now we count their society, give them the first honors in the synagogue, call them up to hear the law recited which anathematizes the Sabbath-violator. We dread the moment that the finger of innovation should erase anything from the ceremonial code; but calmly we behold the hand of sacrilege destroying the Ten Commandments."

The Nature of the Battles

Isaacs was also very involved in the struggle against Reform in this country. With the beginning of the 1840's, a massive influx of German Jewish immigrants flooded into America, swamping the existing predominantly English Jewish community. Some of these Jews brought with them Reform ideas which were greatly strengthened by the arrival of radical reform "Rabbis" from Germany, such as Isaac M. Wise and Max Lilienthal. Isaacs, an articulate English writer and speaker, devoted much energy to fighting these ideas.

In 1857 he founded *The Jewish Messenger*, first as a semi-monthly and later as a weekly newspaper, for which he served as editor and wrote most of the articles, assisted by his son and his students. In the very first issue he wrote: "Our principles are based upon the strictest orthodoxy." Nostalgically, he wrote of former times in which "the Rabbis were faithful to their charge, the flock fed on such mental food from which they might eat and live forever; there was no scoffing at religious exactions; no deriding Divine principles as unsuited to the spirit of the age, the violator of the Sabbath and festival did not ask others to join him in the unholy alliance."

Throughout his career as editor of *The Jewish Messenger*, which continued until his death, Isaacs remained a strong opponent of Reform. Many of his articles were well-written, with a sharp satirical bent. Some are quite topical today and can still be read with profit. Thus he described Reform as "that curious plant, which has of late shot forth with lamentable luxuriancy in some congregations, to the derogation, if not subversion, of our time hallowed faith." In analyzing the various Reform prayer books produced in America, Isaac commented "Charleston, Cincinnati, Baltimore, New York, have each and every one its own form of prayer. Which of them has the best, we do not know, as we confess we never had sufficient curiosity to open the pages of one, being perfectly satisfied with the Liturgical exercises laid down for our guidance in Israel's code of laws."

The pages of *The Jewish Messenger* reveal much information about Jewish religious life in America. In 1858, Isaacs noted that Rabbi Abraham Rice of Baltimore had called his attention to the chaotic situation of *kashrus* in New York saying he "was actually paralyzed" by the violations rampant in the city.

"The above charge," Isaacs wrote, "is literally true ... how pliant some men's consciences are on a matter in which they jeopardize their future bliss ... Are we to purchase meat from butchers who have three Hebrew letters in their store without making any inquiry whether they are Israelites, are deserving of our confidence, or whether they should not be doubted, seeming that they violate the most holy rites of our religion?"

Isaacs called for mandatory re-examination of New York *shochtim*, noting that many had never been tested since their departure from Europe. "The smallest community in Europe takes every care that their co-religionists are provided with proper men ... while we, having twenty thousand Israelites in our midst, are actually careless on a matter which affects body and soul". Unfortunately, due to the lack of any central authority this chaotic situation continued with regard to *kashrus*.

Isaacs was active in charitable and welfare activities of the

New York community. In 1843 he formed the Bnai Jeshurun Ladies Benevolent Society, the first Ashkenazic Women's Chevra Kadisha in New York, which did *taharos*, sewed shrouds, and paid the funeral expenses of poor Jews. In 1845, he was among the founders of the Jewish Publication Society of America, dedicated to publishing books of Jewish interest. In 1859, as a result of the outcry in the Jewish world concerning the kidnapping of Edgar Mortara, Isaacs led in the formation of the Board of Delegates of American Israelites. It was his hope, unfortunately never fulfilled, that this organization would grow into an American national *kehillah*. Again, in 1873, he played a central role in starting the United Hebrew Charities in New York to centralize and coordinate all charitable activities in the city.

Isaacs was closely connected with the Jews' Hospital, which in 1852 was the first such institution in America. Until that time, Jewish patients were treated in Christian hospitals where they had no kosher food, and in their weakened condition were subject to constant attempts at conversion. Isaacs, as the hospital's first vice-president, exerted all his influence to see that this institution fully conformed to halachah. Thus in 1859, after much discussion in the pages of the *Occident* and other American Jewish periodicals, he wrote to Chief Rabbi Nathan Marcus Adler in London with a halachic query as to the permissibility of post-mortem examinations and autopsies at a Jewish hospital. Rabbi Adler's response, which was publicized in the American and British Jewish press, allowed such an examination only if the life of another person, present at the time, depended on it. The Jews' Hospital later became the present Mt. Sinai Hospital.

Isaacs also devoted much energy, together with Isaac Leeser, to the establishment of Maimonides College, an Orthodox seminary in Philadelphia in 1866, as an Orthodox training school for *chazanim*, *shochtim*, teachers, and preachers. He also devoted much energy to raising funds for this school, to put it on a firm foundation. Unfortunately, the college was never a success and it was closed in 1868, soon after Leeser's death.

The Turning Tide Against Torah

Indeed, by the 1860's the tide had turned decisively against Orthodoxy in America. More and more congregations were abandoning their Orthodox principles and accepting the new Reform gospel. There remained only a small group of individuals and congregations faithful to Torah, holding out for Orthodox

Judaism. Isaacs continued his sharp attacks on Reform in his newspaper — as in 1866, when he noted that what was needed was not "the unauthorized tampering with the tenets of our blessed faith, not the manufacture of a convenient religion"; but he seems to have been less and less effective.

Isaacs gave further expression to these developments in an article in *The Jewish Messenger* in 1868, commenting on the absolute disorder that prevailed in the field of Jewish marriage and divorce. He realized that only a true halachic authority could stop the descent of the American Jewish community into assimilation and disappearance, and therefore advocated the formation of a proper *bais din*, noting that there were "Fifty thousand Israelites in our city, twenty-six synagogues, and not one properly constituted *Bais Din*, to whom questions of the greatest importance might be entrusted." He eloquently described the situation whereby parties who desired a Jewish divorce went to a charlatan who, "without any compunction of conscience, readily yields to the wishes of the applicants, and they are divorced contrary to Jewish law, but agreeably to his understanding of its principles." Isaacs pointed out how this led to the chaotic situation affecting the permissibility of marriage with thousands of Americans, who were the product of unions following such illegal divorces. "As far as our experience extends," he noted, "and it is upwards of a quarter of a century in this city, that there is everything to deplore and nothing to approve, as it regards our religious supervision."

The currents of change sweeping the American Jewish world also began to affect Isaac's congregation. Shaarei Tefila, when formed in 1845, was located on Wooster Street, between Spring and Prince Streets, north of Canal Street, then a well-to-do Jewish area. In 1869 the synagogue moved, with the shift in Jewish population, to Forty-fourth Street between Sixth Avenue and Broadway. As is often the case, change in location introduced pressure on Isaacs for change in the synagogue ritual. The old generation of founders had passed away and a new, Americanized group was in control. Despite all his efforts, Isaacs was forced to agree to some minor changes — such as omission of the *piyutim* and later time for beginning services — to ward off basic halachic violations. Despite this, the pressure for Reform continued to mount even within his own congregation. Isaacs, however, succeeded in maintaining halachic standards for the rest of his career until his death in 1878. However, shortly after that time, with the erection of a new building yet further uptown, Shaarei Tefilla became completely Reform, introducing an organ and the Reform prayer book. In a sense, the members had to wait for Isaacs to die before severing their links with Torah Judaism.

Although the life of Samuel Isaacs seems in retrospect to be singularly unsuccessful, we still can find much to respect and admire in it. It is true that most of what Isaacs built and attempted to build did not stand the test of time. It was heartbreakingly difficult to plant Torah in the soil of America, yet the couragous attempts of this authentic Torah pioneer to raise Torah observance and knowledge in the country surely were not totally wasted. He plowed up the earth and prepared it for later more successful plantings, and a delayed but magnificent flowering of Torah in America.

A Chief Rabbi for New York City

*the ill-fated
struggle to unite
New York
Jewry under one
leader*

Rabbi Jacob Joseph זצ״ל
5603/1843-5662/1902

A BASIC characteristic distinguishing the Jewish community of the United States from that of Europe is in the nature of organization. The Jewish community in Europe was often well organized, especially in the religious sphere. There was an official religious hierarchy leading up to the communal spiritual head, the chief rabbi. This hierarchy included *dayanim* (religious judges), *shochtim* (ritual slaughterers), and often congregational rabbis and preachers. Each member of the communal organization had a well defined-position in that organization and he attemped to fill it as required. The communal network was held together and maintained its authority over the general populace by virtue of communal self-discipline — a discipline maintained by both the religious functionaries and the laymen. It is this organizational structure and accompanying self-discipline that is absent from the Jewish community in the United States. One attempt to introduce it took place in 1888 when New York appointed its own chief rabbi.

The idea of establishing a chief rabbinate was not new to America. The respected position of Nathan Marcus Adler as Chief Rabbi of the British Empire served as a constant spur to the

American Jew. The official government recognition of the British Chief Rabbinate and the real religious authority it exercised over British Jewry were constantly before the eyes of American Jewry. As early as 1845, Isaac Leeser wrote in *The Occident* of the necessity of establishing an American chief rabbinate on the English model; nothing, however, was done. The idea had to wait for the influx of Eastern European immigrants who began arriving in small but increasing numbers, especially after the Civil War.

⊷§ Wanted: One Chief Rabbi

The oldest and most prominent Russian-Polish congregation in New York was Beth Hamedrash Hagadol on Norfolk Street on the Lower East Side. It had been established in 1859. Rabbi Abraham Ash, an East European immigrant, served as rabbi to the congregation from 1860 on. Rabbi Ash had a stormy relationship with his congregation. He was criticized by his congregants for continuing to engage in business while occupying a rabbinical position. They were becoming Americanized and wanted a full time "clergyman." In addition, Rabbi Ash was of Chassidic background, and thus naturally tended towards *Chassidus*. This caused an even greater schism with his synagogue members. They were primarily Lithuanian Jewish immigrants of a strong *misnagdish* tradition and had little sympathy for Chassidim or *Chassidus*. Thus when Rabbi Ash resigned his position in 1877, his departure was not mourned.

Immediately thereafter the Beth Hamedrash Hagadol resolved to import a distinguished foreign scholar to be its new rabbi. It also decided to ask other congregations to join in the venture. In 1879, a meeting, attended by delegates of thirty-two congregations, was held, resolving to appoint a chief rabbi and a *bais din* (rabbinical court) to assist him. An organization called the Board of Delegates of the United Hebrew Orthodox Congregations was set up. It was also resolved that the position of chief rabbi would be offered to the famed Rabbi Meir Leibush Malbim. The offer was to be made as soon as the sum of five thousand dollars was raised.

A circular was sent to all the East European congregations in New York describing the importance of appointing a chief rabbi. The new spiritual head would stop the *chilul Shabbos* which was rampant among the immigrants and seemed to be growing worse. He would bring some measure of control to the field of *kashrus* where absolute chaos reigned. And he was to present religion in a favorable light to the youth and bring them back to religion. In the interim, however, Rabbi Malbim died. Rabbe Ash had meanwhile reconsidered his resignation and was again willing to assume his former duties as rabbi of the Beth Hamedrash Hagadol. He was soon reappointed to this position. There was now no need, as far as the Beth Hamedrash Hagadol was concerned, for bringing a new European rabbi to New York, and it left the projected union of synagogues. With the departure of the largest and richest congregation, the newly-formed United Hebrew Orthodox Congregations fell apart. For a time the attempt to appoint a chief rabbi was abandoned.

The need for a chief rabbi in New York became apparent again in 1887 when Rabbi Ash died. During the 1880's, the previously small stream of East European Jewish migration to America had become a flood. There were now thousands of newly arrived Jews in New York with no effective spiritual leadership.

A meeting was held at the Beth Hamedrash Hagadol, resolving that letters be sent to all other congregations to meet on appointing a chief rabbi for all New York. Naturally the idea was ridiculed in the Reform-controlled Anglo-Jewish press. Nevertheless, there was a swift response: within a month an annual sum of twenty-five hundred dollars had been pledged by various congregations, and the Association of American Orthodox Hebrew Congregations was formed. This was to be the new Chief Rabbi's kehillah.

Advertisements concerning the position were placed in the Russian-Jewish press. In addition, eight leading European scholars were asked for their recommendations on filling the position with the hope that one of them might accept it himself. The rabbis queried were Rabbi Yitzchok Elchonon Spektor of Kovno, Rabbi Hillel Lifshitz of Suwalk, Rabbi Eliyohu Chaim Meisels of Lodz, Rabbi Jacob Joseph of Vilna, Rabbi Ezriel Hildesheimer of Berlin, Rabbi Eliyahu Levinson of Krottingen, Rabbi Yehoshua Leib Diskin of Brisk, and Rabbi Chaim Berlin of Moscow. In the letters to these sages, the Association wrote that they did not expect to maintain separate rabbis for each congregation, but they wanted one central authority. This authority would be especially necessary for kashrus. A minimum annual salary of three thousand dollars was promised (an enormous sum in those days).

Rabbis Meisels and Lifshitz expressed willingness to come if the Chief Rabbi would have official government recognition. They were obviously thinking of the British Chief Rabbinate. The others all had no interest except for Rabbi Jacob Joseph, who expressed cautious optimism.

Control of the Association was in the hands of wealthy businessmen. They wanted a Talmudical scholar, but they also desired a rabbi who had secular culture as well. They thus first turned to Rabbi Hillel Lifshitz. He had a reputation of being a great Talmudist, as well as in fluent command of the German language; also he was conversant with modern ideas. An official invitation was sent to him. Meanwhile, however, Rabbi Yaakov Halevi Lipschitz, secretary to Rabbi Yitzchok Elchonon Spektor, wrote to the Association stating that Rabbi Zvi Hirsch, the son of Rabbi Yitzchok Elchonon, was the choice of leading rabbis for the position. Rabbi Lipschutz carried on an active campaign for his candidate and got Rabbi Hillel Lifshitz of Suwalk to withdraw his candidacy. The Association in New York, however, refused to have a candidate forced on them. They resolved to offer the position to the only other possibility who had shown some interest. This was Rabbi Jacob Joseph.

⊷§ The Choice is Made

Rabbi Jacob Joseph had studied in Volozhin, where his sharpness of mind had earned him the title of "Rav Yaakov Charif." He was serving as the *dayan* of Vilna at the time of his appointment. Since Vilna had no official rabbi, Rabbi Joseph had discharged rabbinical functions there as well. He was also the official city *magid*, and as such was famous for his powerful and effective preaching.

Rabbi Joseph was not too anxious to go to America. It was well known that America was a "*treifah medinah*," and only the less religious of the Eastern European masses emigrated there. Rabbi Joseph, however, was unable to maintain his family on his meager salary in Vilna, and thus had little choice but to accept the offered position in New York.

The Association was elated by Rabbi Joseph's acceptance. In April, 1888, a constitution and by-laws for the organization were drawn up: Each participating congregation was to send delegates to the Association. No congregation was to be allowed more than ten delegates. A president, vice-president, and treasurer were to be elected as well as a twenty-one member board of trustees. The Chief Rabbi was expected to appoint *dayanim* to assist him. No member congregation was allowed to choose a rabbi without the approval of the Chief Rabbi. These local rabbis were forbidden to have *hechsheirim* (kashrus certifications) without the authorization of the Chief Rabbi.

Chief Rabbi Joseph arrived from Europe on July 7, 1888. The ship landed at Hoboken and an enormous crowd gathered to greet the Chief Rabbi. He was escorted to a house provided for him at Henry and Jefferson Streets on the Lower East Side.

The arrival of the Chief Rabbi was attacked vigorously in the Reform-controlled Anglo-Jewish press, asserting that he was a foreigner with no understanding of America and with no possibility of success here. Even such native American Orthodox spokesmen as Rev. Henry P. Mendes and Dr. Sabation Marois attacked Rabbi Joseph. These men feared that the newly established Chief Rabbinate would draw support away from their struggling school, The Jewish Theological Seminary, which was still Orthodox at that time.

The Chief Rabbi gave his first public sermon on *Shabbos Nachamu*. The Beth Hamedrash Hagadol was packed and large crowds who were unable to get in stood in the street to catch a glimpse of the Rabbi as he entered the building. Police had to be called to restrain the crowd. The sermon was a huge success, and was even favorably reported by the anti-Orthodox press.

✎§ Cleaning Up the Slaughterhouse Mess

When the Chief Rabbi had arrived in New York, he found kosher cattle slaughtering done in approximately fifteen small butcheries. Many of these establishments employed *shochtim* whose learning, piety and skills were highly questionable. In most of the slaughterhouses, rabbinical supervision was non-existent. The *shochtim* were simply employees of the abattoirs and were completely controlled by the owners. In most slaughterhouses, the external examination of the lungs, required by halachah, was dispensed with because the owners would not allow the *shochtim* time to perform this function.

Rabbi Joseph was able to eliminate these evils. He tested all the *shochtim* and replaced unqualified ones with newly arrived European *shochtim*. He also ordered the hiring of more *shochtim*, and was responsible for increasing by thirty or forty the number of active *shochtim* in New York. The Chief Rabbi also ordered that all lungs be examined visually, and that lead seals be attached to all kosher carcasses, to avoid confusion. Two rabbis were appointed as *mashgichim* (supervisors) to visit the various slaughterhouses and inspect the knives of the *shochtim*.

Rabbi Joseph also came to grips with the chaotic conditions reigning in the chicken markets. In these establishments, rabbinical supervision had been virtually non-existent. The Chief Rabbi ordered the *shochtim* to attach a lead seal to identify every bird they killed. The seal was to be irremovably fixed to the leg of the fowl.

The supervision Rabbi Joseph had introduced into the chicken markets involved the cost of five cents per fowl. The Associated Congregations hesitated to impose the full cost on the kosher consumer. It had entertained establishing a central abattoir for the killing of all fowl, where great economies in slaughtering and supervision could be instituted. This, unfortunately, was not to be achieved.

The system of *kashrus* set up by the Chief Rabbi was for reasons of practicality confined to the downtown neighborhoods. Pious Jews living uptown wanted the Chief Rabbi's system extended to their own vicinity. Thus in February, 1889, a meeting was held at Bloomingdale's Rooms, 60th Street and Third Avenue. Among the sponsors of this meeting were the two leaders of uptown Orthodoxy, Rabbi Bernard Drachman and Rev. Henry Pereira Mendes. An advertisement was inserted in the Anglo-Jewish press stating, "Uptown Kosher Meat Supply — Wanted Retail butchers for the above, East or West Side. Any willing to open stores under regulations of the Board of Shechita will please apply by letter to the Rev. Dr. Drachman."

Rabbi Joseph was not only active in the field of *kashrus*; he was also interested in education. The Chief Rabbi took an active role in the young yeshiva, Etz Chayim (forerunner of the Rabbi Isaac Elchanan Theological Seminary), which had been founded on the Lower East Side in 1866. This was the first yeshiva established in America. It was an elementary school that later expanded into a high school, which taught both Hebrew and secular subjects. Rabbi Joseph periodically visited the school and gave oral tests to the older classes to check on their progress. He was also actively involved in aiding immigrant scholars, granting them *semichah* and helping them find rabbinical positions.

Despite all its accomplishments and all the forces supporting it, the Chief Rabbinate and its Associated Congregations organization was not destined to last. In the end, it succumbed to the cumulative opposition of self-seeking, anti-religious elements. A prolonged struggle preceded this doom.

As a source of support for the Association, the Chief Rabbi

announced a tax on *shechitah* of chickens. The buyer would pay an additional penny at the purchase of each chicken slaughtered. This penny would go towards covering the expense of supervision of the *shochtim* and general *kashrus*.

The proposed tax ran into immediate difficulties. Housewives protested against the extra expense. The butchers and *shochtim*, who were previously able to do as they chose and were now subjected to strict supervision, joined the attack. The other rabbis on the Lower East Side who were losing their income from independent *hashgachos* also joined in. The tax was assailed as being "*carobka*" — the Czarist government tax on *shechita*. Once this emotional charge was injected, reasonable discussion became impossible. Naturally, the Socialist and atheistic Yiddish Newspaper writers, who had been waiting on the sidelines, enthusiastically joined in the attack. The Chief Rabbi was assailed as robbing from the poor to maintain himself and wealthy businessmen in luxury.

The butchers formed a Butchers' Association at a meeting addressed by local rabbis, who were losing their *hashgachah* income. A new *bais din*, composed of these anti-Chief Rabbi rabbis, was formed. The butchers and *shochtim* pledged that they would only accept the *hashgachah* of this new *bais din*.

Rabbi Jacob Joseph fought back. He obtained the support of the two prominent uptown American Orthodox leaders — the afore-mentioned Rabbi Bernard Drachman and Rev. Henry P. Mendes. In response to their initiative, the butchers made peace with the Chief Rabbi and dissolved their new organization.

A new problem soon arose, however. The Chief Rabbi attempted to introduce *hashgachah* on matzah flour for the Pesach of 1889. The cost of the *hashgachah* was minimal, less than a quarter of a cent per pound of matzah. Nevertheless, the Socialist press seized this and made it into a major issue. The Chief Rabbi was painted as the defender of capitalist interests....These constant quarrels and disputations completely destroyed the dignity and respect so necessary for an office such as the Chief Rabbinate.

⋖§ The Geographic Split: Another Chief Rabbi

In addition, another problem emerged. East European Jewry consisted of groups from various sections — such as Lithuanians, Poles, Galicians, Rumanians and Hungarians — all represented on the Lower East Side. It was alleged that the new *kehillah* was totally controlled by the *Litvaks* (Lithuanians). Not only was the Chief Rabbi from Lithuania, but so were the newly appointed *dayanim*. Indeed, it was because of awareness of this problem that the Association had already in June 1888 offered the position of *av bais din* (head *dayan*) to Rabbi Yehoshua Segal, known as the Sherpser Rav. Rabbi Segal had immigrated from Galicia to New York in 1875, and was one of the leading rabbis on the Lower East Side. He, however, had refused the offer; he had felt that by reason of his seniority in America, he was entitled to the Chief Rabbinate.

Rabbi Segal had a large following among Galician Jews specifically, as well as among all those immigrants who came from Chassidic areas. As discontent with the Chief Rabbi grew, Rabbi Segal put in his bid for authority. In 1889, he was declared "Chief Rabbi of New York" by two Lower East Side congregations. Soon a new organization — Congregation Sons of Israel, Men of Poland and Austria — was created. Other congregations soon joined. There were now two rival *kehillos* with two Chief Rabbis in New York. Each undertook supervision of *kashrus*, and the chaos increasingly worsened.

Thus, in 1894, the large packing form of Weston and Levi fired the *shochtim* approved by the Associated Congregations and replaced them with *shochtim* approved by the rival Chief Rabbi. Rabbi Joseph inserted an advertisement in the Yiddish press denouncing this move. It read in part:

> "Upon the basis of qualified witnesses, we have es-
> tablished that the shochet, Moses Kemilhar, who is now
> employed by Weston and Levi on East 44th Street, had been
> found guilty of knowingly and willfully passing treifah meat
> for kosher. Our verdict is that he is a disqualified shochet
> and that it is forbidden to eat of the meat he slaughters."

This announcement was signed by Chief Rabbi Jacob Joseph and the *Bais Din*.

A few days later a paid rejoinder appeared in the Yiddish press. It read:

> "To inform all buyers of meat that the wholesale meat
> firm of Weston and Levi, East 44th Street, employs two
> shochtim *learned in Torah, pious, and competent in*
> shechitah. *Slaughtering is conducted under my scrupulous*
> supervision. Every Jew, even the most religiously exacting,

may eat of this slaughtering."

It was signed Chief Rabbi Joshua Segal.

On top of this, conflict broke out again between the butchers and Chief Rabbi Joseph. The conflict over matzah supervision had also taken its toll. The Association eventually found itself unable to financially maintain the Chief Rabbi and his office. Finally, an agreement was reached with the butchers whereby they would pay the Chief Rabbi's salary in exchange for his supervision of their work. Although the Association still remained in existence on paper, it was now a dead body. Rabbi Jacob Joseph had moved from Chief Rabbi of New York to a simple *mashgiach* of the New York butchers.

Throughout all these attacks and tribulations, Rabbi Joseph attempted to maintain his dignity. He refused to allow his opponents to be attacked in the same low, vicious manner in which he was being assailed both orally and in the Yiddish Press. Indeed, he went so far as to protest to the leaders of his *kehillah* when they attempted to publicly brand the supervision of the rabbis opposing his as being *treifah*. "They need their *hashgachah* for *parnasah,"* was the Chief Rabbi's protest. Perhaps Rabbi Joseph was too modest and too humble for survival in the rough and tumble of the New World....

The Chief Rabbi retained his title, but even this was disputed when Rabbi Y. Vidorowitz of Moscow arrived in America in 1893. He immediately announced himself as Chief Rabbi of the United States and Canada. He was of Chassidic background, and succeeded in gathering a number of tiny *shtieblach* together and also became a Chief Rabbi. By this time, the title had become a mockery.

The final blow came in 1895. The butchers refused to continue paying Chief Rabbi Joseph's salary. The congregations also refused to accept the burden, and he was thus left penniless. Soon after, the Chief Rabbi suffered a stroke which left him bed-ridden for the rest of his life. He became a forgotten man and spent the last five years of his life as a paralyzed invalid in squalid misery. In 1902, when Rabbi Jacob Joseph passed away, he was all of fifty-nine years of age. His sufferings had taken their toll. Thus ended the tragic attempt at establishing a European style chief rabbinate in New York.

His Title Was "Hillel HaKohen"

*he successfully
led New York
Jewry for thirty-
five years*

Rabbi Dr. Hillel Klein זצ״ל
5608/1849-5686/1926

W E YEARN for great personalities to admire, often unaware
that the American landscape of not-too-long-ago provided
us with a number of outstanding individuals. One such figure
was Rabbi Hillel Klein.

Two years after Rabbi Jacob Joseph had become Chief Rabbi
of New York, he found the responsibility too vast to handle
alone. He heard that Rabbi Klein had just been forced out of his
position as Rabbi of Libau, Latvia. Rabbi Klein seemed to possess
an unusual combination of attributes that made him a most attractive candidate for an American assignment, so upon Rabbi
Jacob Joseph's recommendation, a leading congregation in New
York invited Rabbi Klein to serve as its Rav. In 1890 he arrived
on these shores.

What had made this deposed rabbi so attractive to the Chief
Rabbi that he had him brought to America to serve as his assistant? What were the remarkable ingredients in his background
that made him so suitable for this task?

❧ The Unusual Combination

Hillel HaKohen Klein, born in Baratcka, Hungary in 1849,

was endowed with unusual abilities. By the age of eleven, he knew *Tanach* completely by heart and was familiar with the entire *Seder Nezikin* of the Talmud with commentaries. At the uncommonly young age of twelve, he went to Pressburg Yeshiva as a *talmid* of Rabbi Avraham Shmuel Binyamin Sofer, the *Ksav Sofer*. He left four years later to enroll in the yeshiva of Rabbi Ezriel Hildesheimer in Eisenstadt, Hungary.

The Eisenstadt Yeshiva was unique in that it not only taught *limudei kodesh* (sacred studies), but devoted time to German and classical languages as well as to mathematics. To combat the spread of assimilation and the Reform movement, Rabbi Hildesheimer thought it necessary to produce young *rabbanim* and laymen with a fundamental knowledge of secular subjects. Here Hillel Klein was introduced to secular knowledge in service to the higher pursuit of spiritual goals.

Recognized as an exceptional *talmid*, Klein was presenting a *shiur* (lecture) to thirty students before a year had passed. Two years later, Klein left for Vienna, where he entered the *Gymnasium* and later the university. Rabbi Zalman Spitzer, son-in-law of the *Chasam Sofer*, invited the young man to give a daily *Gemara* class in the well-known Schiffshul — a celebrated fortress of Torah and *yiras shamayim* (fear of G-d) in Central Europe.

When Rabbi Hildesheimer left Eisenstadt in 1869 to establish his seminary in Berlin, he asked some of his most accomplished disciples to help him — among them Hillel Klein and David Zvi Hoffmann, who was to become famous as *rosh yeshiva* of the Hildesheimer Seminary in Berlin.

In Berlin, Hillel Klein received *semichah* in 1871 from Rabbi Binyamin Zvi Auerbach of Halberstadt. Rabbi Auerbach, with Rabbis Ezriel Hildesheimer and Samson Raphael Hirsch, had been among the foremost leaders in the battle against Reform in nineteenth century Germany. Hillel Klein also received *semichah* from his rebbe, Rabbi Hildesheimer, and in 1873 he received his doctorate from the University of Berlin.

This was only part of the background that seemed to make Rabbi Hillel Klein so eminently suitable for his position of leadership in the teeming New York City of the turn of the century.

Rabbi Klein moved to Kiev in 1875, to become a tutor to the son of Israel Brodsky, a well-known religious industrialist and millionaire who had contributed the necessary funds to establish the *kollel* of the famous Volozhiner Yeshiva. During his five years in Kiev, Hillel HaKohen Klein became familiar with the vibrant world of Eastern European Jewry and came into constant contact with leading rabbis of Russia and Lithuania who were frequent visitors to the Brodsky home.

In 1880, Rabbi Klein accepted the appointment to the rabbinate of Libau, Latvia, a large commercial center of some 10,000 Jews on the Baltic Sea.

At this time there were two rabbis serving every Jewish community in Russia: The government had established official seminaries to produce assimilation-minded "rabbis." The local communities refused to accept these ignorant, irreligious young men as spiritual leaders. Thus every town had an official crown rabbi, who had graduated from one of the government-sponsored rabbinical seminaries or from a recognized European university, and the true Rav of the city, who answered all rabbinical queries and was responsible for the community's Torah institutions. Rabbi Klein was exceptional in that he could serve Libau in the double capacity of both Rav and rabbi. Because of his unusual background, he was acceptable to both the government and the people of Libau.

In 1881, Rabbi Klein married Julie Hirsch, daughter of Mendel Hirsch, principal of the Frankfurt *RealSchule*, which had been founded by *his* father, Rabbi S.R. Hirsch.

Rabbi Klein's rabbinical service to Libau was abruptly terminated in 1890 when he was forced to leave the community on the grounds that he was a foreign national — most likely a ruse to cover up the government's real complaint: that *this* crown rabbi was not like the others and would not serve as a tool of the regime to promote Jewish assimilation.

The New York Assignment

The fame of Rabbi Klein had reached New York City, and he struck Rabbi Jacob Joseph as possessing just those qualities that the community needed. He suggested that the Congregation Ohab Zedek on the Lower East Side offer the position of rabbi to Rabbi Klein. The congregation followed the advice and sent a *ksav rabbanus* (rabbinical contract) to Rabbi Klein.

Soon after his arrival in New York in 1890, Rabbi Klein was appointed by Chief Rabbi Jacob Joseph as one of his *dayanim* (rabbinical judges) and became his untitled assistant. Rabbi Klein was deeply involved in Rabbi Joseph's efforts towards centralization of *kashrus* supervision in New York City and was in charge of all supervisory undertakings of the *kehillah*, especially after the Chief Rabbi's stroke, when Rabbi Klein became the unofficial Chief Rabbi of New York City.

Observant Jews in New York City in the 1890's faced severe problems. The greatest difficulty was the seven-day work-week, which was the rule in all industries. Those with at least a bit of feeling for the day rose early on Shabbos mornings to *daven* with the first *minyan* before going to work. Only elderly retired folks and a few hardy exceptions among the active workers truly observed Shabbos.The harm of this situation cannot be over es- timated. Children grew up without ever seeing Shabbos observed. No wonder the young generation began to assimilate so com- pletely!

Rabbi Klein joined Rabbi Dr. Bernard Drachman and Rev. Dr. Pereira Mendes, the leaders of native American Orthodoxy, to remedy this terrible situation, founding Agudas Shomrei Shabbos in 1894 to foster Shabbos observance among the Jewish masses. Manufacturers were approached to close their factories on Satur- day. *Shomer Shabbos* workers were then directed to these fac- tories. A list of other Shabbos observant employers was also com- piled ... An educational campaign was launched to convince Jewish housewives not to shop on Shabbos, and then the league would pressure stores in Jewish areas to close on Shabbos. Lastly, the organization advertised in the Yiddish press that all laborers seeking *Shomer Shabbos* employment contact the organization. While this plan did not fully succeed in completely solving the *Shmiras Shabbos* problem in New York, it did alleviate it somewhat. There was at least an address for religious Jews to turn to for help in this matter.

Rabbi Klein's intellectual background and university train- ing helped him in his fight against the Reform Movement in the United States as it had in Europe. He attacked Reform in many of his public addresses, and endeavored to persuade the youth that only Torah Judaism was authentic. Reform leaders feared him more than other Orthodox rabbis, for they felt that he disproved their contention that Orthodox Judaism was ancient and out- dated. Isaac Meyer Wise, founder and leader of the American Reform Movement, wrote a scathing article in his newspaper against Rabbi Klein, expressing doubts as to whether Rabbi Klein truly possessed a doctorate. (Still unanswered by modern historians is: did Isaac Meyer Wise ever receive the doctoral degree he claimed for himself after his arrival in America?) Rabbi

Klein responded with a letter to the newspaper: *"In order to save you from error, I am enclosing herewith a copy of my diploma, in which I take but a modest pride. There is but one title that I bear with a conscious pride, and that is Hillel HaKohen."* This brief note ended the controversy.

◆§ The Slaughterhouse Battles

As Rabbi Jacob Joseph's right hand, Rabbi Klein was actively involved in the fight to centralize *shechitah* (ritual slaughter of animals) in New York and bring it under proper control. All declarations in the Yiddish press concerning *kashrus* were signed by the Chief Rabbi, his *bais din*, and also *"Hillel HaKohen hamechuneh (also known as) Doctor Klein."*

After the passing of Rabbi Joseph and the collapse of the centralized New York *kehillah*, Rabbi Klein retained a number of the cattle *shechitah* houses in Manhattan under his supervision. When Judah L. Magnes and other important Jewish figures attempted to establish the New York *kehillah* in 1914, they turned to Rabbi Klein for help in *kashrus* supervison. The New York *kehillah* was an endeavor to link all Jews in the city into one organization with subdivisions dealing with education, charity, and *kashrus*: the *kashrus* committee would license *shochtim* and provide *mashgichim* for the slaughter houses, eliminating the plague of unreliable pseudo-rabbis and *shochtim*. The final authority in all New York *kashrus* matters would be a supreme *bais din* consisting of five leading rabbis of the city including Rabbi Klein. The supreme *bais din* was also to organize forty-one additional New York rabbis into local *batei din* of three *dayanim*, providing every district in the city with a local *bais din*.

As can be easily surmised, this plan was never completely operational. The big meat packers objected to any arrangement that would restrict their control of the slaughterhouses. In addition, many local rabbis opposed interference with their personal *hashgachos*. The crucial blow was the failure of the whole *kehillah* idea when money and inspiration dissipated with the end of World War I, and the dream quietly vanished into thin air.

Rabbi Klein was also concerned over the welfare of the *shochtim* (ritual slaughterers). Their working conditions were truly horrible — extremely long hours, sometimes extending from 3 a.m. to 9 p.m.! The working areas were sheds, open at both ends to the cold, wind, and snow. In 1892, the *shochtim* revolted against these harsh and humiliating conditions. The encouragement of Rabbi Klein and Chief Rabbi Joseph aided the *shochtim* in organizing the Meleches Hakodesh Society, which struck for better conditions. This strike and succeeding ones eventually brought the *shochtim* great improvements by the beginning of the twentieth century.

Rabbi Klein was again involved in *kashrus* matters in the spring of 1911, when the matzah bakers in New York struck against long working hours and low salaries. With Pesach fast approaching, an acute shortage of matzos threatened New York and indeed much of the United States, since most matzah bakeries were in the city. Rabbi Klein organized a *bais din* to arbitrate the labor dispute. They resolved the strike and the Jewish community's matzah supply was assured for the year.

◆§ A Torah Institution for New York

Torah education was primary among Rabbi Klein's concerns, mainly to aid the only advanced yeshiva in the United States at the time, Yeshiva Rabbi Yitzchak Elchanan. This *bais hamidrash* had been established in 1896 on the Lower East Side. Rather than educate Americans, it provided further Torah study for European yeshiva boys who had immigrated to the United States. These *talmidim* would eventually receive *semichah* (ordination) and serve as rabbis in their new country. The financial burden of this yeshiva was crushing, especially for the masses of poor immigrants who were the only potential supporters for a European yeshiva in this country. Thus the yeshiva had no permanent quarters, and moved from *shul* to *shul* on the Lower East Side.

Rabbi Klein agreed to serve as president of the yeshiva in 1902. He recognized the yeshiva's need for a building of its own to maintain its dignity and optimum function. He thus immediately launched a building campaign fund, and by 1904 the yeshiva purchased a building on the Lower East Side. Rabbi Klein simultaneously led a campaign to clearly establish that the Jewish Theological Seminary was not a yeshiva, or for that matter an Orthodox institution at all. By this time, the Seminary had strayed from a Torah-true course, and it was necessary to publicize this — especially since it had been an Orthodox establishment but a decade before. Rabbi Klein succeeded in having a clear line of distinction drawn in the Yiddish press between the seminary graduates and the *musmachim* of his yeshiva.

In 1906 Rabbi Klein formed the Semichah Board of the institution together with Rabbi M.Z. Margolies and Rabbi S. Wien. Under their supervision, the first students of the yeshiva, and perhaps the first *talmidim* to be ordained on American soil, received *semichah* that year. Rabbi Klein resigned from his position as president of the yeshiva in 1908, but remained one of the yeshiva's *masmichim* until his death. In that capacity he was responsible for assigning a host of rabbis, both Eurpean immigrants and native Americans, to positions all over the United States.

Tzeddakah Campaigns and Communal Activism

Some of Rabbi Klein's greatest achievements were in the field of *tzeddakah*. In 1914 the first World War broke out, enveloping most of Europe. The main Jewish population centers ran along the Russian-German and Russian-Austrian borders, which became the most heavily contested battlefields. Old established communities and yeshivos were uprooted. The Jewish population of entire regions fled into the interiors of their countries, and those that did remain were subject to impoverishment and persecution by constantly advancing and retreating armies. The yeshivos suffered most, for they were deprived of their means of support, and the future of Torah learning in Europe hung in the balance.

Realizing that something had to be done, Rabbi Klein, together with other Orthodox activists and rabbis, organized the Central Relief Committee to aid the suffering Jews of Europe by raising large sums of money. Rabbi Klein was careful to set up this organization with only Orthodox supporters. He thus was able to direct funds and food supplies to the responsible *rabbanim* and community leaders in war-torn Europe, rather than to anti-religious elements who would have used the shipments for their own purposes. In this manner he was also able to channel a substantial share of the money to the European yeshivos. Eventually the secularists set up their own relief organizations, but it should be noted that Rabbi Klein and his colleagues were the first workers in this field. Ultimately the various relief organizations consolidated to form the Joint Distribution Committee. Rabbi Klein was able to maintain his influence on the JDC and assure that a fair share of aid was sent to Orthodox circles.

Rabbi Klein continued to exert his influence on the JDC after the war as well, dispatching much financial aid to help the European yeshivos in their reconstruction. He was particularly active on behalf of the Hungarian yeshivos, devoting time and effort to his former yeshiva in Pressburg. Without Rabbi Klein's work, the existence of the yeshivos in Lithuania, Poland, Czechoslovakia, and Hungary would have been precarious indeed.

Rabbi Klein was also actively interested in the Old *Yishuv* in *Eretz Yisrael.* In 1892, Rabbi Klein joined a number of prominent Jewish figures, including the Orthodox newspaper publisher, Kasriel Sarasohn, in forming the *Agudas Hakehillos Letziyon* — to unite all activity in this country on behalf of the old *Yishuv.* Rabbi Klein headed the (Hungarian) Kollel Shomrei Hachomos in Eretz Yisrael until his death. He regarded his activity on behalf of the *Kollel* as a serious obligation, working late into the night, signing receipts and answering correspondence so money would not be spent on secretarial help. These arduous activities eventually led to serious eye trouble, which necessitated an eye operation.

Rabbi Klein also helped found Ezras Torah, a much-needed fund devoted entirely to supporting Torah scholars in Europe during and after World War I. He lent his full efforts and prestige to Ezras Torah, serving as treasurer for fully ten years.

In 1918 a delegation of great Torah leaders, including Rabbi Aaron Walkin of Pinsk and Rabbi Dr. Meir Hildesheimer of Berlin, came to New York on behalf of the fledgling World Agudath Israel Movement. A second delegation, with Rabbi Hildesheimer, Rabbi Meir Don Plotzki and Dr. N. Birnbaum followed in 1920. These delegations were warmly received by Rabbi Klein, but nearly all prominent rabbis and lay leaders in the United States were followers of the Mizrachi movement, with only one exception, Rabbi Klein. Indeed, Rabbi Klein was appointed president of the newly founded American branch of Agudath Israel, a position he retained until his death. Unfortunately, the time was not yet ripe for an Agudath Israel branch in America. The attempt ended in failure and Rabbi Klein's demise closed the episode.

Until his death Rabbi Klein remained the spiritual leader of Congregation Ohab Zedek. When he was installed as rabbi there in 1890, this *shul* was located on Norfolk Street on the Lower East Side. Later the congregation moved to 116th Street in the then-fashionable Jewish neighborhood of Harlem. From 1909 to 1922, Rabbi Klein had as his assistant rabbi the well known, native born American *ba'al teshuvah*, Rabbi Dr. Bernard Drachman. During this same period, the famous Yosele Rosenblatt served as the *shul's chazan.*

Rabbi Klein died on March 21, 1926, leaving a solid record of Jewish achievement in this country. At the time of his death he was honorary president of the Agudas Harabanim, president of Agudath Israel of America, treasurer of Ezras Torah, the *nassi* of Kolel Shomrei Hachomos in Jerusalem and vice-president of the Union of Orthodox Jewish Congregations of America. One can whole-heartedly agree with the Yiddishe *Tageblatt's* eulogy: "There was practically not one important thing done in New York in the last thirty-five years foreign to HaRav Klein."

"He Who Saves a Soul in Israel"

*his heroic
rescue work
during the
Holocaust and
its aftermath*

Elimelech Gavriel Tress ל"ז
5670/1909 — 5727/1967

*On The first day of Rosh Chodesh Tammuz, 5727
(1967), Elimelech Gavriel Tress, Administrative President of
Agudath Israel of America, was called to the* Yeshiva Shel
Ma'aloh. *His short life spanned a period in American Jewish
life which went from utter despair that Torah would ever
take root in the alien soil of this continent, to the development and growth of scores of Torah institutions, built and
surrounded by a growing community of committed
Orthodox Jews. But his life and work not only spanned this
period — Elimelech Gavriel Tress was in a large measure
responsible for raising American Orthodoxy from the
darkness of despair to the spiritual prosperity it now enjoys.*

*Elimelech Gavriel Tress, functioning on the highest
levels of Torah leadership, was the personification of
authentic humility, not the least bit compromised by the
great dignity of his bearing. He was known to many as
'Mike,' an unusual familiarity for a man of his stature; yet it
did not in the least compromise the deep respect and even
reverence felt by all who knew him.*

The story of his life, which must one day be written, is

*the story of a revitalized American Orthodoxy — which must
also one day be written. The debt which Orthodoxy owes to
'Mike' Tress is being repaid by the untold numbers of
American men and women who are today Torah Jews
because of his efforts. But American Orthodoxy owes it to
Elimelech Gavriel Tress that his life and works be made
known — not for his sake alone, but for the glory of Torah.
Toward that goal, the following sketch of one aspect of his
work — his monumental rescue achievements — by one who
worked closely with him, offers an insight into the total personality of Elimelech Gavriel Tress.*

IT WAS in a small room in the house of his aunt, somewhere in
the section of old Williamsburg that has since given way to the
Brooklyn-Queens Expressway. 'Mike' had been ill for a few days
and we had come to visit him. He had made us newcomers feel at
home the first moment we had entered the local branch of Zeirei
Agudath Israel, searching for some bridge, some continuity with
the Jewish ideals that had shaped our world in the past. It was
then, months before the outbreak of World War II, that 'Mike'
Tress outlined the bold, broad-scope plan that showed his near-
prophetic vision, his alertness to the needs of the hour, and his
ability to see with the heart and with the soul, rather than with a
cool, sober, cautious mind.

The world was still at peace, watching idly as Hitler turned
ever tighter the screws of torture and destruction on the Jewish
masses under his control, as he prepared his campaign of persecution and extermination that was to dwarf the worst recorded in
the annals of human inhumanity, by the Teutonic thoroughness
of his attack.

In retrospect, it seems almost uncanny how this young
American Jew, not quite a full-product of the Yeshiva world,
realized the role America — particularly from a Jewish viewpoint
— was to play in the perpetuation or perhaps the survival of
human freedom and dignity. Most of us were Europeans,
graduates of years of intensive Agudist leadership-training. Yet
we were deeply affected by the vision and keen understanding of
the meaning of what was going on that was revealed to us by a
young man who, as we had quickly learned, stood in the
mainstream of American life — a young man with a thorough college education, with business connections that seemed beyond
our grasp at the time.

In materialistic America, the land supposedly void of idealism, 'Mike' Tress spoke of the urgent need to organize Orthodox Jewish youth; to bring them close to Torah *chinuch* when the fountainheads of Jewish scholarship seemed in danger. He spoke of the gathering clouds of war, when so many more of the heartlands of Jewish life might come under the heel of war and catastrophe, and when America would be the only place that could offer some chance of help and rescue. Trained to think of the New World as a place where everybody lives and works for himself, we watched with growing admiration as this young man spoke of the need to set up an organization that would tie together the isolated Orthodox Jewish energies, and provide some form of systematic help for the mass of Orthodox Jewry that was threatened by the growing German steamroller of military might and brutality. It was an eye-opener, even to those of us who had personally witnessed some of these historic developments, but were caught up in our own limited and limiting perspective. It was time to forget about ourselves, about our own careers — if there was any meaning to our Agudism. Now — he said with his warm, persuasive voice — was the time to start moving, organizing, so that we would not be caught unprepared when and if, *chas vechalilah*, the need arose.

'Mike' sketched in broad outlines what later proved to be one of the least-known, least-publicized feats of Orthodox Jewish rescue work that hinged solely on heart, iron will, raw courage, and sheer guts — to be more exact, on 'Mike' Tress, Michael G. Tress, or Elimelech Gavriel, as he became known to many thousands of Jews throughout the Jewish world. The result of it was — it may seem gross exaggeration at this time, decades and a generation later — one of the most important bridges from the Old World of Torah Judaism to the New World that was to arise on what had before seemed arid, hopeless ground. Across it flowed the human and spiritual resources that were salvaged from the worst catastrophe modern Jewish history has known. And the man solely responsible for it, for its scope, for its spirit, for its unlimited vitality was 'Mike' Tress.

He had no illusions. There was little chance for glory, for monetary rewards or other incentives that motivate the less idealistic. His was a strength of conviction, with a heart that flowed over with compassion for anyone in need; with love and enthusiasm for anything Jewish. This was the secret of the success of all the work done by 'Mike' Tress in those tragic, yet heroic years when he single-handedly created an apparatus to save Jews from the burning *Gehinnom* of Hitler Europe; to help them come to these shores, and to offer them a chance to reweave some of the strands of a normal human and Jewish existence in a new and fertile soil.

Soon after this first planning session by his bedside, we opened the office of Zeirei Agudah Israel in the then recently-acquired building at 616 Bedford Avenue in Brooklyn — an address that was soon to become a beacon of light and hope in a world shrouded with hopelessness and abject tragedy. We started with an old desk and Mike's own typewriter — he had given up a promising business career to dedicate himself wholly and wholeheartedly to the task which he had so vividly outlined for us, perhaps not even realizing himself the historic function of this initial effort. From it grew a strong Agudist youth movement, with a spreading and tightening net of Pirchei and Bnos branches. From it originated numerous campaigns and activities to bring the wider masses of Jewish youngsters to the yeshivos that had begun to spread, and to give support to communities where hope had long been abandoned for Jewish survival beyond the Last Minyan of Elders.

'Mike' was everywhere. He gathered groups of inspired young *chaverim* about him, who carried his spirit everywhere. They brought trainloads of youngsters from other cities and towns to Williamsburg, to the *yeshivos* and *mesivtos;* gave them a feeling of the beauty and significance of *yiddishkeit.* He ignited the spark of *mesiras nefesh* wherever he went, with his warm talks, his tireless efforts for old and young, for anyone who called on him for help day or night.

But most important of all, there was the effort that 'Mike' Tress lavished in preparation for the massive rescue work that emanated from the office at 616 Bedford Avenue, until he built it into an efficient organization that achieved so much more than other organizations — larger, better qualified, and richer in personnel and resources. There were no office-hours, no vacations, no time for routine or relaxation. There was only that restless drive to save and help the innocent victims of a growing tragedy day in, day out, wearing hour after hour. There was a constant coming and going of people seeking and giving help. Cables to and from all parts of the collapsing Jewish world, seeking to open doors that were closed or closing by the minute. And there were the *chaveirim* who gave up so much of their time, of their limited means, all of their efforts inspired by the example and the limitless zest of 'Mike' to get affidavits, to collect sorely needed funds, to find jobs and opportunities for rescue, for medical care, for replanting what human bestiality had brutally uprooted. The methods and means were unorthodox, far different from the bureaucratic routines of other relief and rescue organizations. They defied the rigidities and inflexibilities which hampered or blocked so much that might have been done by other more powerful organizations set up for this purpose in the Jewish and non-Jewish world. With the weak, limited resources at his disposal 'Mike' molded the office of Zeirei Agudath Israel, later on Agudath Israel of America, into a powerful center, whose work has not been recognized or even recorded amidst the trumpets and publicity of the larger relief organizations.

It would be preposterous were one to attempt even to outline the extent and scope of this work initiated and executed under the guiding hand of 'Mike' Tress. One can merely touch on a few highlights, some of the breathtaking historic moments, encounters, and experiences that turned each day and night of our activities in those early years during and after World War II into a kaleidoscope of tireless toil, frustration — and undreamed of success ... The first batches of affidavits procured and shipped out and the first men and women brought over ... the opening of the Refugee Home on the top floor of 616 Bedford Avenue ... 'Mike' himself ordering food, calling friends and business associates for clothes, beds, jobs for the young and older men who came there because they had no place else to go that would give them shelter and help them to build a new future ... 'Mike' buying an old truck to establish a business for some of these young men ... 'Mike' flying to Washington several times a week, back-and-forth, pleading, cajoling, using the most impossible, hopeless ways to open doors ... flying to Washington even on Shabbos at the urging of the *gedolim* who had soon turned to 'Mike' to guide them and help those who turned to them ... the first telephone call to Reb Aharon Kotler in Japan ...Reb Aharon arriving in the U.S.A. ... Frank Newman travelling to Japan at Mike's request to bring the first large contingent of the Mirrer Yeshiva to these shores, and helping to get them settled ... the coming and going of the world's foremost *gaonim, rabbonim, gedolei haTorah* who helped compile lists of those who had to be helped ... *roshei yeshivah* who arrived in this country turning to 'Mike' to help them organize or reorganize their yeshivos in the new land under strange conditions ... Rabbi Elya Meir Bloch, Rabbi Motel Katz Rabbi Reuven Grozovsky, Rabbi Avraham Kalmanowitz, and all the other famous personalities to whom 'Mike' was a constant source of aid and guidance, until they were ready to make their greatness felt in creating a renaissance of Torah and Torah life in this country unexpected even by the most daring visionary ... the Chassidic *rabbe'im* ... the Kapitshenitzer, the Lubavitcher, the Boyanner, the Skwerer Rebbe, and so many others who have since been taken from us, to whom 'Mike' had become a personal friend and advisor ... famous men like Chazzan Kwartin ... the hundreds of ordinary men and women looking for help and advice ... the woman whose husband had been caught in Finland, for whom even the Red Cross had not been able to do anything. 'Mike' sent a cable to the King of Sweden, and today the man lives in Brooklyn with his family ... and thousands of others who may have forgotten what 'Mike' did for them, for their parents, their children ... the *gadol haTorah* who came into an executive meeting to express the gratitude of the Mirrer Yeshiva for the help 'Mike' had given them — this token of appreciation was a first act of duty carried out with tears of joy and appreciation ... an endless parade of men and women who owe so much to one warmhearted, seemingly inexhaustible Jew.

Books could be filled with all that 'Mike' Tress initiated, organized or guided during those early years of frantic rescue work. 'Mike' did not stop there. He grew far beyond all of us and our amateur efforts, as he answered the challenge to ever larger and wider tasks thrust upon him by Divine Providence. He was called upon to work with world rescue and relief organizations on a global basis. He began to travel the continents, and his name and the name of Agudath Israel were respected and beloved far beyond the confines even of his own keen vision. We who had the privilege to accompany him during those first inspired and inspiring years of preparation and building knew that he was and always wanted to remain just a *chaver* among *chaverim*, a Jew who felt the call of the time and the hour of need, whose heart was big enough to feel the pain and sorrow of his fellow brethren, and who sacrificed all he had and could give for them.

When we printed our first letterhead, 'Mike' said: "Let's put on the bottom the slogan: *'Hamekayem nefesh achas beYisroel, k'ilu kiyam olam molei'* (He who saves a single soul, is considered as having saved a whole world). Let it be the *leitmotif* of our rescue work." This 'Mike' did in the fullest sense of the word. He gave all of his strength, and all of his health, and wealth, so that others could live and continue to build a Torah-true Jewish life, to use his favorite words. Only to him they were not words, they were a reality which he helped build and perpetuate, in one of the most glorious phases and chapters of recent Jewish history, written with the blood of his heart and his inspired soul.

In the Footsteps of a Gadol*

*an outstanding
tzaddik and
authority on
halacha of our
time*

Rabbi Yoseif Eliyahu Henkin ל״צז
5655/1891—5733/1973

FOR FORTY successive years, I had an extremely intimate
relationship with Rabbi Henkin. I knew him well. And he was
— as we all knew — a man of singular greatness.

He not only shielded the true measure of his *gadlus* from the
public, but he managed to "hide himself" from his immediate
family and closest acquaintances, as well. Throughout our entire
relationship, I never imagined that this frail human being recited
"*Tikun Chatzos*", in mourning for the *Bais Hamikdash*, every
midnight. In fact, I did not become aware of this fact until after I
had known him for many years, and then only by chance. Night
after night he would sit in his house lamenting over the
desecration of the Torah and the dispersion of *Klal Yisrael*,
sharing the *Shechinah's* grief. But this was only one of the myriad
acts of *tzidkus* he concealed from us all.

Rabbi Henkin carried on his shoulders the plight of literally
tens of thousands of families throughout the world — their daily
well-being was his daily personal concern — yet he never revealed
to a soul who these families were except on the occasion of a
government audit.

* based on a eulogy by the late Rabbi Naftoli Zvi Yehuda Riff

Rabbi Henkin never turned anyone away without a suitable sum of money. In those few instances when the recipient felt that what he received was not sufficient, he did not react as others might: by telling the beneficiary that his case was not the only one, that there are hundreds of others just as needy. Rather, Rabbi Henkin would send the man or woman away with tears, explaining that he understood how great the need was, only wishing there were additional funds to do more.

□ *Rabbi Emanuel Gettinger of the Young Israel of Upper Manhattan recalled: A wizened old man approached me in Tsfas. "Are you from America?" he asked. "I have a father there."*

A father? The man appeared to be over eighty himself! "Yes, a father who takes care of me. His name is Rav Eliyahu Henkin."

His weekly salary as the director of Ezras Torah was $50 — a paltry sum, by any standard. At one of our meetings, a resolution was raised to increase Rabbi Henkin's salary. He immediately rose from his chair and declared: "Must I leave Ezras Torah?"

The less his personal benefit from Ezras Torah, the greater the aid for *talmidei chachamim* in distress.

He was a *baki beShas* (thoroughly knowledgeable in the entire Talmud) — both *Bavli* (Babylonian) and *Yerushalmi*, as well as the four tracts of the *Shulchan Aruch*. Once, in my presence, he received an urgent phone call from *Eretz Yisrael* and he resolved the problem, which apparently defied easy solution to those who called him, relating to marriage laws, without reference to single *sefer*.

Rabbi Henkin could never be found sitting at home without a *sefer* in his hand — often a volume of *Shulchan Aruch*, or the Responsa of the *Chasam Sofer*.

On several occasions I noticed Rabbi Henkin refer to a mysterious small notebook. He once revealed to me that in this notebook he kept a log of those minutes during the day that he did not utilize for Ezras Torah. He was not involved with his own personal business during those minutes, but when someone came to his office at Ezras Torah to discuss *divrei Torah* or if he received a telephone call, as he often would, from anywhere in the world requesting his opinion on a particular problem or *sha'aila*, he immediately looked at the time and noted in his record how many minutes he had borrowed from Ezras Torah. He would then know how many minutes to "make up" on behalf of Ezras Torah-related work.

When Rabbi Henkin was a boy of 15, he traveled to the city of Slutzk hoping to be accepted into the Yeshiva Gedolah of Reb Isser Zalman Meltzer. (One of the *maspidim* noted that he left for Slutzk when he was only fourteen, but he was detained on the way for a year. During that year of delay he reviewed the entire *Masechta Eruvin* forty times!) Upon meeting him for the first time, Reb Isser Zalman asked him why he had come all the way to Slutzk. The youngster replied that he wanted to attend the Yeshiva. To the other *talmidim* standing there this seemed absurd. They were young men already accomplished in their learning, *talmidei chachamim* in their own right, and here was a mere boy of 15 seeking to join their ranks!

Reb Isser Zalman continued: "Tell me, my son, what have you learned?"

"*Masechtos Shabbos* and *Eruvin*."

Astonished that a young boy had learned these difficult tractates, he asked: "Are you prepared for an examination?"

"Yes," the youngster replied, whereupon Reb Isser Zalman questioned the boy on the entire breadth of the two *masechtos*. He answered all challenges with ease, exhibiting an extraordinary knowledge and understanding of every *Rashi* and *Tosefos*. Rav Isser Zalman was flabbergasted: "This child knows these *masechtos* better than I do!" Rabbi Henkin was immediately admitted to the Slutzker Yeshiva.

His superior acumen notwithstanding, Rabbi Henkin possessed great humility as a *talmid* and this characteristic remained with him his entire life. Although his knowledge of Torah spanned all basic Talmudic literature as well as the responsa of the latter day sages (*Acharonim*), Rabbi Henkin always preferred to remain in obscurity.

He was an exceptionally good-hearted and pleasant person, loved by young and old. Yet, when the occasion called for it, Rabbi Henkin asserted his authority.

☐ *He once became aware of a certain dispute and intervened. He reprimanded both parties with sharp words. The mere sight of Rabbi Henkin stepping out of character to intercede immediately put an end to the conflict.*

I remember well the *hesped* given by Rabbi Henkin for the *Chazon Ish*, wherein he resolved a seeming contradiction between a statement in the *Midrash* and a passage in *Masechta Rosh Hashanah*. The *Gemara* compares the passing of *tzaddikim* to the destruction of the *Bais Hamikdash*, while the *Midrash Eichah (Lamentations)* declares that the death of the righteous is an even greater calamity. Rabbi Henkin explained that the *Gemara* in *Rosh Hashanah* alludes to the death of Gedalia ben Achikam whose authority and dominion was accepted by the entire nation — his death was comparable to the destruction of the *Bais HaMikdash*.

The Midrash, on the other hand, refers to the passing of a *tzaddik* whose leadership is not openly manifest, whose authority has not been generally proclaimed by the congregation. This *tzaddik* prefers to remain obscure, closeted with his *sefarim*; yet his influence clearly and unmistakably permeates all rabbinical assemblages and lay gatherings. Although he does not personally appear, his convictions and standards are articulated through the expressions of those he has touched, moving heaven and earth in the process. The loss of such a *tzaddik* is an even greater tragedy than the loss of our Holiest of Holies ...

His words apply equally to himself: He never sat at the dais at conventions or meetings; he never voiced his opinion in public; nor did he even express the worry or apprehension he harbored deep in his heart over the plight of tens of thousands of families throughout the Diaspora. And yet, it was Rabbi Henkin who, from a distance, was the prime mover in many undertakings (such as the establishment of the vast Ezras Torah apartment complex for needy *talmidei chachamim* in *Eretz Yisrael*).

□ *"All my years I thought that Rabbi Henkin would lead our generation to greet Moshiach,"* said Rabbi Yaakov Kaminetzky. *"Now, who will lead us?"*

This past summer, before I left for *Eretz Yisrael*, I went to take leave of Rabbi Henkin. He asked me when I would return to America because there was so much work to be done. Our parting was marked by tears flowing down Rabbi Henkin's cheeks over the misfortune of the families he carried in his heart.

Just as he was an advocate for one and all on this world, may he continue to be a *meilitz yosher* for all of *Klal Yisrael* from his place in *Gan Eden*.

The Seattle Legacy

*a rabbinical
couple and their
imprint on the
Jewish
community of
America's
Northwest*

Rabbi and Mrs. Baruch Shapiro

*I haven't visited my native city of Seattle in many
years — except mentally during occasional moments of
nostalgia. But I have maintained steady contact with doings
there, through travelers and students in Eastern yeshivos,
and I find that much that has transpired there during my
years there and since has left a strong imprint on its other
sons as it has on me — much as the Warsaw experience
marked all of that city's native sons, as Lodz did the Lodzers,
and Tiktin the Tiktiners. The almost total geographic isolation of the Northwest community of 10,000 Jewish souls
certainly made the Seattle experience a definable one — especially in view of some of the outstanding personalities that
were there during those years. For besides being the last stop
on the grand transcontinental tour for many a meshulach
and lecturer (and some settled there either in delight or exhaustion), it was also first touch-down for many who left
Europe through Siberia, and decided not to travel further
East.*

Two who stayed were Rabbi Baruch Shapiro and his Rebbitzen. The Rav was a talmid (disciple) of both Reb Meir Simcha of Dvinsk (who gave him semichah) and the Rogatchover. He had been touring America on behalf of Mizrachi during the first decade of the 20th Century, and stayed on in Seattle to help raise funds for the construction of the impressive Bikur Cholim Synagogue. There he met his Rebbitzen, Hinda Gershonovich, daughter of a family that had settled in Seattle to earn a livelihood by supplying Alaskan gold-miners with victuals. For over half a century, he was few people's rabbi, but everyone's Rav, while she was the Rebbitzen of Seattle.

I. The Rav

Rabbi Shapiro's training in Dvinsk prepared him for the classical role of stodt-rav, but Seattle was no European shtetel. This did not faze him, and his career was typified by his own interpretation of the Chazal: "Royal leadership can only exist with one of who has a kupas shratzim (a chest of creeping things) behind him" — referring, he said, to rabbinical positions abandoned out of principle: He helped build the Bikur Cholim and then left it, allegedly because he refused to take the president's daughter in marriage. A dissident group set up another congregation with the improbable name "Theodore Herzl," which he led; but he left again (Herzl turned Conservative) to lead the newly-founded congregation Machzikei Hadas for the next forty years.

A succession of distinguished rabbis headed the 500 families of the Bikur Cholim in a variety of styles — some frenetic, others phlegmatic; some scholarly, some folksy; occasionally, combinations of all. The community ran the shechitah, built a mikvah, founded a Talmud Torah, a "yeshiva," a Hebrew Day School. Through all the vicissitudes of community life, Rabbi Shapiro seemed to make immersion in Torah study his primary and all encompassing occupation, pausing now and then to comment or goad, instruct or object as the occasion demanded ... When the butchers were not faithful to their schedule of washing the meats, he spoke up to chastise them ... When the Hebrew school's lay committee wanted to experiment with non-traditional approaches to education, or to dismiss an "old-fashioned" but competent staff member, he intervened — and no one dared disagree ... The townspeople were overwhelmingly Mizrachi-affiliated, but when Agudath Israel came to the fore as the organizational arm of leading *gedolei Torah*, he formed an Agudah branch (one could almost say a "cell") in his Machzikei Hadas. ... His *Chevrah Shas* that met regularly to study *Gemara* was a delight to novices for his clarity of exposition, and to seasoned *lomdim* for the sprinkling of depth-charging probes he would drop ... Rabbi Shapiro taught *Gemara* privately to select boys of high school age, and instructed them to continue their yeshiva studies in the East.

One of the first to leave on his direction was my oldest brother. Rabbi Shapiro announced the time of his departure from the *bimah* on his last Shabbos in town, urging the congregants to be at the rairoad station to send off their delegate to the Torah center in the East. Several *minyanim* of people were in Seattle's Union Station that next evening ... Whenever yeshiva students returned home for vacation, they were invited to address the congregation on Shabbos. There we were, fourteen-year olds and twenty-year olds, reporting to our friends and elders on our experiences and changing philosophies ... Not surprisingly, some yeshiva students who had returned to Seattle had standards of conduct and halachic practice that went beyond the limits set by Rabbi Shapiro in his "extremism," but he seemed to accept this with an unspoken approval.

He wrote the *gittin* (documents of divorce); all the complicated halachah problems came to his desk; and he, in turn, was in correspondence with Rabbi Chaim Ozer Grodzensky, and with his close colleague, Rabbi Eliezer Silver... "Shapiro's Shul" may not have appeared to be stage-center in Seattle, but in many ways it was.

Neighborhoods shifted in Seattle, as elsewhere, and while for many years scores of Jews would walk several miles over the famed hills of the city to their cherished Bikur Cholim, eventually the new neighborhood of the 60's was too far away for the long trek. The Bikur Cholims (there are two — the Ashkenazic and the sizable Sephardic congregations) relocated in another area. Machzikei Hadas hesitated, and finally dissolved. The Rebbitzen had long passed away, but Rabbi Shapiro, a neatly tailored figure, gray beard closely cropped, walking-stick in hand, was a familiar sight as he made his way to the nearest *shul* in the new neighborhood.

When he passed away, Seattleites felt that the Age of Rabbi Shapiro, for a while in twilight, had come to an end. But it had not. Rabbi Shapiro left a will, written in Yiddish in 1962, that reminded his *landsleit* that he was not forgetting them, and that they would not easily forget him and what he had stood for.

In addition to a bequest of several hundreds to local institutions, Rabbi Shapiro left sizable sums to surviving relatives, and charitable institutions, as well as:

☐ *$1,000 each to the following: Agudas Harabanim, Agudath Israel of America, Mesivta Torah Vodaath, the Lubavitcher Yeshiva, The Satmar Yeshiva, Hagaon Rabbi Moshe Feinstein's Yeshiva, and Rabbi Aharon Kotler's Yeshiva.*

☐ *$1,000 each to: Chinuch Atzmai, Batei Avos in Bnei Brak*

— reflecting a very individual understanding as to what will perpetuate Jewry.

More fascinating, and more revealing, was point 11 in his will:

☐ *Whatever remains from my estate after burial expenses etc., I leave to the local congregation ... in Seattle, for the purpose that it engage as* Rav *a gadol (an eminent Torah authority) of* Shas-and-Poskim *type, contingent upon the approval of three* gaonim: *Rabbi Eliezer Silver, Rabbi Aharon Kotler, and Rabbi Moshe Feinstein. According to the shul's current income, it could not afford an adequate salary to pay a qualified individual; thus up to 50% of the salary could be drawn from the remaining funds of my estate. The* rav *who succeeds me will find better circumstances than I encountered ... The impact of his tenure will not only be for the betterment of the shul he serves, but other parts of the community would also profit. They will come to understand that as vital as it is to have English-speaking rabbis, and as effective as they may be, it is even more essential to have a* rav *who is a gadol of* Shas-and-Poskim *type. Not only for the enhancement of K'vod haTorah (the prestige of Torah) — which is as essential for Yiddishkeit as is air to one's breath — but also for rendering authoritative halachic decisions on the many complicated queries that arise here in this country with even more frequency than in the old country.*

The community embarked on its search for a *rav* to satisfy his stipulations, and engaged a graduate of American yeshivos who shares Rabbi Shapiro's general communal aspirations and personal goals. The major beneficiary of Rabbi Shapiro's will was to be the Congregation Bikur Cholim, from which he had broken away in his youth, returned to in his old age, and did not really leave after his death.

II. The Rebbitzen

PEOPLE described her as a typical Rebbitzen — neatly combed *sheitel*, modestly styled clothes, full of good wishes and *Baruch Hashem*s. I remember her more as a typical mother.

They had no children of their own. According to the story that was commonly accepted in town, Rabbi Shapiro had asked his wife after several childless years of marriage if she would want a release from their marriage. "No," was the purported reply. "I don't need children, you will be my child." She devoted herself to fully freeing him from any and all outside distractions and disturbances, giving him opportunity for maximum involvement in Torah. She arranged their house with his study in a front room walled in by windows on three sides. "If anyone wants to come in to waste his time," she explained, "they should first realize how busy he is and then maybe not disturb him." ... After her passing, the Rabbi was often seen pushing a shopping cart in the aisles of a local supermarket. He preferred not to ask anyone else to help him on personal matters. But during the forty-plus years until then, one can hardly recall seeing him at a non-rabbinical function.

In a sense, the Rebbitzen was mother to the larger Jewish community. If something was amiss, she did not hesitate to pick up her famous telephone to inquire after general welfare, and then get to specifics. These "telephone calls from the Rebbitzen" were well known, and frequently touched my close circle of friends, and we viewed her as a "mother" to a steadily growing group.

An older brother of mine had already joined the Rebbitzen's *Shabbos* afternoon study group, and I could hardly wait for a junior class to start. When I was eight, she did form a new circle of four or five boys of my age ... During the summer, we would sit around her old oak dining table, sip lemonade, and recite and discuss *Pirkei Avos* ["Ethics of the Fathers"] from *Siddurim* with

English translation. During the rest of the year, we would learn seemingly random selections from *Rashi's* commentary on *Chumash*, actually selected by her for their moral message — I still hear Bernard shrilly declaiming: "*Af anu yodeem shebamidbar haya* — we always *knew* that Moshe was in the desert ... But to tell us praise for Yisro, who was sitting at the height of the world and left it all to be closer to Hashem."

☐ *During August, when we were on vacation from summer sessions in Hebrew School, we'd report to her house for Shacharis at 9 in the morning, to pick cherries from her trees ... to learn* Chumash *and* Rashi.

The printed text was more than adequate. But her personal comments often hit with greater impact. After reading that "the world is but an anteroom ... ," the Rebbitzen added, "Mr. Ginzberg — you know, the furniture man — once sent his helpers to measure our house for carpets. I chased them out. — Who needs it? Another time he tried to deliver a truck loaded with a brand new dining room set. Look, kinderlach, at this one. Is anything wrong with it?"

Jerry smiled, "It's not exactly Better Homes and Gardens.*"*

"Feh!" she said, wrinkling her nose. " 'Va'avadtem eitz va'aven - and you will worship wood and stone!' There's nothing wrong with this set; one shouldn't make idols out of furniture!"

☐ *On another occasion she told how yet another person had offered the Rav a large sum for no reason other than admiration. "Gelt iz begimatriya blotte (the numerical value of 'money' is equal to 'slime') Ver darf es? (Who needs it?)"*

We believed her — for her scornful smile, for her kindly eyes, and for her reputation. She had told the Rav during their courtship that she thought a diamond engagement ring a waste of money. The Rav bought her one anyway so she sold it and sent the money to his impoverished sister in Russia.

☐ *She had a different approach with each boy, but the common denominator was a lavishing of praise and love. To one, she constantly said: "I always tell your mother how lucky she is; you're the best boy in all Seattle." — Usually followed by, "So how could you think of doing ... ?" With this policy, she talked him and his anxious mother into turning* down a scholarship to a co-ed Jewish summer camp in Canada.

☐ Nachum was president of a youth group, led by Dovid P., a Jewish soldier from New York City stationed nearby. She asked Nachum how he could expect to get inspiration from Dovid, when he isn't even religious. "But he knows so much about the Jewish people and about Eretz Yisrael," Nachum protested. "I'm sure he's as religious as he can be in the army!"

"Does he put on tefillin?" she asked
"I'm sure he does!"
"If he doesn't — "
"Then I agree. — But he does, I'm positive."
"Well," she said quietly, "I asked him ... He's a very fine boy. He dropped his eyes in shame when I asked him about tefillin, and he told me the truth. The answer was 'no'. — He is a fine boy, yes. But you need a better inspiration."

☐ When the Sefer Torah was taken out for reading on Shabbos, some of the boys used to kiss the Torah and run out to play. The Rebbitzen once admonished, "When we open the aron we say: Veyanusu mesanecha — When the ark travels, Your enemies will run away, — Hashem's enemies, not boys like you." That was the end of Kriyas HaTorah recess.

☐ Holding the Torah scroll after reading was a privilege. Once Bert seized the privilege, but found it a weighty one — that day, the Rav delivered an unusually long drashah before it was returned to the ark. She later told Bert, "You know how I always listen closely when the Rav speaks. But today I couldn't take my eyes off you. You held the Torah with so much love, like someone holds a baby." Bert seemed to see himself as some kind of royal bearer of the scroll since then, and we had trouble wresting our turns from him.

☐ When I neared Bar Mitzvah, I dropped my membership in the Rebbitzen's Shabbos afternoon sessions, and younger boys stepped in. (Strange as it seems, none of us had sisters in that age group, so there were no comparable girls' sessions.) But her influence did not end. She convinced me to join the shul's daily 6:45 Shacharis minyan, and — to accommodate my schedule — she would bring me a hot breakfast.

*(She once told me, "The walk to shul is exactly 'MaTovu'
until 'Rabbi Yishmael,' " referring to the prayers she recited
as she accompanied her husband on the morning trek to
shul.)*

☐ *When one of the boys would read the Torah, she never
failed to tell us how immensely she enjoyed it. Once Bert
read parts of* Eichah *for practice. "I could feel all of Yir-
miyahu's sorrow," she said, "in the way you read three
words: 'Bacho sivke balayla — you will cry in the night.' "
And she had him repeat the phrase several times, while she
shut her eyes in tearful concentration.*

☐ *She took sick several weeks before I left for a yeshiva in
the East. My Gemara rebbe used to poke gentle fun at the
way adolescent boys revered "the Rebbitzen." After he
visited her in the hospital, he also confessed to an awe over
her mastery of* Tanach. *("My husband refuses to teach me
Gemara. He tells me there is still enough for me in Tanach,
and he must be right.")*

When we heard of her passing several months later, we
thought that Seattle would never be the same. That was not exactly so. Those who had known her would *always* feel her influence
... It was those who didn't know her who would really miss her.

Glossary

ACHRONIM
Torah scholars of the last 500 years (approx.)

ADMOR (ADMORIM)
title given Chassidic *rebbes;* acronym of the Hebrew for, "our master, our teacher, our rabbi"

AFIKOMEN
last piece of matzoh eaten at the conclusion of the Passover seder meal

AGGADAH (AGGADOS)
sections of the Talmud not directly relating to halachah

AHAVAS CHESSED
lit., love of kindness; selfless generosity

AHAVAS YISRAEL
love for one's fellow Jews

AISHES CHAYIL
lit., an accomplished woman; opening words of Proverbs 31:10-31, recited Friday evening before *Kiddush*

AKEIDAH
binding of Isaac

ALEPH-BAIS
the Hebrew alphabet, named for the two first letters א and ב

ALIYAH (ALIYOS)
lit., ascending; 1. call to ascend the bimah to read from the Torah; 2. emigration to *Eretz Yisrael*

ALTER
(Yid.) aged one; a title of respect

AMORA (AMORAIM)
sage of the *Gemara* era (approx. 1500-1700 years ago)

AMUD
lectern; especially cantor's lectern

ANI MAAMIN
lit. I believe; thirteen articles of faith recited by some individuals after the daily morning service

APIKORSIM
non-believers; atheists

ARBA'AH MINIM
four species: esrog, lulav, myrtle and willow, used in the Succos service

AREI HAKODESH (sing. IR HAKODESH)
holy cities

ARON
1. *aron hakodesh* 2. coffin

ARON HAKODESH
lit., holy ark; the ark containing the Torah scrolls; also called *aron*

ASERES YEMEI TESHUVAH
lit., ten days of penitence; from Rosh HaShanah until Yom Kippur

ASHAM TALUY
a sacrifice brought in the Holy Temple by one who has reason to suspect that he may have sinned inadvertently but cannot be sure

ASKINU SEUDASA
lit. prepare the east; a hymn, written in Aramaic, heavy with Kabbalistic overtones, sung at each Sabbath meal

AVODAH or AVODAS HASHEM
service of G-d, especially through prayer, charitable acts, kindness, Torah study, etc.

BA'AL
lit. master; used as an author's title relative to his works

BA'AL HABAYIS (BA'ALEI BATIM)
layman

BAAL MOFES
miracle worker

BA'AL MUSSAR (BA'ALEI MUSSAR)
ethical master

BA'AL TESHUVAH (BA'ALEI TESHU-VAH)
penitent; one who has either strayed from Orthodoxy and returned or has not been raised according to Orthodox tradition but has found his way back to the time-honored path

BACHUR (BACHURIM)
post-adolescent unmarried man; especially, *yeshivah bachur,* student of a yeshivah

BAIS DIN (BATEI DIN)
court of Torah law

BAIS HAMIDRASH (BATEI MIDRASH)
study hall; especially a synagogue used for both prayers and study

BAIS HAMIKDASH
the Holy Temple

BAKI BESHAS
one thoroughly versed in the entire Talmud

BAMAH
private sacrificial altar

BARUCH HASHEM
lit., G-d be Blessed; a common expression of thanks to the Creator for any bit of good fortune one may enjoy

BE'CHAVRUSA
with a study partner

BEFARHESYA
in public

BEGLAIT
(Yid.) escort

BEKI'US
far-flung knowledge

BENTCH
(Yid.) to bless; especially to recite Grace After Meals (*bentchen*)

BEN TORAH (B'NEI TORAH)
lit. son of Torah; one who strives to follow the Torah in all its detail, consequently spending much time in study, and putting his lessons into practice

BEREISHIS
the first book of the Torah, so called because its first word is *bereishis*, "in the beginning"

BIALYSTOKER KUCHNS
(Yid.) Bialystoker cookies; a nickname for the inhabitants of Bialystok, home of the chewy rolls popularly called "bialys"

BIKUR CHOLIM
visiting the sick

BIMAH
platform in center of synagogue where Torah is read; also used for communal announcements after or during a pause in the synagogue service

BIRCAS HAMAZON
Grace After Meals

BIRCAS KOHANIM
the blessing given the nation by the *Kohanim*

B'NEI YESHIVA
yeshiva students

B'NEI YISRAEL
the Children of Israel; Jewry

BOBBE
(Yid.) Grandmother

BOKER TOV
"Good morning!"

BORCHU
prayer recited at morning and evening services and at public Torah readings; may be said only in the presence of a *minyan*

CHACHAM (CHACHAMIM)
wise man; in Sefardic circles the equivalent of "Rabbi"

CHACHAMAH
wise woman

CHALITZAH
the legal act which unbinds a *yevamah* from undergoing levirate marriage

CHARIF
lit., sharp; brilliant

CHASSAN
bridegroom

CHASSIDISHE YID
(Yid.) Chassidic Jew

CHASSIDUS
chassidism

CHAS VECHOLILAH
"G-d forbid!"

CHAS VESHALOM
"G-d forbid!"

CHAVER (CHAVERIM)
companions; comrades; fellow travelers

CHAZAL
Talmudic sages; a statement by the sages

CHEREM
excommunication; banishment

CHESHBON (CHESBONOS)
calculation

CHESSED
deeds of kindness

CHEVRAH (CHEVROS)
society

CHEVRA KADISHA
lit., Holy Society; group organized to carry out the religious needs of a community, especially, care of the dead

CHEVRAH SHAS
a group organized for study of the Talmud

CHIDDUSHIM or CHIDDUSHEI TORAH
novellae; new insights in Torah intrepretation

CHILUL SHABBOS
desecration of the Sabbath

CHINUCH
education

CHITZONIUS
exterior; outward appearance, as opposed to *p'nimius*, inner character

CHOK
popular name for *Chok L'Yisrael*, an anthology of *Chumash*, Prophets, Holy Writings, *Mishnah*, *Talmud*, *Zohar*, *Gemara*, *mussar* and *halachah*, divided into daily portions to be studied throughout the year

CHOLAS AHAVAH
lit., lovesickness; especially, yearning for nearness to G-d (*Song of Songs* 2:5 and 5:8)

CHOL HAMOED PESACH
the Intermediate Days of Passover

CHUMASH
set of the five books of the Torah; any of the five books

CHUPAH
bridal canopy; the marriage ceremony

CHURBAN
destruction; especially *Churban Bayis*, destruction of the Holy Temple; and *Churban Europa*, the devastation caused by the Nazis ש״ימ

CHUTZ L'ARETZ
lit., outside the land; any place outside the Land of Israel

CHUTZPAH
audacity

DAF YOMI
a Talmudic study regimen in which one folio of the Talmud is studied each day, the entire Talmud being completed in about seven and a half years

DATCHA
(Russ.) summer vacation house; by extension, summer vacation

DAVEN
(Yid.) pray

DAYAN (DAYANIM)
judge

DERECH HALIMUD
method of study; approach to education

DIN TORAH
case brought to *bais din* for adjudicaton according to Torah law

DRASHAH
learned discourse

DVAIKUS
cleaving to G-d

DVAR TORAH
a Torah thought

EINIKEL (EINIKLACH)
(Yid.) grandchild

EISAV
Esau

EMES
absolute truth

ERETZ HAKODESH
the Holy Land

ERETZ YISRAEL
the Land of Israel

EREV
eve

ERUV
lit. combination; a Rabbinically prescribed legal fiction which has various forms, used to evade certain Rabbinically ordained Sabbath restrictions by extending their parameters

FRUM
(Yid.) religious

FRUMKEIT
(Yid.) religiosity

GABBAI (GABBOIM)
1. beadle; 2. synagogue officer; 3. overseer of charity funds

GADLUS
greatness; especially Torah greatness

GADOL (GEDOLIM)
lit. great one; used in reference to outstanding Torah scholars (see *gadol baTorah*)

GADOL BATORAH (GEDOLEI TORAH)
an outstanding Torah scholar

GADOL HADOR
the greatest Torah scholar of his generation

GALUS
exile; Diaspora

GAN EDEN
Garden of Eden

GAON (GAONIM)
lit. brilliant one; a title given Torah scholars of the post-Talmudic period; also used of anyone possessive of a brilliant mind dedicated to Torah study

GARTEL
(Yid.) sash or belt worn by some men, especially *Chassidim*, during prayer or other religious service

GAZZE
(Yid.) kerosene

GEHINNOM
Hell

GEMARA
1. section of Talmud which elucidates the Mishnah; 2. a Talmudic tome

GEMATRIA (GEMATRIOS or GEMAT-RIOT)
numerical equivalencies of the Hebrew alphabet

GEMILAS CHESSED
act of kindness

GET (GITTIN)
divorce document; divorce in general

GROBBE KOP
(Yid.) thick head; stupid

GUTTEN SHABBOS
(Yid.) "A good Sabbath!"

G'ZEILAH
robbery

HADASSIM
myrtle branches

HAFTARAH
portion of Prophets read at the completion of the public Torah reading on the Sabbath and festivals

HALACHAH
Torah law

HAMECHUNEH
alias; also known as

HARBOTZAS HATORAH
spreading of Torah ideals and study

HASHEM
lit. The Name; a respectful reference to G-d and His Ineffable Name

HASHGACHAH (HASHGACHOS)
1. supervision; especially, *hashgachah peratis*, Divine supervision and intervention in the affairs of the individual; 2. *kashrus* supervision

HASHKAFAH
outlook; philosophical view of life

HASKAMOS
letters of approbation, usually printed at the beginning of books

HASMADAH
diligence

HECHSHER (HECHSHEIRIM)
certification of *kashrus*

HEFKER
ownerless

HEIVN
(Yid.) yeast

HEKDESH
shelter for the indigent, elderly, and incurable

HESPED
eulogy

HOSHANA (HOSHANOS)
special prayers for salvation recited during the Succos festival

HOSHANA RABBAH
last day of Succos, so called because of the many *hoshana* prayers recited that day

IKVESA D'MESHICHA
lit., footsteps of the Messiah; the period immediately preceding the advent of *Moshiach*

IR HANIDACHAS
city led astray; city led to idolatry by some of its own citizens (*Deuteronomy* 13:13-19)

KADDISH
prayer of praise to G-d, recited by mourners, and on the anniversary of one's parent's death, among other times

KAH RIBBON OLAM
lit., G-d, Master of the world; name of a Friday night hymn

KALLAH
bride

KAL V'CHOMER
lit., weak and strong; an *a fortiori* argument

KAMEYAH (KAMEYOS)
scrolls containing mystical inscriptions usually written by Kabbalistic masters for various curative or preventive purposes

KANO'US
zeal

KAPOTA
(Yid.) frockcoat

KASHRUS
kosherness

KAVANAH
intent; concentration; purpose

KAVOD
respect; honor

KEDOSHIM
lit., holy ones; a title given to those who died for their religion, especially by the hands of the Nazis ימ״ש

KEDUSHAH
1. holiness 2. a prayer recited during the repetition of the *Amidah*; may be said only in the presence of a *minyan*

KEHILLAH (KEHILLOS)
organized community

KEHUNAH
priesthood

KIBBUTZ
gathering; especially close circle of disciples

KIBUD AV V'EIM
honor of father and mother

KIDDUSH
1. sanctification blessing recited over a cup of wine at the onset of the Sabbath or a festival; 2. festive collation served to mark a happy event

KIDDUSH HASHEM
santification of G-d's Holy Name; martyrdom

KINDERHEIM
(Yid.) children's home

KINDERLACH
(Yid.) little children

KIPOT S'RUGOT
crocheted skull caps; used to describe the modern, yet Orthodox, Zionist oriented youth who are given to wearing them

KLAL
community

KLAL YISRAEL
the community of Israel, i.e., all of Jewry

K'LAYIM
forbidden mixtures

KLEI KODESH
lit., holy vessels; religious functionaries

KOHEN (KOHANIM)
one descended from the male line of the priestly family of Aaron

KOLLEL (KOLLELIM)
post graduate yeshiva, usually with a student body of young married men supported by scholarships and stipends granted by the *kollel*

KOL MEKADEISH
lit., whoever hallows; name of Friday evening hymn

KOLNER PEKLACH
(Yid.) a nickname for inhabitants of Koln

KORBAN (KORBANOS)
sacrifice; Temple offering

KOSEL MA'ARAVI
lit., Western Wall; the last remaining wall of the Temple Courtyard in Jerusalem; popularly called "The *Kotel*"

KOVEYA ITTIM
set aside time; especially for Torah study

KRECHTZ
(Yid.) sigh of yearning

KRIYAS HATORAH
public Torah reading

KRIYAH
tearing one's garments in mourning

KSAV RABBANUS
lit., document of Rabbinate; credentials of a chief rabbi

KUSHYA (KUSHYOS)
question

KVITTEL
(Yid.) note; especially one handed to a *tzaddik* requesting his blessing or his intercession in Heaven for the benefit of the sick, poor, or otherwise troubled

KVIUS
set time of Torah study

LANDSLEIT or LANDSMAN
(Yid.) fellow townsman

LAMDAN (LAMDANIM)
Torah scholar

LASHON HARA
evil talk, i.e., slander, gossip, etc.

LECHAYIM
lit., "To life!"; traditional toast over a glass of spirits

LESHALOM
in peace

LEVUSH
raiment

LICHT
(Yid.) lights; especially the Sabbath candles

LIMUDEI KODESH
sacred studies, as opposed to *limudei chol*, secular studies

LOMDIM
scholars

LOMDUS
Torah scholarship

LOMZER BALONIM
(Pol.) Lomza's shoppers; a nickname for the inhabitants of Lomza who were reputed to be willing to buy anything offered

LUCHOS
tablets; especially the twin tablets upon which the Ten Commandments were inscribed

LULAV (LULAVIM)
palm branch; one of the four species used in the Succos service

MA'AMAD HAR SINAI
lit., the station at Mount Sinai; the receiving of the Torah

MAARIV
west; back wall of a synagogue; evening prayer

MA'ASE SATTAN
work of Satan

MA'ASER
tithe

MACHMIR
one taking a stringent approach in halachic matters

MACHZOR (MACHZORIM)
prayer books; especially for the festivals

MAGID
preacher; especially the officially recognized preacher of a city

MALKOS
flogging

MAMZER (MAMZEIRIM)
offspring of an illicit union

MA'OS CHITTIM
lit., money for wheat; charity given expressly to offset the expenses of matzoh and other Passover necessities

MARROR
bitter herbs eaten at the Passover Seder

MASECHTA or MASECHES (MESECHTOS)
Talmudic tractate

MASHGIACH (MASHGICHIM)
1. dean of students in a yeshiva who acts as guide and advisor; 2. *kashrus* supervisor

MASKILLIM
lit., enlightened ones; followers of Reform Judaism

MASMICHIM
rabbis who ordain others

MASPID (MASPIDIM)
eulogizer

MATZEIVAH
tombstone

MAZEL
good fortune

MAZEL TOV
"Good-luck!"

MA ZOS
lit., What is this?; a euphemism for a simple person, based on the simple son's question in the *Passover Haggadah*

M'DANAY ASA
myrtle; mentioned in Friday evening *zemiros*

MECHALEL SHABBOS
desecrator of the Sabbath

MEDINAS YISRAEL
State of Israel

MEFORSHIM
commentaries

MEILITZ YOSHER
advocate; especially, a departed *tzaddik* who intecedes in heaven on Israel's behalf

MENUCHAH VESIMCHAH
lit., contentment and gladness; name of a Friday evening hymn

MESHULACH
lit., messenger; itinerant collector for a charitable institution

MESIRAS NEFESH
self-sacrifice; especially in refusal to renounce a principle of religious faith; devotion to a cause beyond the call of duty

MESIVTA (MESIVTOS)
intermediate Torah school, equivalent to high school

MIDOS
character traits

MIFLAGOT
political parties

MIKVAH
ritual bath

MILAH
circumcision

MINHAG
custom

MIN HASHAMAYIM
of Divine origin

MINYAN (MINYANIM)
quorum of ten adult males needed in the performance of certain religious practices; also used as a unit of counting people in general

MI SHEBEIRACH
lit., the One who blessed; the traditional prayer for the sick which begins, "May the One Who blessed the Patriarchs Abraham, Isaac, Jacob, Moses, Aaron, David and Solomon, also bless and heal the sick person ... "

MISHMAR
lit., watch; an all night Torah study session, usually Thursday nights

MISNAGED
opponent of *Chassidus*

MISNAGDISH
opposing *Chassidus*

MISPALLEL (MISPALLELIM)
v. prays; n. one who prays

MITZVAH
1. a commandment of the Torah; 2. any good or exemplary act

MIZRACH
east; front wall of the synagogue housing the *aron hakodesh*

MOFES (MOFSIM)
miracle

MOHEL
circumcizer

MOREH DE'ASRA
chief rabbi of a community

MOREINU
lit., our teacher; title bestowed upon Moreinu Yaakov Rosenheim

MOSHE RABBEINU
our teacher Moses

MOSHIACH
the Messiah

MU'AD
a animal which has been known to inflict damage on three separate occasions; the owner must guard this animal more carefully

MUSMACH
ordained rabbi

MUSSAR
ethical instruction

MUZINIK'L
(Pol.) youngest child in a family

NASSI
president

NAZIR
one who has taken nazirite vows, i.e., not to consume any products of the grape vine, not to cut his hair, not to become contaminated by the contact with a dead body(*Numbers* 6:1-21)

NE'ILAH
final, additional prayer of Yom Kippur

NESHAMAH (NESHAMOS)
spirit; soul

NETUREI KARTA
lit., Guardians of the City; followers of the Satmar Rebbe's views on the State of Israel

NIGGUN
song; tune

NUSACH
1. liturgy; 2. mode of prayer

OHEIV
lover; especially one who loves G-d and his fellow Jew

OLAH
a burnt offering completely consumed by the altar fire in the Temple Courtyard

OLAM
lit., world; a large assemblage of people

OLAM HABA
World-to-Come; the reward awaiting the righteous as the fruits of their labors in *Olam Hazeh*, this world

OLAM HAZEH
this world, as opposed to *Olam Haba*, the World-to-Come; often used as a metaphor for material assets

OMEIN
Amen

OMER
49 day period, beginning the second day of Passover ending the day before Shavuos; each night during this period a special blessing is pronounced followed by the count of that day, e.g., "Today is the 20th day, making two weeks and six days of the Omer."

ONAN
a bereaved relative prior to the deceased's burial

PANIE
(Pol.) sir

PARNASAH
sustenance; income

PARNES (PARNEISIM)
lit., supporter; community head

PARSHAH
Torah portion

PARTAYEN
(Yid.) political parties

PASUK
verse of Scripture

PAYOS
sidelocks

PIDYON (PIDYONIM) or PIDYON GELT
lit., redemption (money); given to a *tzaddik* for charitable distribution, usually accompanying a *kvittel*

PIKE'ACH
wise man

PINKES
record book; ledger

PINTELE YID
(Yid.) lit., point of the ׳, the smallest letter in the Hebrew alphabet; the tiny spark of *Yiddishkeit* lying dormant within every Jewish soul no matter how alienated from his people

PIYUTIM or PIZMONIM
liturgical poems

P'NIMIUS
interior; inner character, as opposed to *chitzonius*, outward appearance

POILISHE YIDDEN
(Yid.) Polish Jews

POLUSH
(Yid.) entrance hall

PORETZ (PRITZIM)
(Yid.) land owner

POSEK (POSKIM)
halachic authority

POSEK ACHARON
final authority; last word

P'SAK (P'SAKIM)
halachic decision

PSAK-GELT
(Yid.) legal fee

RABBANUS
rabbinate

RABBEINU
our teacher; a title given to Moses

RASHBA
acronym of *Rabbi Shmuel ben Aderes*; a *Rishon*

RAV (RABBANIM)
Rabbi

R'CHILUS
gossip

REB
sir; mister; a title of respect

REBBE (RABBEIM)
rabbi; especially, a Torah teacher, or a Chassidic leader

REBBITZEN
(Yid.) wife of a Rabbi

REDEN IN LERNEN
(Yid.) lit., speaking in learning; discussing Talmudic subjects

RIBBIS
interest; usury

RIBBON HA'OLAMIM
Master of the World; a prayer recited Friday evening, following *Shalom Aleichem*

RIBONO SHEL OLAM
Master of the Universe

RISHONIM
Torah scholars of about 500-1000 years ago

ROSH BAIS DIN
head of a rabbinical court

ROSH CHODESH
lit. the new moon; the first day of each month, celebrated as a quasi-festival

ROSH HAKAHAL
community president

ROSH YESHIVA (ROSHEI YESHIVA)
dean of a Torah academy

RUACH HAKODESH
lit., Holy Spirit; Divine knowledge which falls just short of prophecy

SEFER (SEFARIM)
book

SEFER TORAH (SIFREI TORAH)
Torah scroll

SEMICHAH
ordination into the Rabbinate

SEUDAH
meal

SEVARA
rationale

SHA'AILAH (SHA'ALOS)
halachic queries

SHABBOS (SHABBOSOS)
the Sabbath

SHABBOS HAGADOL
lit. The Great Sabbath; the Sabbath preceding the Passover festival; usually marked by a scholarly lecture-sermon, of long duration, pertaining to the laws of Passover

SHABBOS HAMALKAH
the Sabbath Queen

SHABBOS NACHAMU
lit., Sabbath of Assuagement; the Sabbath following the ninth of Av, named for the first word of the *haftarah* reading of the day

SHABBOS TESHUVAH
lit., Sabbath of Repentance; the Sabbath falling between Rosh HaShanah and Yom Kippur; usually marked by a scholarly lecture-sermon of long duration on the theme of repentance

SHACH
abbreviation for *Sifsei Kohen*, by Rabbi Shabsi Kohen, a halachist who wrote a large commentary to the *Shulchan Aruch*

SHACHARIS
morning prayers

SHALOM ALEICHEM
1. "G-d be with you!"; traditional greeting 2. hymn sung Friday night upon greeting arriving home from the synagogue

SHALOSH REGOLIM
the three pilgrimage festivals: Passover, Shavuos, Succos

SHALOSH SEUDOS
lit., three meals; the third Sabbath meal, usually begun just before sunset and lasting until nightfall or later

SHAMASH or SHAMMOS
synagogue caretaker; rabbi's assistant

SHARFE
(Yid.) sharp

SHAS
the Talmud

SHAS-AND-POSKIM
lit., Talmud and halachic authorities; in-depth study of the Talmud with its ramifications in modern society

SHECHINAH
manifestation of the Divine Presence

SHECHITAH
slaughter of animals according to Torah law

SHE'EILOS NASHIM
halachic inquiries regarding the menses, the term of pregnancy and the post-partum period

SHEIM HASHEM
Tetragrammaton

SHEITEL
(Yid.) wig

SHIRAYIM
lit., leftovers; morsels of food from a tzaddik's plate, usually eaten by the Chassidim

SHITAH (SHITOS)
approach to and method of determining halachic decisions

SHIUR
lit., lesson; a Torah lecture

SHIYUR
measure

SHLIACH
messenger; emissary; proxy; often a great sage sent by the community in Eretz Yisrael to raise funds in the Diaspora

SHLIACH TZIBBUR
lit., messenger of the congregation; prayer leader; cantor

SHLICHUS
assigned mission of the shliach

SHMAD
apostasy

SHMIRAS HALASHON
lit., guarding the tongue; restraining oneself from gossip, falsehood, slander, etc.

SHMIRAS SHABBOS
Sabbath observance

SHMITTAH
the Sabbatical year; each seventh year the earth in Israel must not be worked (Leviticus 25:1-7)

SHOCHTIM
slaughterers of animals, following Torah law

SHTENDER
(Yid.) lectern; used during study in lieu of a desk

SHTETEL
(Yid.) village, as opposed to a large city

SHTIEBEL (SHTIEBLACH)
(Yid.) lit. small room; small local synagogue

SHTREIMEL
(Yid.) fur hat worn by Chassidim on the Sabbath and festivals

SHTUB
(Yid.) room

SHULCHAN ARUCH
compilation of practical Torah law

SHUTFIM
partners

SICHAS CHULIN
ordinary conversation, as opposed to divrei Torah, talk about Torah

SIDDUR
prayer book

SIMCHAH B'LEV NISHBAR
rejoicing with a broken heart

SLICHOS
penitential prayers recited before and during the Yomim Noraim and on fast days

STODT-RAV
(Yid.) village rabbi

SUGYOS
topics; especially topics discussed in the Talmud

TAHARAH (TAHAROS)
lit., purities; by extension, the cleansing of the deceased and their preparation for burial

TAKANAH (TAKANOS)
ordinance

TALLIS GADOL
a large tallis, fringed shawl, usually worn draped over one's outer garments while praying, as opposed to a tallis katan, small fringed shawl worn beneath one's outer garments the entire day

TALMID (TALMIDIM)
1. disciple; 2. student

TALMID CHACHAM (TALMIDEI CHA-CHOMIM)
Torah scholar

TALMID MUVHAK
a disciple who is extraordinarily close to the master from whom he received the greater part of his knowledge

TANACH
Scripture

TANNA (TANNAIM)
Sage of the Mishnah

TAYNES
complaints

TCHEPPEN
(Yid.) teasing

T'CHIAS HAMEISIM
resurrection

TEFILLAH (TEFILLOS)
prayer

TEFILLIN
phylacteries

TEHILLIM
Psalms

TEKIAS KAF
a formal agreement sealed by a hand shake

TEKUFAH (TEKUFOS)
period; era

TESHUVAH (TESHUVOS)
1. responsum; 2. repentance

TIKTINER YACHSONIM
(Yid.) Tiktin's aristocrats; a nickname for the inhabitants of Tiktin who considered themselves a cut above the masses

TIKUN CHATZOS or CHATZOT
midnight prayers for a rebuilt Temple

TISCH (TISCHEN)
(Yid.) lit. table; a Chassidic gathering around their Rebbe's festival or Sabbath table during which the Rebbe usually leads his disciples in songs of praise to G-d, expounds on the Torah, and distributes *shirayim*

TIRUTZIM
answers

TOCHACHAH
admonishment

TORAS EMES
truthful Torah; Torah as given on Sinai

TREGERS
(Yid.) porters, stevedores

TREIFAH
non-kosher

TREIFAH MEDINAH
lit., unkosher state; irreligious place; a nickname for America before the post World-War II mass immigration of Orthodox Jews

TSEMACH
sprout

TZADDEIKES
feminine form for *tzaddik*

TZADDIK (TZADDIKIM)
lit., righteous one; used of Chassidic *rebbes* and other extremely pious and caring people

TZADDIKEI-EMES
true *tzaddikim*

TZADDIK NISTAR
hidden *tzaddik*; a righteous one whose modesty and humility mask his righteousness so that his virtuous deeds are performed anonymously and without a trace of fanfare

TZAROS
troubles

TZEDDAKAH
charity

TZETLACH
(Yid.) notes

TZIBBUR
congregation; multitude

TZIDKUS
righteousness

TZITZIS
fringes attached to a *tallis*

TZNIUS
modesty

VAIBERSHER SHUL
(Yid.) ladies' section of the synagogue

VARSHEVER GANOVIM
(Yid.) Warsaw thieves; a nickname given to inhabitants of Warsaw, a city famous for pick-pockets

VIDUI
confessional prayers

VORT (VERTLACH)
(Yid.) lit., word; a short novel, explanation of a verse in Scripture

YACHSON (YACHSONIM)
one of aristocratic lineage

YAHRZEIT
(Yid.) anniversary of a death

YARID
international fair

YARMULKA
(Yid.) skull cap; contraction of *yarei mei'Elokim*, fearer of G-d

YAYIN
wine

YENER MACHALAH
(Yid.) lit. that sickness; a veiled reference to cancer

YERUSHALAYIM
Jerusalem

YESHIVA SHEL MA'ALOH
lit., Heavenly Institute; place of *tzaddikim* in heaven

YEVAMAH
a woman whose husband died, leaving her childless; Torah law requires her to marry her deceased husband's brother (levirate marriage) or be released from this bond by the act of *chalitzah*

YIBADEL LECHAIM
lit., "May he be separated for life!"; a blessing preceding the name of a living person if a deceased's name had just been mentioned

YICHUS
lineage

YIDDISHE NESHAMAH
(Yid.) a Jewish soul

YIDDISHKEIT
(Yid.) Judaism

YIRAS SHAMAYIM
fear of Heaven

YISHUV (YISHUVIM)
settlement; especially the inhabitants of *Eretz*

YITZCHOK AVINU
the Patriarch Isaac

YOM HASHISHI
lit., the sixth day; opening words of Friday evening *Kiddush*

YOMIM NORAIM
lit., Days of Awe; the Ten Days of Penitence, beginning Rosh HaShanah and ending Yom Kippur

YOM TOV
festival

YUNGELEIT
(Yid.) young married men

ZALTZ
(Yid.) salt

ZECHUS
merit; reward

ZEIDE
(Yid.) grandfather

Z'MAN TEFILLAH
halachically prescribed time for prayer

ZOGT EPES
(Yid.) "Say something"

ZOCHAH
worthy